DELAWARE AUTO RACING

FRONT COVER: Ken Marriott accepts the checkered flag from flagman Tom Brown at Delmar in 1953. (Courtesy of Charlie Brown.)

COVER BACKGROUND: Cars line up around Georgetown Speedway for the day's feature race. (Courtesy of David Grey.)

BACK COVER: Tom Brown and crew take time to relax next to their No. 6 race car between races. (Courtesy of Charlie Brown.)

DELAWARE AUTO RACING

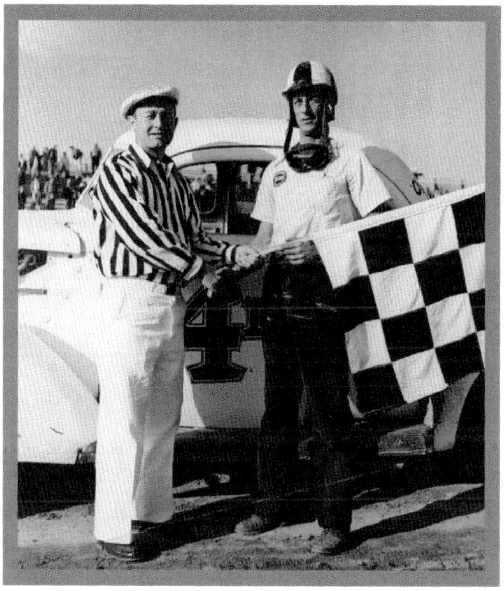

Chad Culver and Wayne Culver
Foreword by Charlie Brown

ARCADIA PUBLISHING

ISBN 978-0-7385-9207-7

Published by Arcadia Publishing
Charleston, South Carolina

Printed in the United States of America

Library of Congress Control Number: 2011933148

For all general information, please contact Arcadia Publishing:
Telephone 843-853-2070
Fax 843-853-0044
E-mail sales@arcadiapublishing.com
For customer service and orders:
Toll-Free 1-888-313-2665

Visit us on the Internet at www.arcadiapublishing.com

To my daughter, Ava Suzanne Culver.
May your life be one big adventure and may all your dreams come true.

To all the drivers, owners, promoters, and fans
who have made racing in Delaware what it is today.
Thank you for the many great memories.

CONTENTS

FOREWORD

The history of dirt track racing in Delaware can be traced back as early as 1919, when the first Kent-Sussex Fair held motorcycle racing on the half-mile horse track. The venue hosted annual events thereafter, including the AAA "Big Cars" that packed the grounds and the stable rooftops. But it was not until our brave young soldiers returned home after World War II that the foundations of racing in the First State were laid.

These veterans were looking for something to give them the adrenaline fix they needed to replace that of combat. They were not lacking in courage by any means, and racing cars provided just the right element of danger and excitement.

Dirt track racing started when a farmer let a group of guys congregate in his pasture on a Sunday afternoon. They staked out an oval, taped up headlights on their "family" cars, and went at it. Thus, dirt track stock car racing was born in Delaware.

Soon, racers were going to local junkyards and buying late-1930s to early-1940s coupes and sedans and turning them into race cars, sparing the family car the abuse from what was often a contact sport.

The venues also changed as speedways began to pop up, leaving the pastures for grazing. The old Delmar Speedway, on the west side of town, and Georgetown Speedway became part of a new racing organization known as NASCAR (National Association for Stock Car Auto Racing).

Today, the sport has evolved. The $100 junkyard specials have been replaced by custom-built masterpieces that cost thousands. Tracks have come and gone since the 1950s and 1960s, but the thrill of watching cars race wheel to wheel, sliding through the turns on a clay oval, remains in Delaware.

—Charlie Brown

ACKNOWLEDGMENTS

The aim of this book is to help preserve and document auto racing in Delaware. Its completion would have been impossible if not for the following people, who provided photographs and information: Burt Quillin, Louis O'Neal, Cy Clendaniel, Snookie Vent, Eric Vent, the Pettyjohn family, Paul Mills, Tom Jerman, Charlie Brown, Don and Linda Allen of D&L Photos, Bill Lawson, Calvin Musser, Betty Wyatt-Dix, Charlie Cathell, Jeff Hardifer, Joe Ann Joseph (representing the Melvin Joseph family), Melvin Joseph Jr., John Snowberger, Helen Banks, Daniel S. Pierce, David Grey, the Delaware Historical Society, Jimmy Messick, Robert Dutton, Bobby Wilkins, Harold Bunting, Walt Breeding, Ken Covey, Sonny Warrington, Butch Warrington, Keith Short, PJ Walker, Horace Williams, Joe Freeman at Racemaker Press, Alan Bradley, Herb Stahl, the Twilley family, and all the fans of Delaware racing who have lent their steadfast support.

In addition, I would like to extend a special thanks to my coauthor, Wayne Culver, who is also my dad. Dad spent countless hours running down photographs, as well as researching information and making contacts for this book. Many thanks also go to my mom, Antonia Culver, for the time spent on the road picking up photographs and mailing them to me. Finally, a big thank-you goes to my wife, April, who proofread and made suggestions for the book while offering her unwavering support and patience.

INTRODUCTION

This is the story of auto racing in Delaware. Although small in size (Delaware is only about 30 miles wide and 90 miles long), the state's auto racing heritage is among the most interesting in the whole country. Although the first automobile race in America took place in 1895, it took a while for racing to catch on in the First State; race cars started speeding around Wawaset Park in Wilmington, Delaware, around 1915. In 1921, race cars first took the place of horse racing at the Delaware State Fair at Elsmere, where a sold-out crowd of 5,000 showed up to witness one of the fastest-growing sports in America. Also in 1921, a record crowd witnessed the first auto races at the Kent-Sussex Fair in Harrington, Delaware.

Throughout the next few decades, until the start of World War II, open-wheel big-car racing and the smaller—but no less exciting—midget cars flourished. Tracks throughout Delaware, such as Elsmere, Hares Corner (in the northern part of the state), and Harrington Speedway (at the Kent-Sussex Fairgrounds), helped lay the foundation for auto racing as it exists today.

Delaware also produced its share of stars during the early years. Perhaps the most successful was Bridgeville's Russell Snowberger, who went on to start in the Indianapolis 500 fifteen times and was ranked fourth among American racing drivers in 1931.

As the United States prepared to enter World War II, a new type of racing found favor in rural towns throughout the country. Stock car racing was exploding, and tracks popped up everywhere to cash in on the craze. In 1941, the Delaware State Fair was moved from Elsmere to the Kent-Sussex Fairgrounds in Harrington, Delaware. The former Kent-Sussex Fair half-mile oval track was the last track in Delaware to host both horse and auto races on the same surface. Unfortunately, all racing came to a halt when the war began and was not cranked back up until the mid-1940s.

Once the war was over, America was looking for an exciting sport to provide entertainment, and stock car racing was there to fill the need. Many new tracks were built in the 1940s, all in the lower part of the state. These tracks included Love Creek, near Midway; Myers Speedway in Bridgeville; Nassau Speedway, which was located in the middle of a farmer's field; Volunteer Speedway (Loves Speedway), near Rehoboth Beach; Old Delmar Speedway; Magnolia Speedway; and the most successful track, Georgetown Speedway. Georgetown was built by Melvin Joseph and offered $500 purses. Thousands of fans lined the fences to see the nation's top drivers compete on the half-mile oval. Popular drivers included Johnny Martin, Bill Steele, Johnny Stoltzfus, Ralph Moody, Bob Burkhart, Lou Johnson, and Russ Bennett. Today, the large half-mile oval on US 113 still holds Modified and Late Model races.

In the 1950s, more tracks were constructed across the state. The half-mile dirt oval of Augustine Beach Speedway and the one-third-mile paved oval of Wilmington Speedway entertained fans in the northern part of the state. Tracks that sprang up in the central part of Delaware were Capital

Speedway in Dover, Blue Hen Speedway in Harrington, and Blackbird Speedway near Grears Corner. The southern part of the state was quickly becoming a hotbed of racing, with many new tracks to accommodate those who wanted to race often; Delaware International Speedway (formerly named US 13 Speedway in Delmar) would become one of the best tracks on the East Coast. This speedway, built by Bill Cathell next to his family's successful drag strip in the 1960s, would host some of the best racing in America. This tradition continues today through Bill's son, Charlie Cathell. During the 1970s and 1980s, the Cathell family often had twin 20-lap features, providing twice the action and giving fans more bang for the buck. As racing continued to gain popularity, other tracks appeared in the 1960s and 1970s. Little Lincoln Speedway in Sussex County, one of the more popular tracks in Delaware, held races until 1975.

When most people think of racing in Delaware, Dover Downs comes to mind. In the mid-1960s, a group of men—including industrialist John W. Rollins, lawyer and politician Davis P. Buckson, and construction guru Melvin L. Joseph—combined forces to purchase a small farm owned by Thomas Murray on the east side of Dover. Joseph, who had long dabbled in motorsports, designed and built the track. Built in 1969, the "Monster Mile" is a one-mile, high-banked, concrete oval that still has two dates on the coveted NASCAR schedule. Both NASCAR and USAC (United States Auto Club) raced at Dover the first year of the track's operation, with A.J. Foyt winning the USAC race and "The King" Richard Petty earning his first of seven wins at Dover. While Dover Downs continues to host NASCAR races each year, most of the dirt oval tracks are history; today, only two dirt oval tracks hold racing for full-sized stock cars—Georgetown Speedway and Delaware International Speedway (DIS).

Racing is more about the people involved in the sport than the tracks or even the race cars. The people of Delaware are a strong and innovative bunch. Nestled on the Delmarva Peninsula between the Chesapeake Bay and the Atlantic Ocean, Delaware is more urban in the north, but the southern part of the state is rural landscape until you near the resorts along the beaches. The racers, owners, and track promoters are some of the most interesting, hardworking, knowledgeable people one could ever meet. The pictures in this book showcase some of the historic cars and drivers who have earned their places in history, from the slightly modified 1940 Fords to the Big Block Modifieds of today.

Racing in Delaware featured owners and drivers who were as unique as the cars they operated. Legendary drivers like Hal Browning drove everything there was to race: Modifieds, Sprint Cars, Late Models, and even NASCAR stock cars. Browning's career started in the 1960s and has continued past 2011. Still racing and still winning, Browning is a racer's racer and has won in just about every class. Early drivers like Johnny Martin set the stage for later Modified drivers. Martin won many races behind the wheel of some of the best-prepared Modifieds of the time. The 1970s and 1980s saw new emerging stars, like seven-time DIS Modified champion Bobby Wilkins. With 118 victories, Wilkins holds the record for most wins in a Modified at DIS.

Harold Bunting is another legendary Delaware driver; Bunting was an 87-time race-winner at DIS and was dominant on the way to capturing three championships at the speedway. One of the most versatile drivers in Delaware racing history is Eddie Pettyjohn. During his long career, Pettyjohn raced in both the Late Model and Modified classes and won over 400 races. He went on to success in both classes, as well as having one of the most memorable race cars in Delaware racing history—the Corvair station wagon–bodied eight-ball. Like in many families involved in racing, the Pettyjohns' love of the sport has been passed down from generation to generation.

Eddie's three sons—Kenny, David, and Mark—all followed in their father's footsteps. Kenny Pettyjohn has won more than 100 races and is a 10-time Delaware International Speedway Late Model champion.

Family ties run deep in Delaware racing. Another historic racing clan is the Vent family, of Milton, Delaware. Snookie Vent, owner of Snookie's Speed Shop, and his family have provided parts and services for racers all over the state. Every week, the speed shop trailer is at the track, fully stocked with parts for racers. This tradition has been handed down to Snookie's son, Snookie Jr., and grandson, Eric Vent.

Delaware is also home to some legendary car owners. Norris "Speedy" Reed always had some of the best-looking and best-prepared cars at the track. Perhaps one of the most "David versus Goliath" moments in racing came when Reed's car, with driver Ramo Stott, won the pole for the 1976 Daytona 500. Others, like Ken Covey, owner of Covey's Car Care, have owned and funded teams and drivers for many years and are mainstays in local racing. Covey fielded the famous No. 21 Modified for many years, winning some of the biggest races with driver Gary Gollub. Banks, Warrington, Dutton, and Mills are just a few of the many families to field cars in the state of Delaware.

Many of Delaware's racing traditions continue today on the few dirt tracks that remain. Support for racing in the First State remains strong, and with this group of racers, promoters, and car owners, the sport is in great hands. My hope is that this book will bring back some memories of racing's rich history in Delaware. Here, readers will find photographs of people and events with one thing in common—a love of racing. Janet Guthrie, the first woman to compete in the Indianapolis 500 and the Daytona 500, once said that "racing is a measure of spirit, not strength." The history of racing in Delaware has a spirit that has endured since the 1900s and will continue for the foreseeable future.

1

Through the Dust

Since the first pieced-together cars sped around the dusty track at Wawaset Park in Wilmington, Delaware, race fans have flocked to see drivers push these machines to their limits. At the Kent-Sussex County Fair, it started with the "Big Motorcycles Race" around the horse track in 1919. Motorcycles gave way to auto racing in 1921 as a young Russell Snowberger started his first race at age 19. Snowberger went on to finish third that day and eventually raced at Indianapolis 15 times. In 1931, Snowberger actually won the pole for the Indianapolis 500 and finished fifth in the final standings.

The big open-wheel cars ruled the dirt tracks until the start of World War II. With no more protection than goggles and a driver's cap, racers roared around horse tracks at speeds that astounded the public. The "Big Cars," as they were called, had no seat belts or roll cages and were driven to the edge by the skilled drivers; they were the pioneers of auto racing, and their bravery and skill entertained thousands across Delaware.

At an automobile race in Harrington, Delaware, in 1947, a record for attendance was set that was not bested until after the construction of Dover Downs Speedway. A crowd of 36,258 race fans gathered around the dusty half-mile oval to witness the races that day. Some made a living at auto racing, while most did it for the thrill and a hope of victory.

Almost all of the tracks are now gone, but the memory and legacy of these racers live on. Harrington Raceway is the last existing track in Delaware to have hosted both horse and auto racing on the same oval, where, for over 70 years, beasts and men sped across the loose surface.

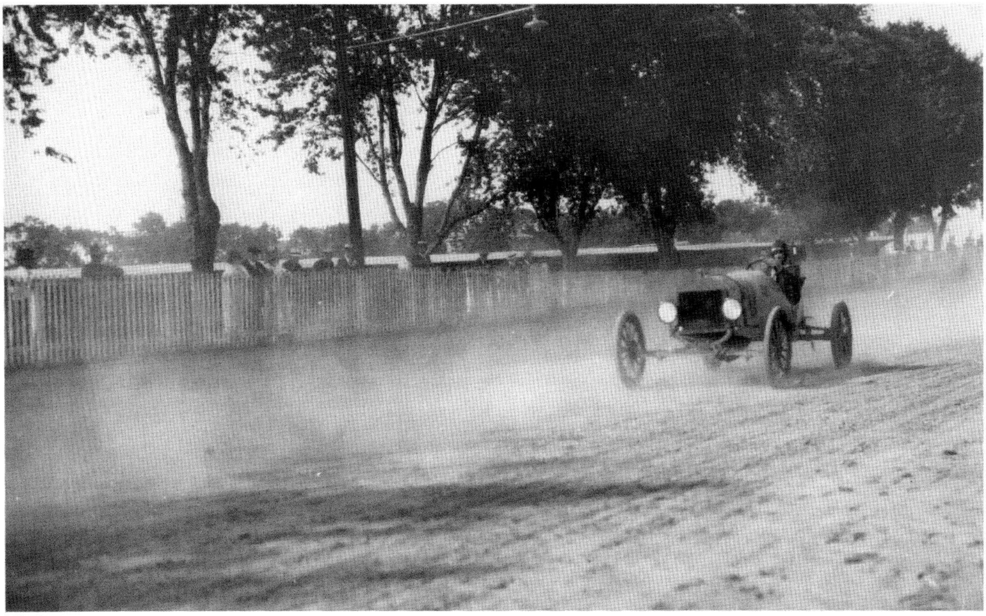

In 1916, a lone racer speeds down the front stretch at Wawaset Park in Wilmington. Races were held at Wawaset Park until 1917, when the Delaware State Fair moved to Elsmere. (Courtesy of the Delaware Historical Society.)

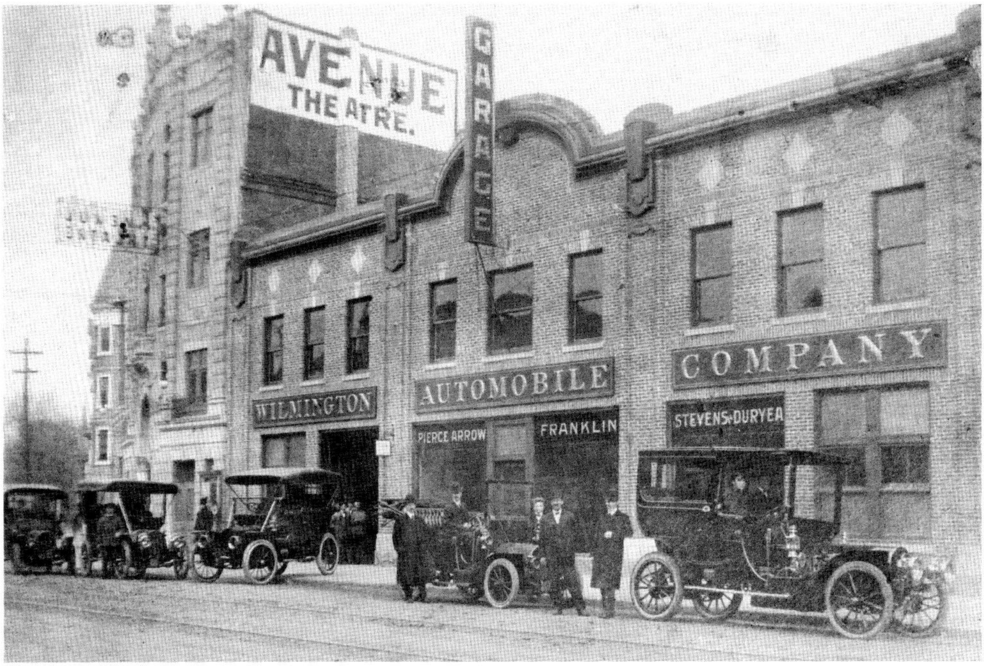

This photograph of the Wilmington Automobile Company, dated around 1910, shows some early cars ready for driving. The first automobile race in America was held on Thanksgiving Day, November 27, 1895. On a 54-mile course, Frank Duryea was first to cross the line with an average speed of 7.3 miles per hour. (Courtesy of the Delaware Historical Society.)

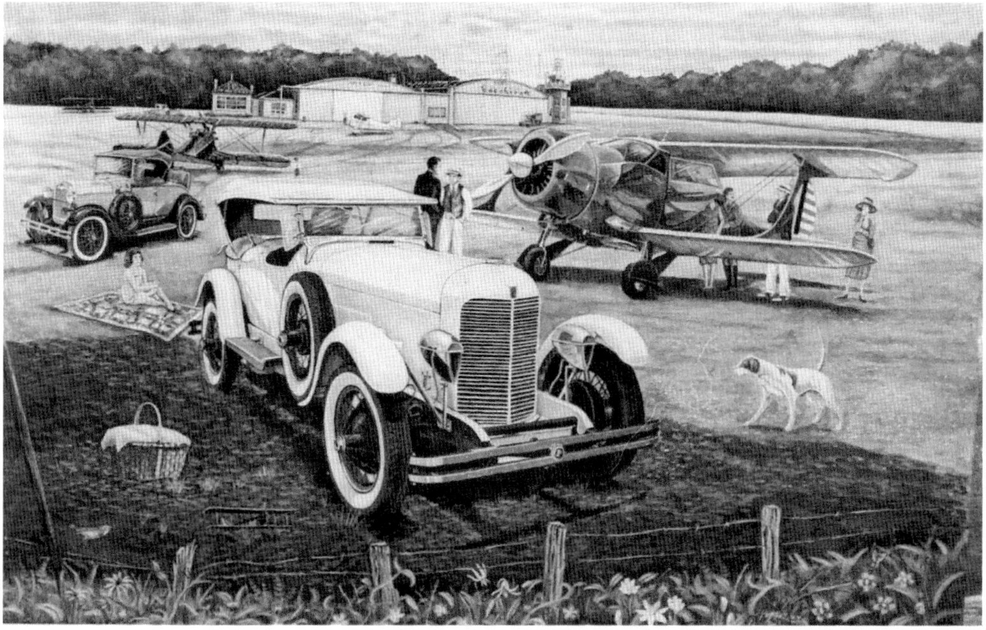

The main subject matter in this painting by John Matassa is a 1929 four-passenger DuPont Le Mans Speedster. The car was built to be raced at the famed French competition, the 24 Hours of Le Mans. At the time, Le Mans was only open to four-seat cars, and the DuPont speedster left the race early with gearbox problems. E. Paul DuPont produced 537 cars between 1919 and 1931. (Courtesy of the Delaware Historical Society.)

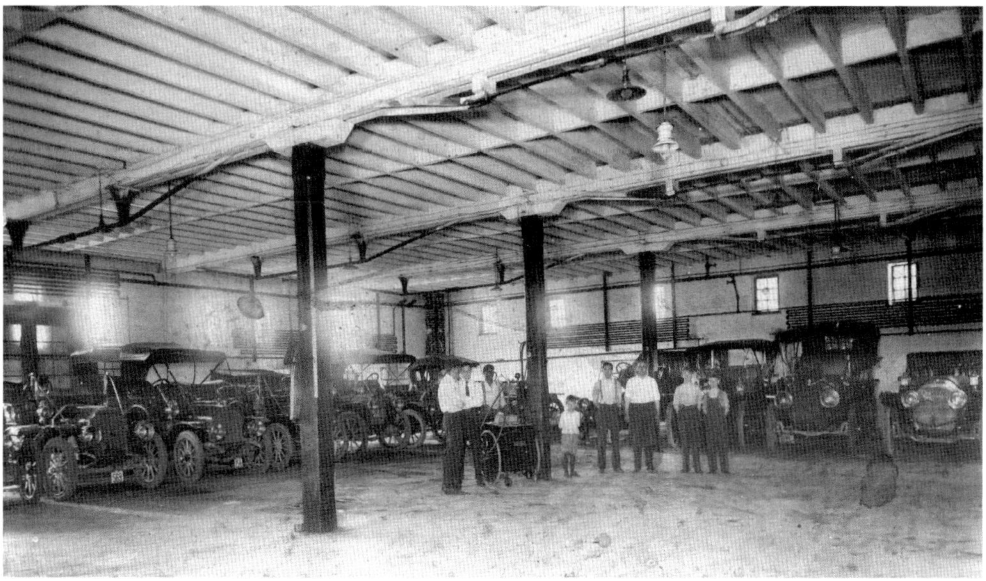

Racing increased in popularity as automobiles became more affordable. Manufacturers used racing to promote the speed and durability of their machines. The old adage "win on Sunday, sell on Monday" remains true to this day. Here, a fleet of new cars awaits potential buyers at a dealership on US Highway 13 in Delaware. (Courtesy of the Delaware Historical Society.)

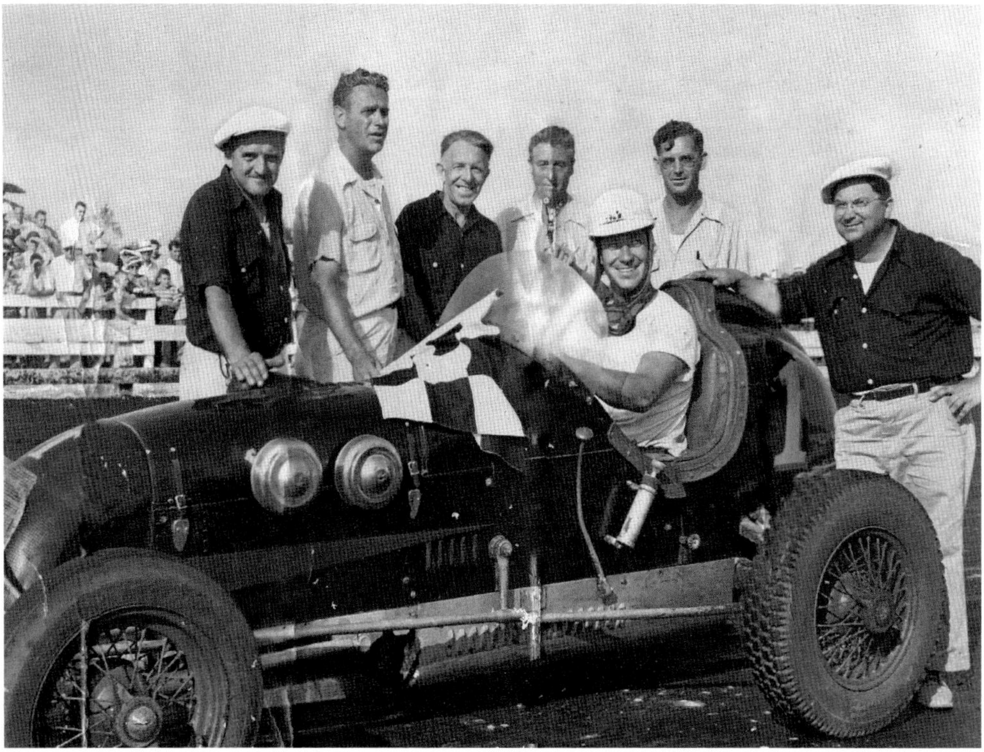

Pictured at Delmar Speedway on September 3, 1950, are, from left to right, Lou Kunz, Harry Johnson, Jules Furslew, Bill Streeter, driver Mike Magill, George Bower, and Charles Garsbgo. The rod located outside the car, next to the driver cockpit, is a hand brake. With no roll bars, these open wheel cars were extremely dangerous. (Courtesy of Louis O'Neal.)

EXECUTIVES

George W. Bower, *Pres.* — Ed Nichols, *Publicity Director*
Iris G. Bower, *Vice Pres.* — Bill S. Streeter, *Promoter*
Rella C. Greene, *Sec.-Treas.*

OFFICIALS

Starter - Harry Johnson, Phila., Penna.
Scorer - Carl Miller and Jerry Smith, Phila., Penna.
Timer - Alvin Fisher, Phila., Penna.
Pit Steward - Joe Armstrong, Phila., Penna.
Announcer - Carl Sweigert, Lebanon, Penna.
Judges - George Bower, Fruitland, Maryland
H. B. Van Auken, Salisbury, Maryland

Del-mar-va Sweepstakes Trophies to be presented to winning driver and car owner of feature race.

ENTRANTS QUALIFYING TIME TRIALS

Car No.	*Driver*	*Residence*	*Make of Car*	*Time*
1	Mike Magill	Haddonfield, N.J.	Riley	______
2	Earl Horn	Needham, Mass.	Hal	______
2	Skip Sherman	Laureldale, Penna.	Frazier	______
3	Buddy Powers	Phila., Penna.	Hal	______
3	Dick Fries	Reading, Penna.	Ford V-8	______
4	Frank Concannon	Phila., Penna.	Riley	______
4	Mel Weidner	Reading, Penna.	Ford 6	______
5	John Hill	Binghampton, N.Y.	Hal	______
5	Ben Smorto	Corona, N.Y.	Norton	______
5	Fred Post	New York, N.Y.	Riley	______
7	Larry Smith	Bloomingdale, N.J.	McDowell	______
7	Sandy Sanford	Johnson City, N.Y.	Riley	______
8	Bill Case	Doylestown, Penna.	Riley	______
9	Bill Holt	Scranton, Penna.	Riley	______
10	Jack Yardley	Haddon Heights, N.J.	Ford	______
18	Bud Phillips	Bloomsburg, Penna.	Riley	______
21	Dick Dowd	Newark, N.J.	Riley	______
33	Mike San Felice	Norristown, Penna.	Ranger	______
39	Bud Olson	Paulsboro, N.J.	Riley	______
44	Eddie Gallione	Schenectady, N.Y.	McDowell	______
46	Steve McGrath	Stamford, Conn.	McDowell	______
51	Mike Zilka	Johnstown, N.Y.	Riley	______
55	George Markie	Schenectady, N.Y.	Hal	______
74	Jim Boas	Plainfield, N.J.	Riley	______
77	Bob Geist	Califon, N.J.	Riley	______

EVENT No. 2

This program insert from September 3, 1950, shows the lineup for the Big Car race at Delmar Speedway. Note the makes of the cars and the hometowns of the drivers. Most drivers of the Big Cars were from up north and traveled with the United Racing Club (URC) series. When stock car racing began, more local racers got involved, and programs started to list more Delaware drivers. (Courtesy of Louis O'Neal.)

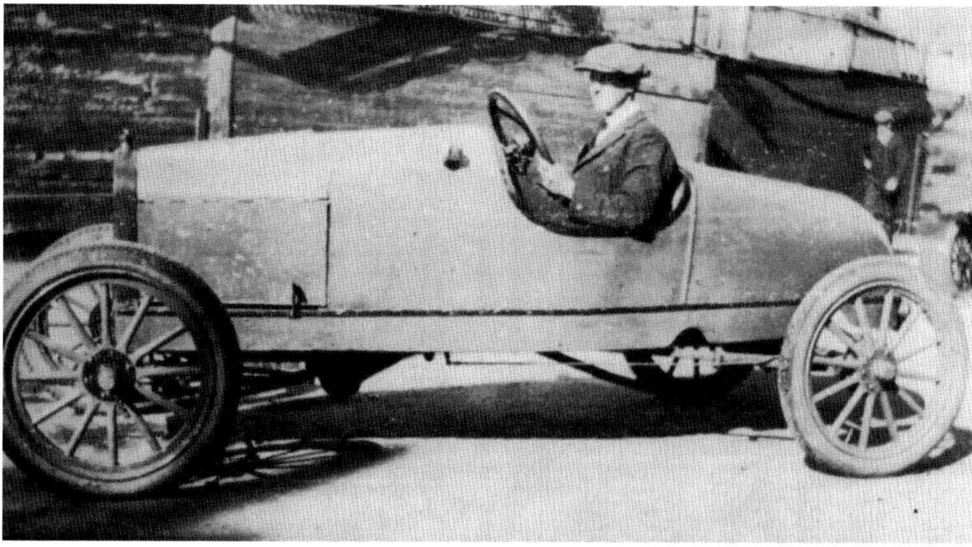

A young Russell Snowberger prepares to make his debut in Harrington, Delaware, at the 1921 Kent-Sussex Fair. He eventually held the track record at Harrington. (Courtesy of John Snowberger.)

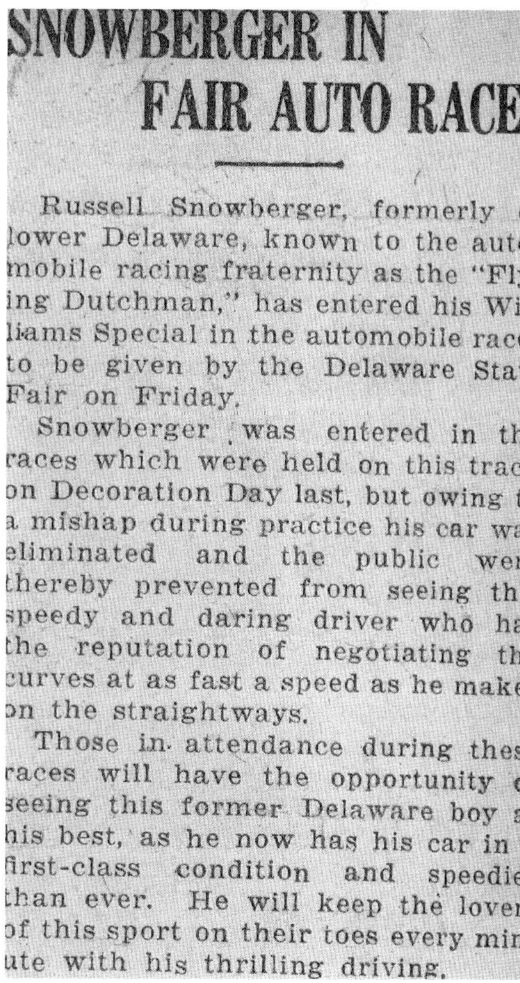

SNOWBERGER IN FAIR AUTO RACES

Russell Snowberger, formerly of lower Delaware, known to the automobile racing fraternity as the "Flying Dutchman," has entered his Williams Special in the automobile race to be given by the Delaware State Fair on Friday.

Snowberger was entered in the races which were held on this track on Decoration Day last, but owing to a mishap during practice his car was eliminated and the public were thereby prevented from seeing this speedy and daring driver who has the reputation of negotiating the curves at as fast a speed as he makes on the straightways.

Those in attendance during these races will have the opportunity of seeing this former Delaware boy at his best, as he now has his car in a first-class condition and speedier than ever. He will keep the lovers of this sport on their toes every minute with his thrilling driving.

In the late 1920s, Snowberger was becoming quite a star, as evidenced by this newspaper clipping. Promoters became aware that Snowberger's records and driving reputation would attract large crowds to the races. (Courtesy of John Snowberger.)

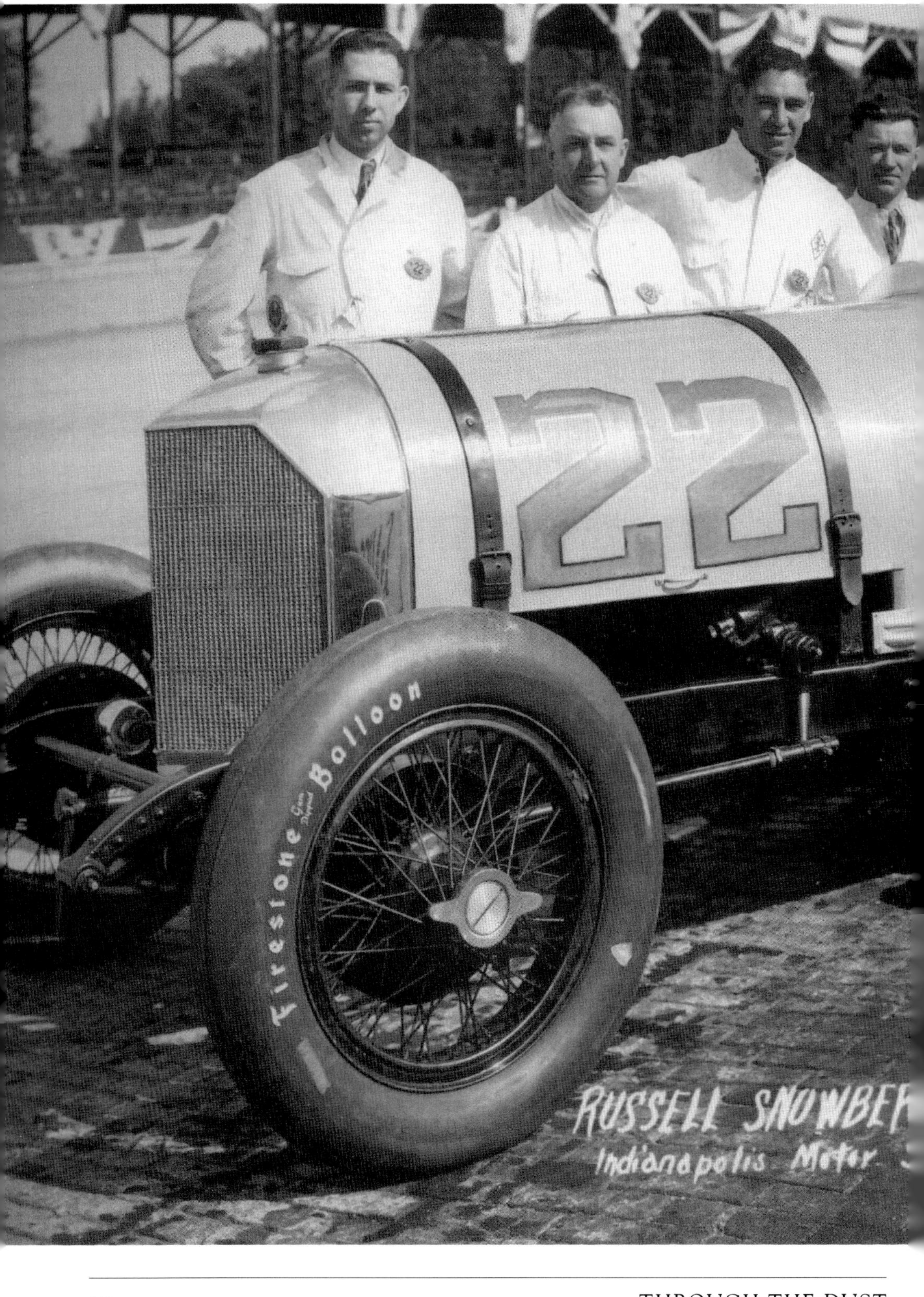
22
Firestone Balloon
RUSSELL SNOWBER
Indianapolis Motor

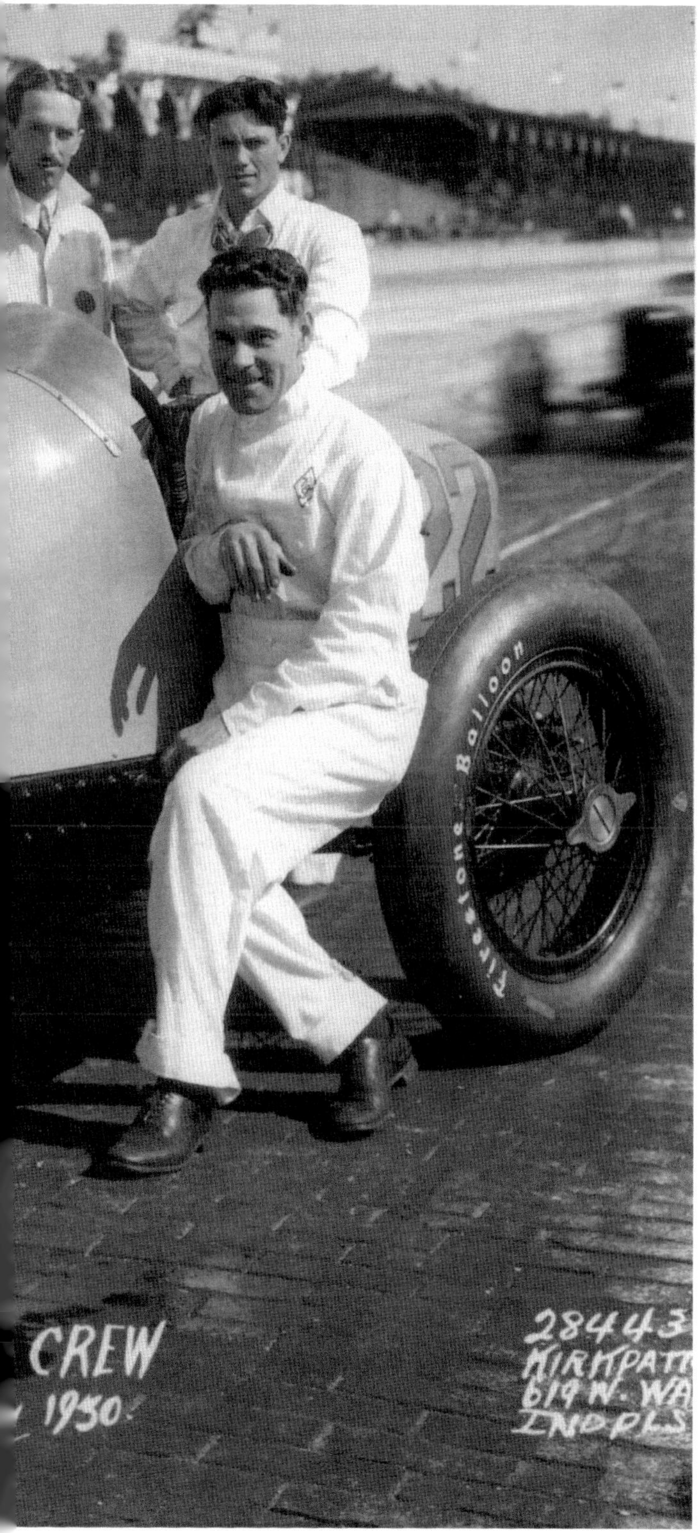

Russell Snowberger, of Bridgeville, Delaware, began his racing career in 1921 at the Kent-Sussex County Fairgrounds in Harrington. At the young age of 19, he finished third in his first race and eventually set the track record at Elsmere with a lap time of 31.3 seconds. Snowberger became one of the most well known and successful drivers to hail from Delaware. He earned a reputation for revamping stock cars into Indy cars and, in 1930, finished eighth in the Indianapolis 500 in a car that he built for $156. Snowberger started the Indianapolis 500 fifteen times and won the pole for the race in 1931. After his retirement from driving, Snowberger became a successful chief mechanic, car builder, designer, and car owner. (Courtesy of John Snowberger.)

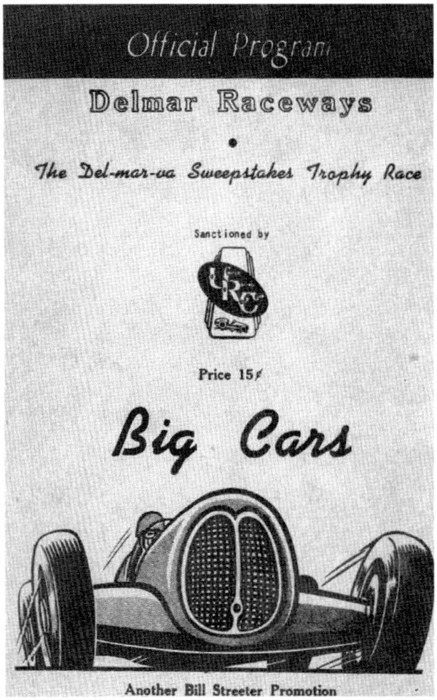

This program is from the old Delmar Speedway that was located on the west side of the town and run/promoted by George Bowers. The Art Deco car on the front is promoting the Big Cars, as they were called. The sanctioning body of the race is the URC, or United Racing Club. The URC has been promoting races from 1948 to the present. (Courtesy of Louis O'Neal.)

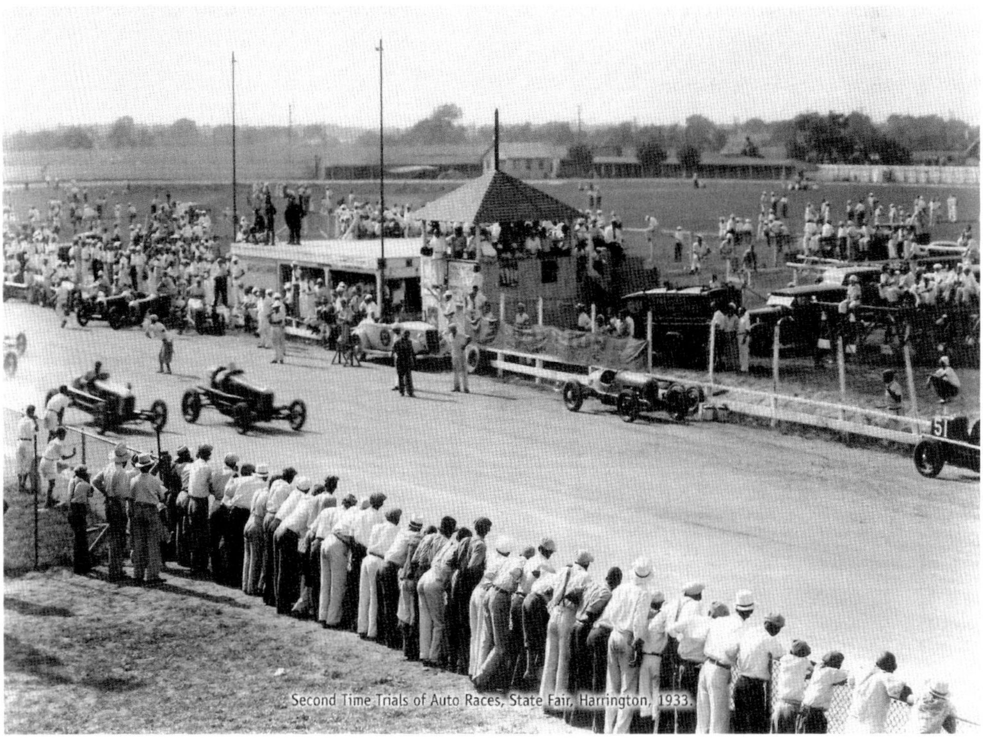

In 1933, crowds line the fence as race cars speed by during the second time-trial event at Harrington. Notice how vehicles and crew members remain on the track during the event, with no protection from the speeding cars. (Courtesy of Horace Williams Jr.)

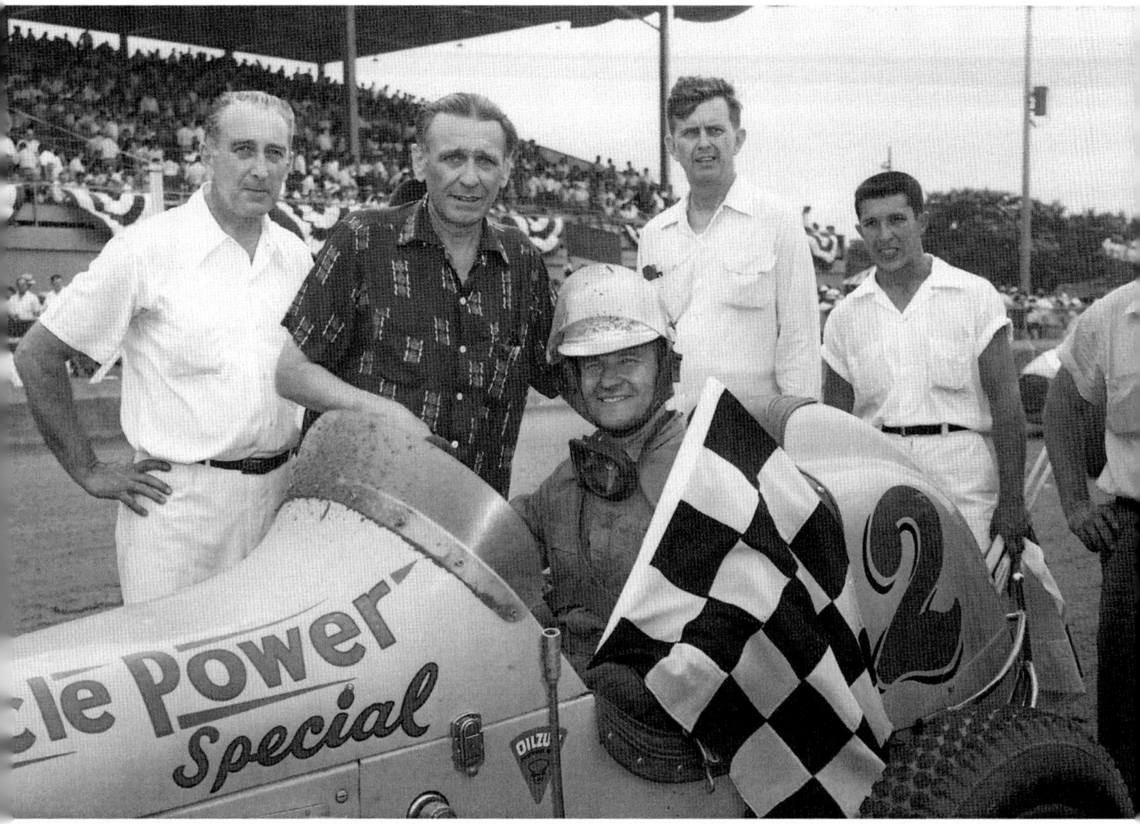

Big Car racing remained a popular attraction even after stock cars burst onto the scene in the 1940s. The winning driver of the June 30, 1955, race at Harrington was none other than "The Flying Farmer," Tommy Hinnershitz. Hinnershitz was one of the most popular Big Car drivers in history and won an amazing seven Eastern Sprint Car Championships. (Courtesy of the Walt Chernokal Collection, Racemaker Archive.)

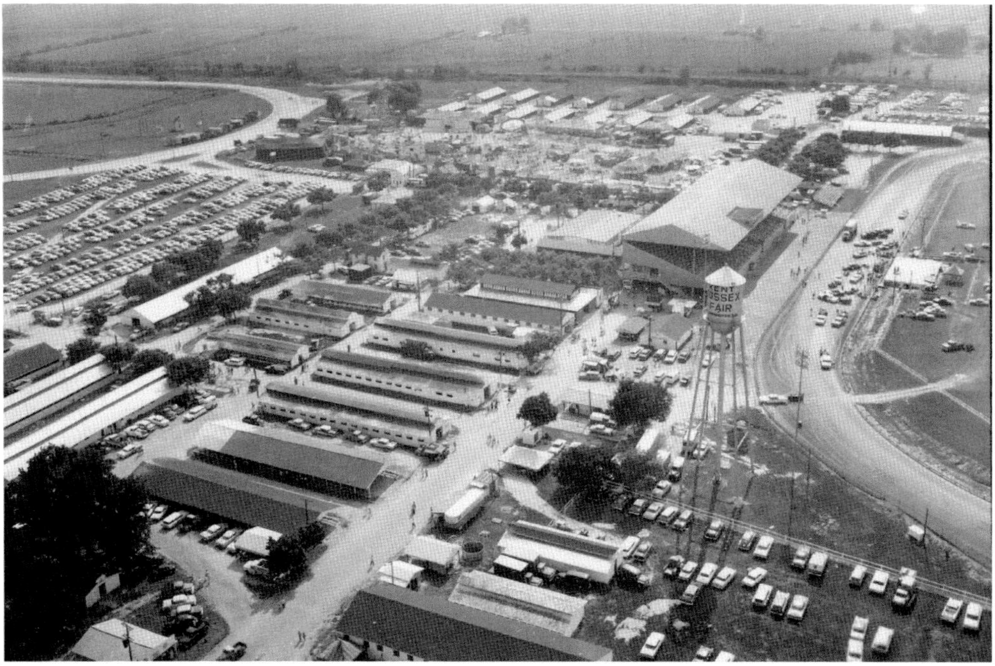

The oval at the Delaware State Fairgrounds has hosted races for over 70 years and is the last existing track to hold both automobile and horse racing on the same surface. This aerial photograph was taken in 1962. The water tower still says "Kent-Sussex Fair." (Courtesy of the Delaware Historical Society.)

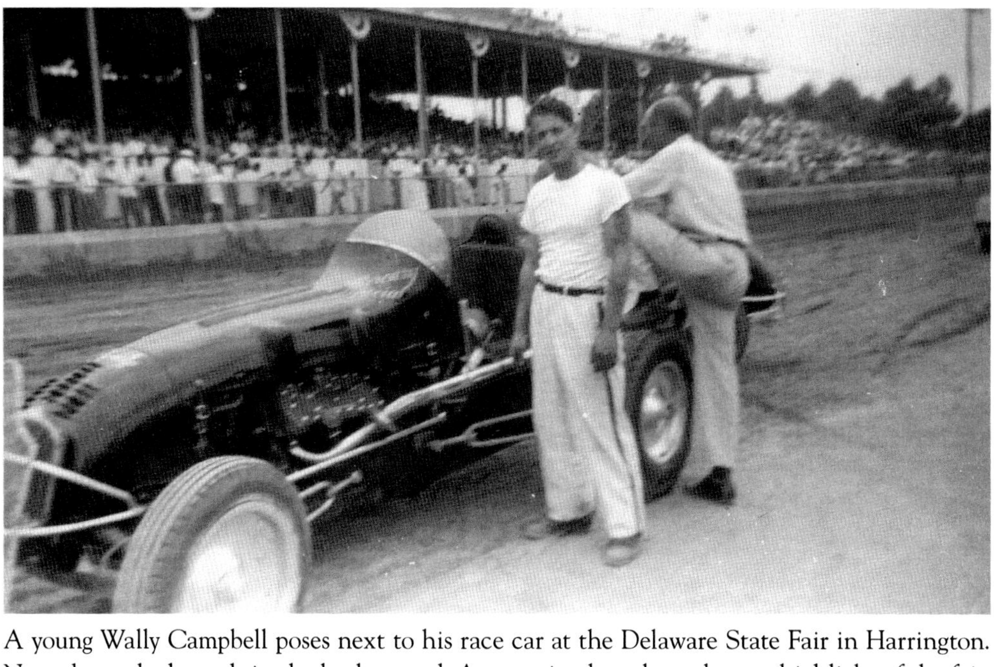

A young Wally Campbell poses next to his race car at the Delaware State Fair in Harrington. Note the packed stands in the background. Auto racing has always been a highlight of the fair. (Courtesy of Charlie Brown.)

Members of the Moody family and the Joseph family gather around the new race car of a young Melvin Joseph Jr. The small Quarter Midget was modeled after the larger race cars of the day. Joseph Jr. won his first race, as a child, in this car and went on to be a successful race car driver. (Courtesy of Melvin Joseph Jr.)

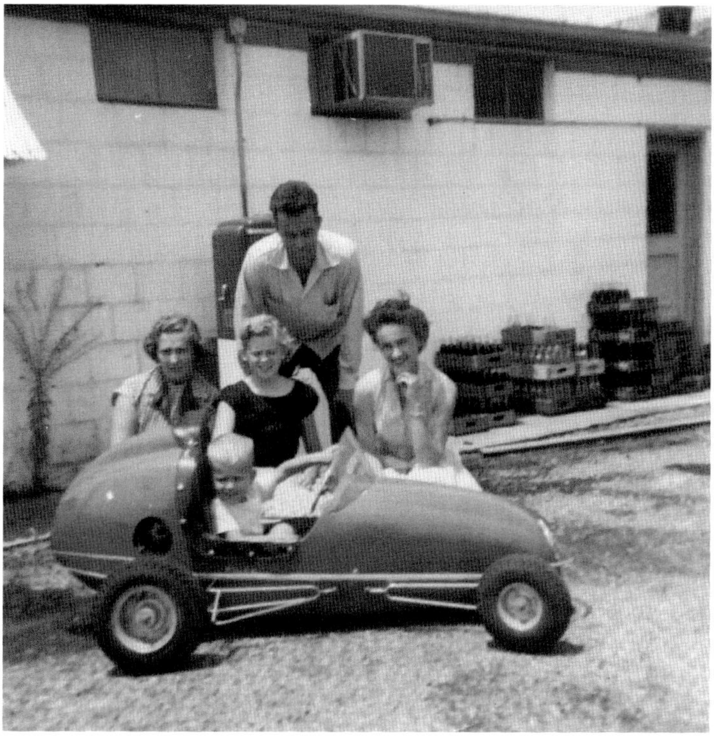

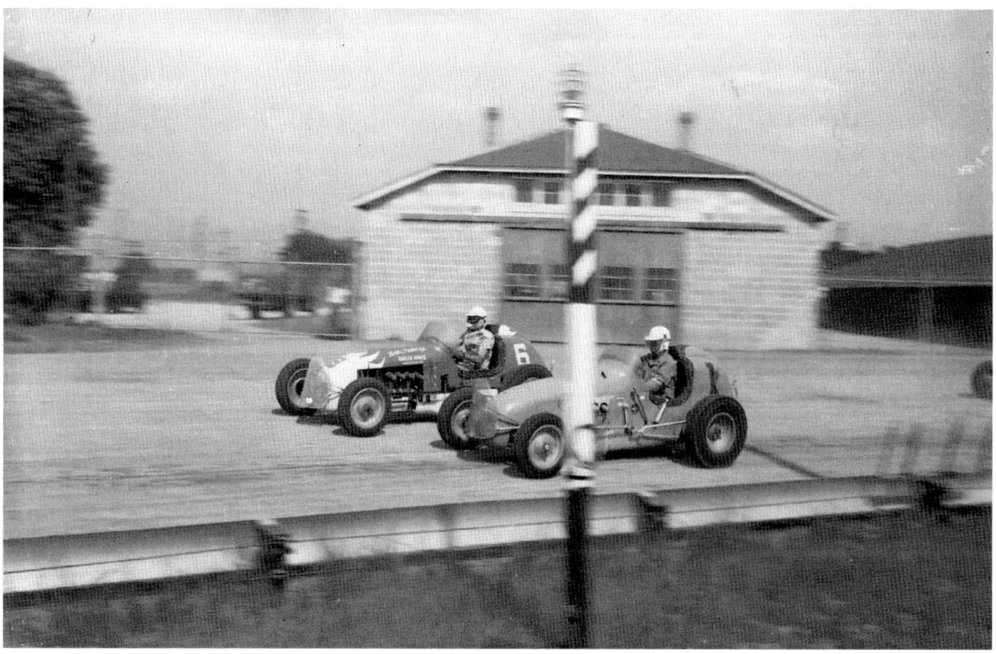

In this 1952 photograph of the No. 6, driven by Johnny Parson Sr., and the No. 1, driven by Tommy Hinnershitz, the viewer can see how dangerously close some of the horse stables at the Harrington Fairgrounds are to the track. (Courtesy of the Walt Chernokal Collection, Racemaker Archive.)

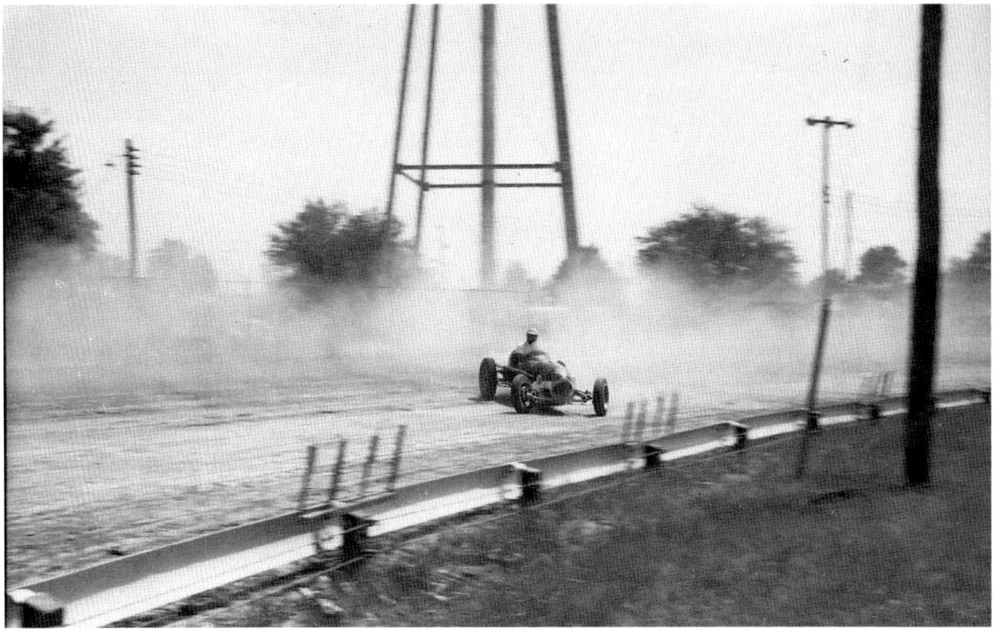

Turning right to go left, Paul Russo, in the No. 22, puts his car into a perfect drift around turns one and two at Harrington. It must have been a thrill for the drivers to push these early race cars to their limits. (Courtesy of the Walter Chernokal Collection, Racemaker Archive.)

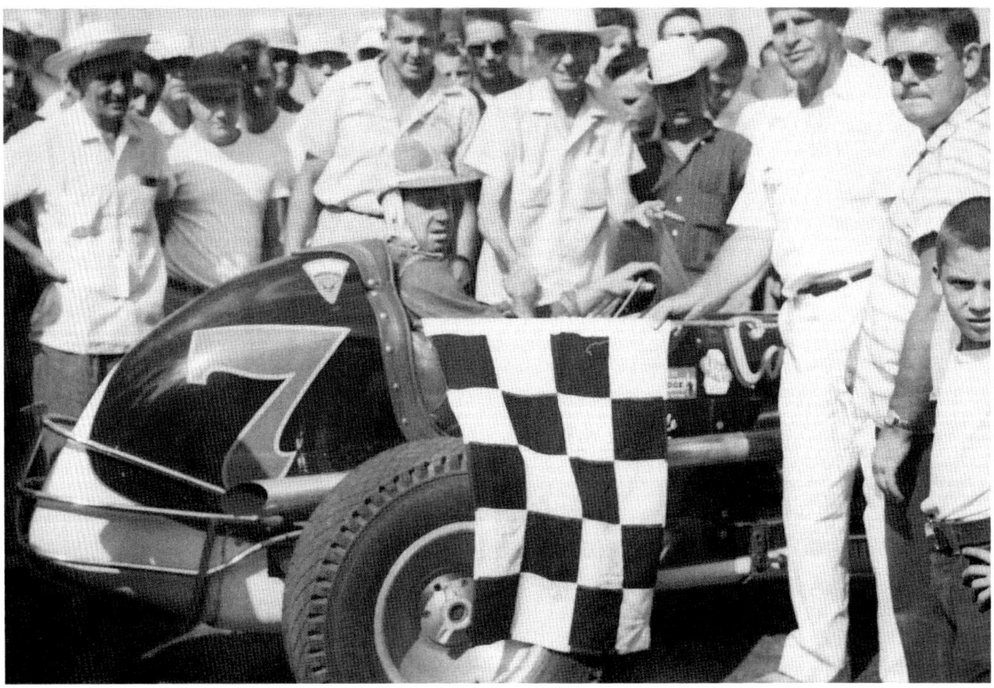

On July 27, 1957, Bert Brooks won the United Racing Club feature at Harrington. Spectators and officials, anxiously anticipating a moment with the hero of the day, surround the winner's car. (Courtesy of the Walt Chernokal Collection, Racemaker Archive.)

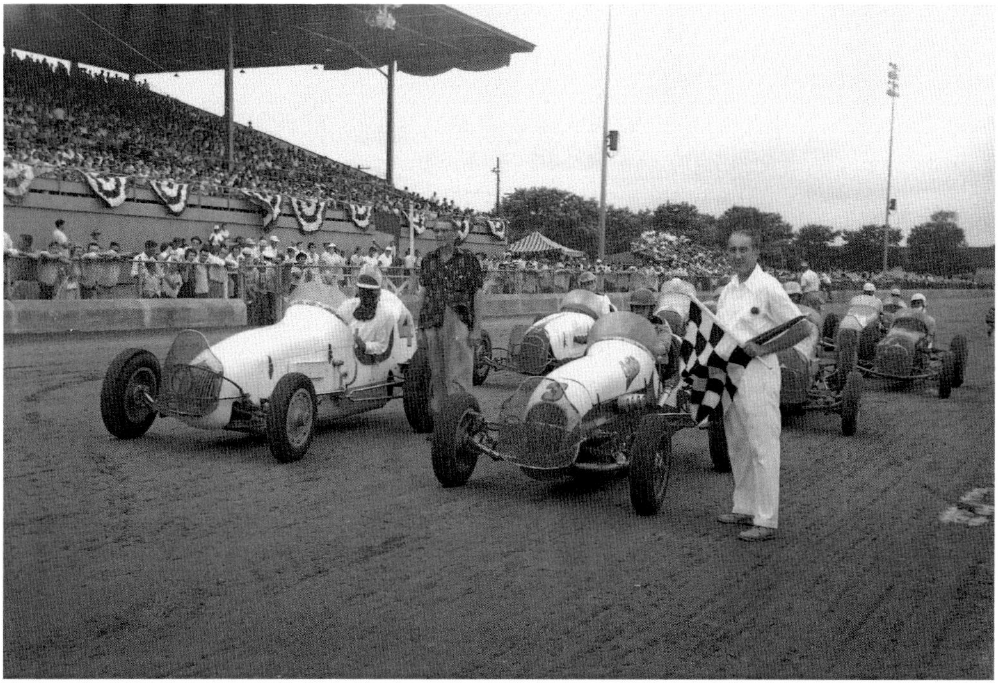

In 1955, the Big Cars line up for the feature at Harrington as a huge crowd watches. Note the screens on the front of the cars, meant to keep loose dirt from clogging the radiators. While the loose surface at Harrington was good for horse racing, it provided quite a challenge for drivers. (Courtesy of the Walt Chernokal Collection, Racemaker Archive.)

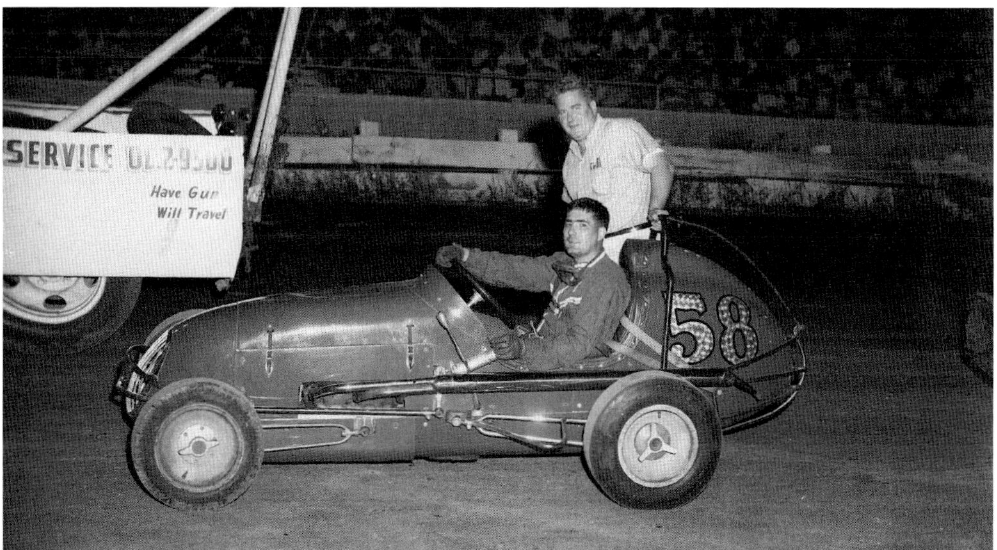

Although smaller than the Big Cars, Midgets provided just as much excitement. Hal Horan poses in his No. 58 Midget at Wilmington Speedway in 1958. (Courtesy of the Walt Chernokal Collection, Racemaker Archive.)

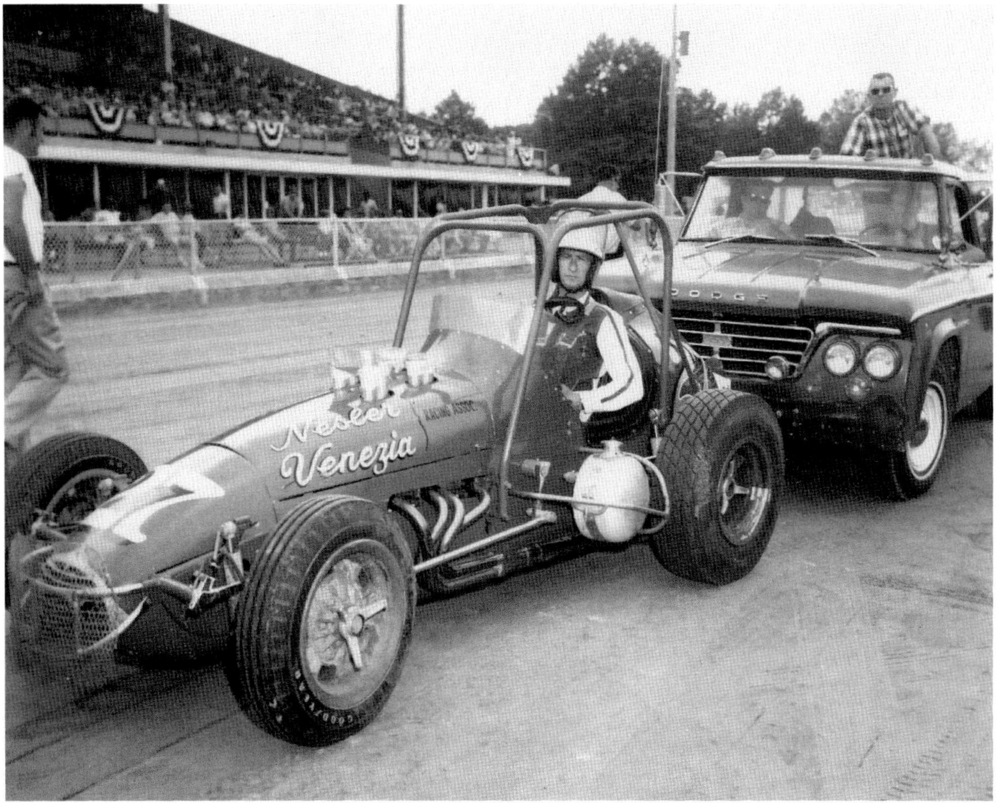

As time progressed, Big Cars began to be called Sprint Cars and started to include cages around the driver for safety. With no clutch, the cars used an in/out box and had to be push-started. Here, Earl Halaquist, in the No. 27, prepares to be pushed off for the feature event. (Courtesy of the Walt Chernokal Collection, Racemaker Archive.)

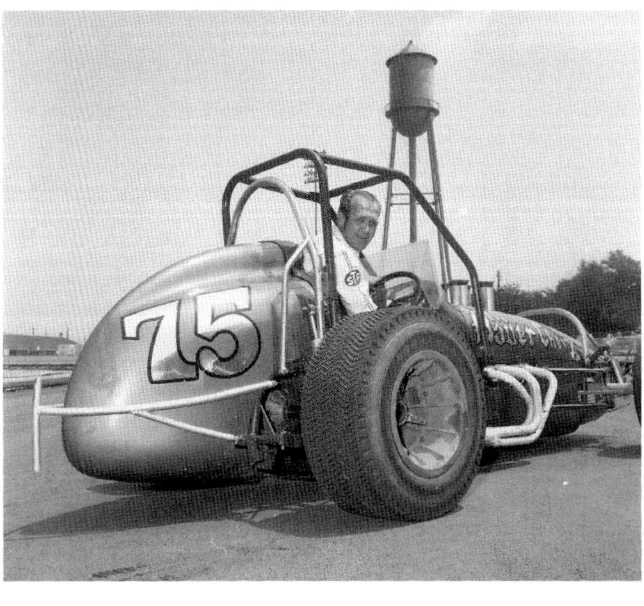

With the fair's water tower in the background, Bill Hughes takes time to pose in his Bill Bauer–owned, Chevrolet-powered Sprint Car before the races in 1970. (Courtesy of the Walt Chernokal Collection, Racemaker Archive.)

2

Delaware Dirt

With the start of World War II, all auto racing came to a halt. However, as servicemen returned home at the end of the war, many looked for a way to feed a need for adventure. These men acquired mechanical skills while in the military, and participating in racing was a great way to get the adrenaline rush they were seeking. Stock car racing was becoming increasingly popular. Cars from the 1930s and 1940s were easily available and could be bought at a reasonable price. Tracks started to spring up all over the state, and the action was intense.

With few rules to follow, drivers started to modify cars for performance and to handle the abuse of the rough tracks. With all the modifications, the cars became more "Modified" than "Stock"—thus, they became known as Modified race cars. Some of NASCAR's first premier drivers raced in Modifieds before the organization's inception in 1949. Sanctioning groups—such as NASCAR, the Delaware Stock Car Racing Association, and the United Racing Club—drafted rules and regulations to help keep costs down and to provide an even playing field for everyone. New classes started to develop at local tracks. Modified, Sportsman, and Sprint Cars are just a few of the classes that developed during dirt racing's infancy. With the rise of racing at so many local tracks, race fans got to see people they knew driving cars at amazing speeds. Seeing local drivers perform instilled a sense of community pride, and drivers soon had many adoring fans rooting for them at the tracks. This period laid the foundation for dirt racing in Delaware. Although many of the tracks and drivers have passed on, the legacy they left behind will last forever.

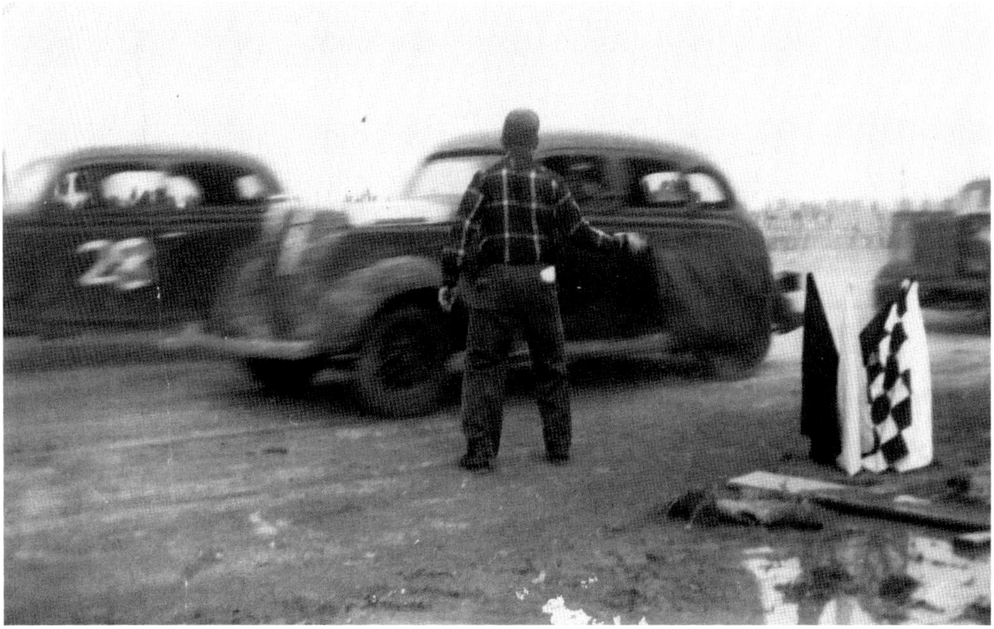

Tom Brown flags his very first event at Love Creek Speedway in 1948. Love Creek, carved out of a farmer's field, was located near Midway, Delaware, between Lewes and Rehoboth Beach. (Courtesy of Charlie Brown.)

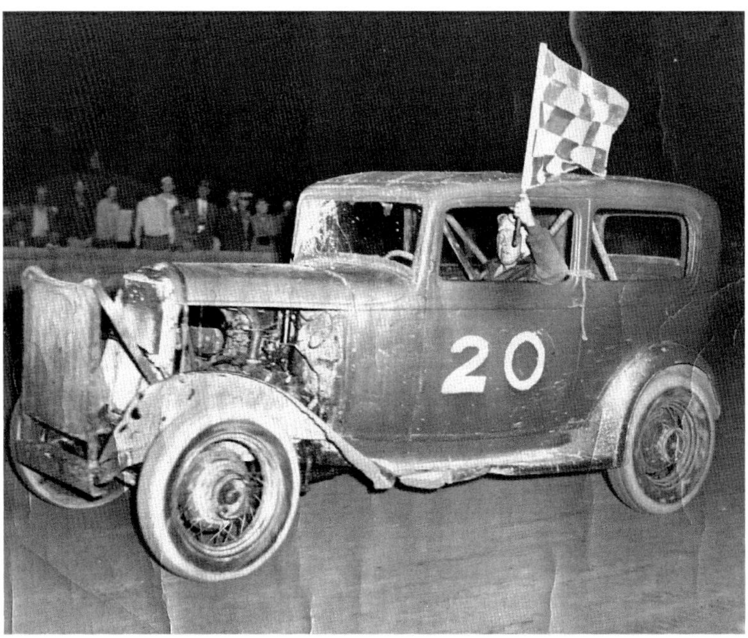

Bill Walker proudly displays the checkered flag after his feature win. Notice the wire wheels and flathead engine. Many drivers would hop up their flathead engines, but none shared what they had done. Wire wheels soon gave way to Wide 5 steel wheels that were much stronger. (Courtesy of Louis O'Neal.)

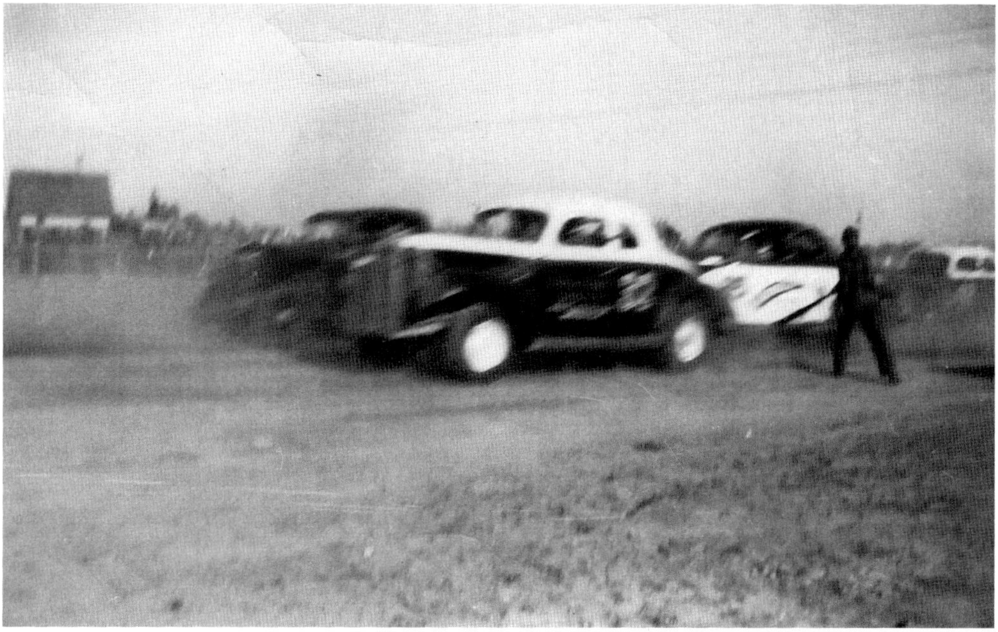

Cars race dangerously close to flagman Tom Brown at Love Creek Speedway. Flagging a race was one of the most dangerous jobs to have in the early years of racing. Bob Harper, a flagman at Hares Corner racetrack, near New Castle, was killed during a race when the dust got so thick that the racers could not see him step on the track to signal the final lap. (Courtesy of Charlie Brown.)

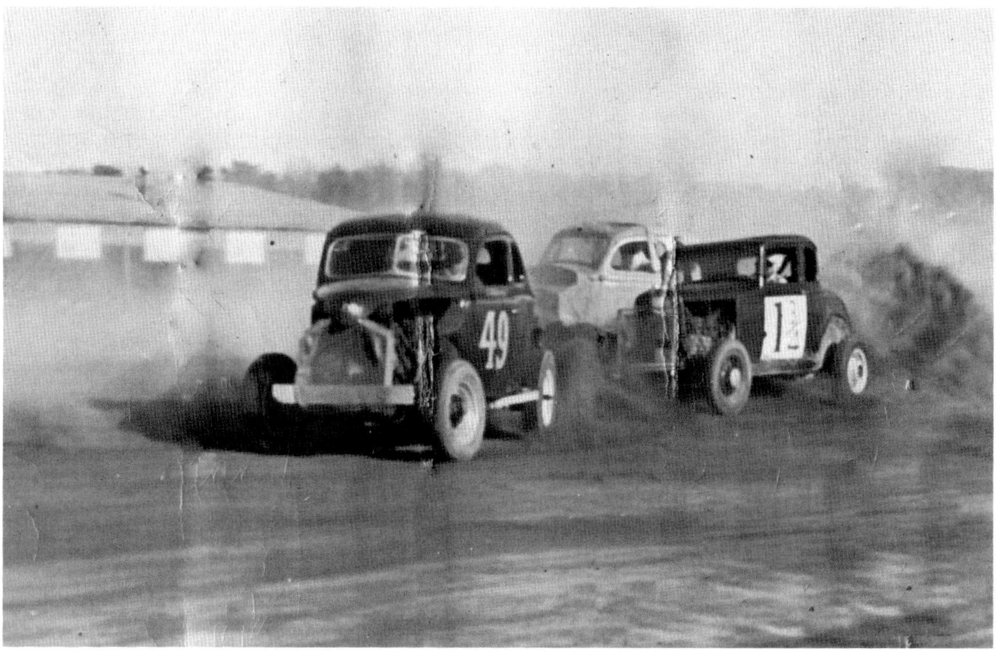

The Melvin Joseph–owned No. 49 leads the pack around the old Georgetown Speedway. This speedway was located on US 9, east of US 113, and was built as a horse and automobile track. The horse stables are visible in the background. (Courtesy of Louis O'Neal.)

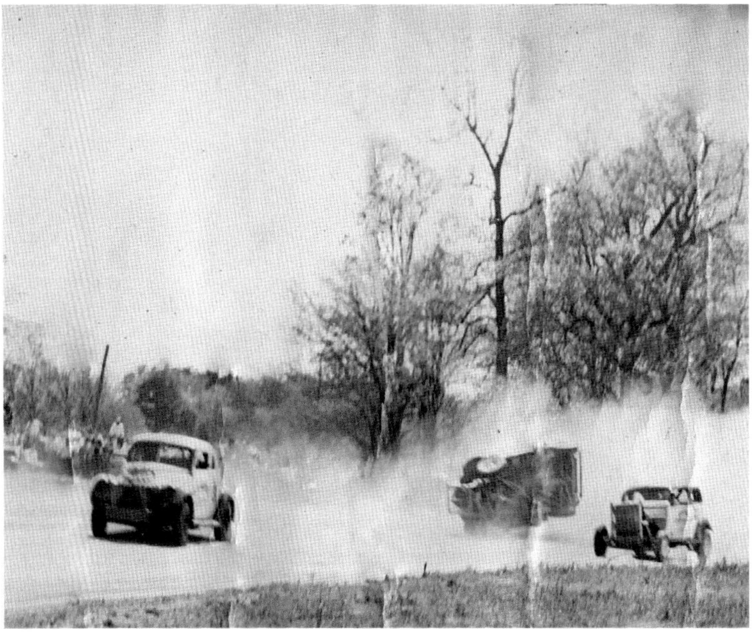

A racer goes for a wild ride at Myers Speedway in Bridgeville, Delaware. Myers was a half-mile dirt oval that operated during the early 1950s. (Courtesy of Louis O'Neal.)

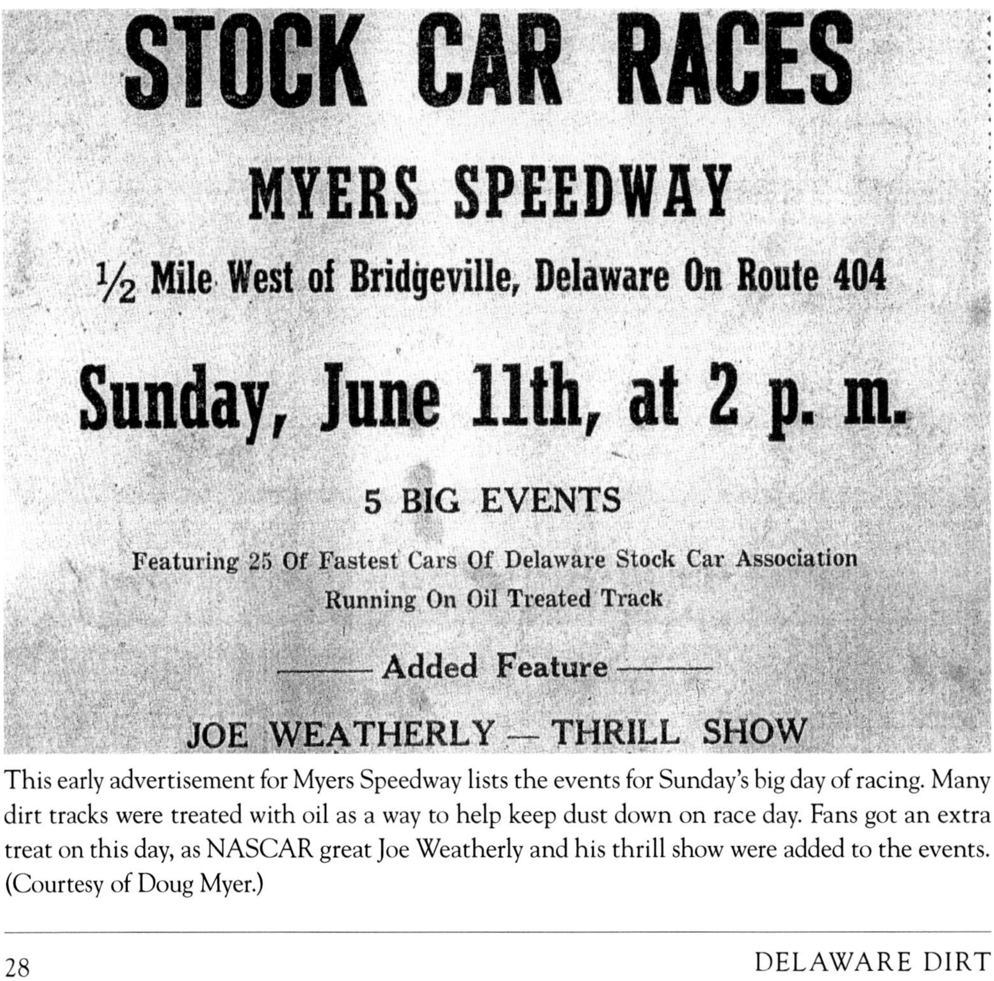

This early advertisement for Myers Speedway lists the events for Sunday's big day of racing. Many dirt tracks were treated with oil as a way to help keep dust down on race day. Fans got an extra treat on this day, as NASCAR great Joe Weatherly and his thrill show were added to the events. (Courtesy of Doug Myer.)

This Wilmington Speedway program from the 1950s shows one of NASCAR's earliest logos. In 1952, the speedway hosted a NASCAR event on the Grand National Circuit. A crowd of 5,360 watched as 50-year old Pappy Hough won the checkered flag. (Courtesy of Louis O'Neal.)

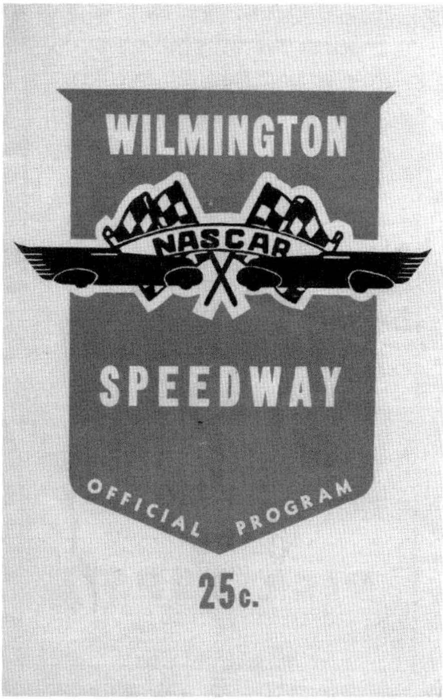

Lou Johnson (left) and Wally Campbell were two of the best racers ever to compete in Delaware. Johnson raced for more than 25 years and went on to win two United Racing Club championships, as well as the 1953 Georgetown Speedway Championship. Campbell won the NASCAR 1951 Modified Championship and was inducted into the Sprint Car Hall of Fame in 2011. (Photograph by Lee Smith, courtesy of the Jeff Hardifer Collection.)

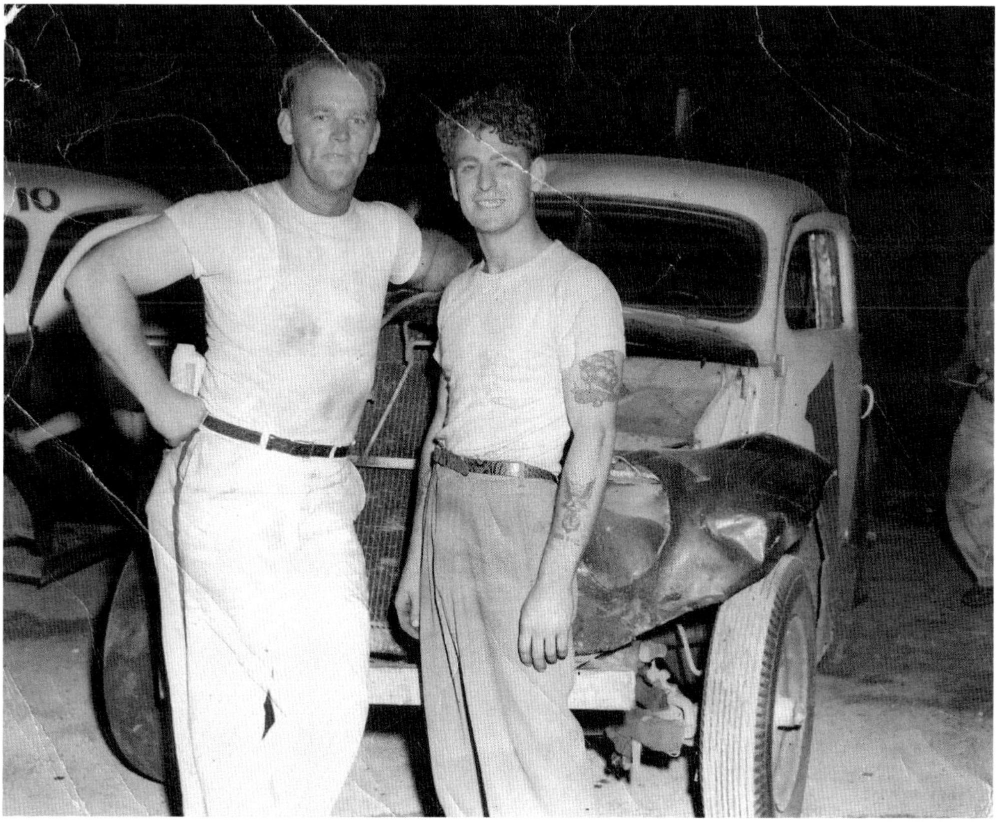

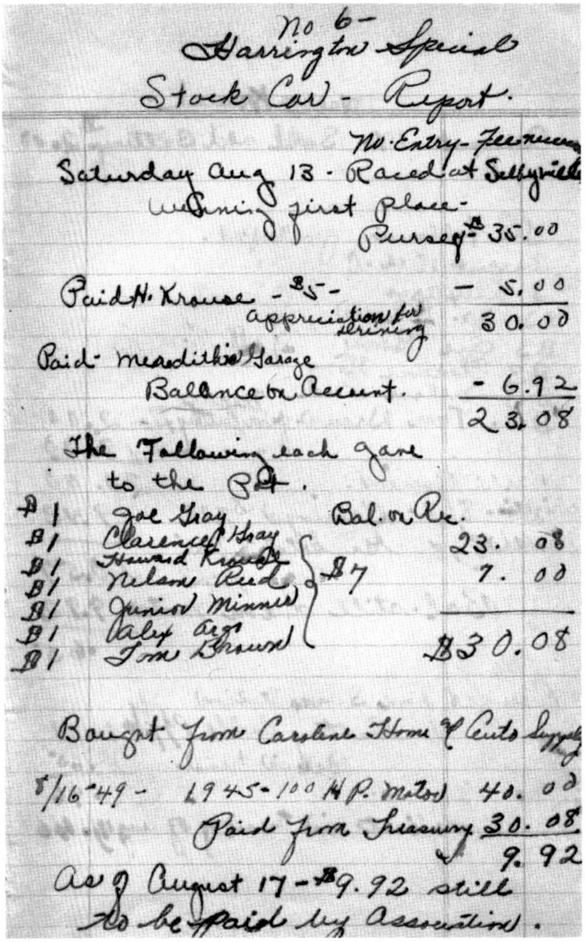

No 6-
Harrington Special
Stock Car - Report.

No. Entry-Fee necessary
Saturday Aug 13 - Raced at Selbyville
winning first place-
Purse $35.00

Paid H. Krouse - $5 - — 5.00
appreciation for driving 30.00
Paid - Meredith's Garage
Ballance on Account. - 6.92
23.08

The Following each gave
to the Pot.
$1 Joe Gray — Bal. on Ac.
$1 Clarence Gray — 23.08
$1 Howard Krouse — $7 — 7.00
$1 Nelson Reed
$1 Junior Minner
$1 [illegible]
$1 Tom Brown — $30.08

Bought from Caroline Home & Auto Supply
8/16-49 - 1945-100 H.P. Motor 40.00
Paid from Treasury 30.08
9.92
As of August 17 - $9.92 still
to be paid by Association.

The log at left shows the beginnings of a race team. In 1949, Tom Brown and family decided to go racing with driver Howard Krouse. The log shows the car winning a purse of $35 from an unidentified track in Selbyville, Delaware. The log also shows the teamwork necessary to compete—all crew members gave $1 to the pot to help defray the cost of racing. Sponsors were hard to come by, and car owners would often pay expenses out of their own pockets and ask friends to help with the cost of running a team. The photograph below shows Tom Brown (with glasses) and proud crew members next to the No. 6, ready to race at Green Tree Raceway. (Both, courtesy of Charlie Brown.)

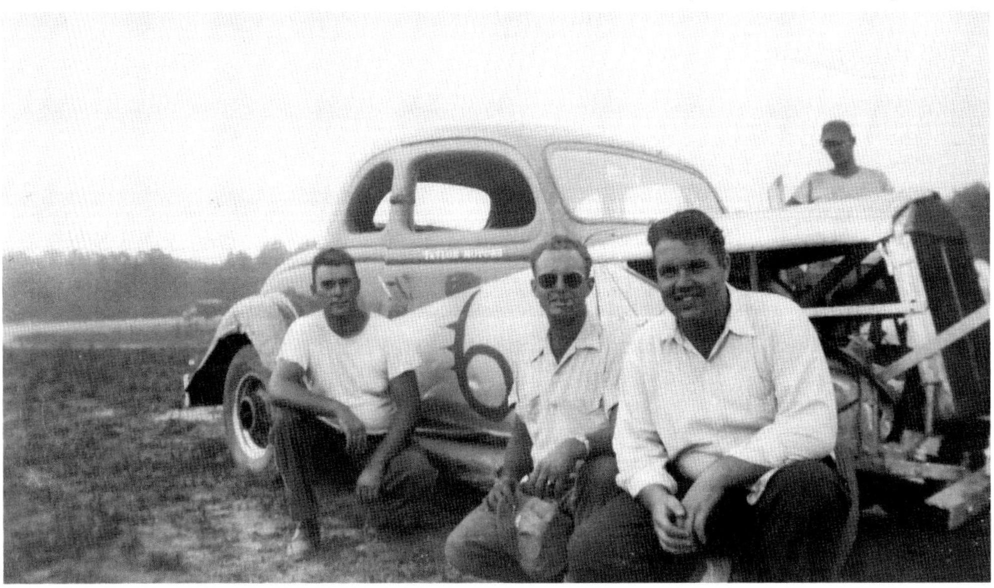

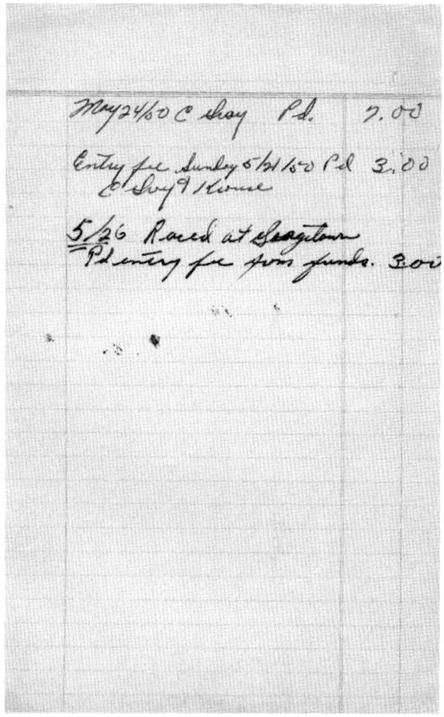

May 24/50 C Gray Pd. 7.00

Entry fee Sunday 5/21/50 Pd 3.00
C Gray 9 House

5/26 Raced at Georgetown
Pd entry fee from funds. 3.00

The last entry in Tom Brown's car log (at right) shows an entry fee of $3 to Georgetown Speedway in 1950. This was the final entry in the log for car No. 6. The photograph below shows crew member Joe Gray looking through the driver's-side window to survey the damage after a horrific wreck at Georgetown Speedway. Amazingly, the driver walked away unscathed; however, car No. 6 was a total loss. Note the lack of safety equipment inside the car. (Both, courtesy of Charlie Brown.)

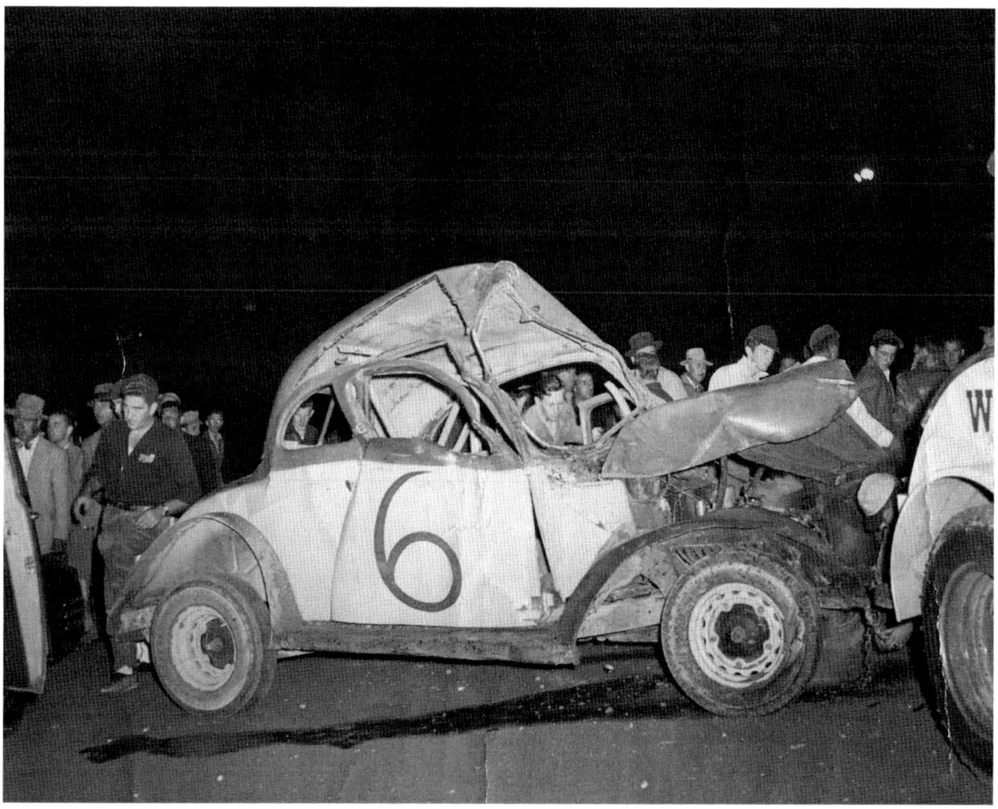

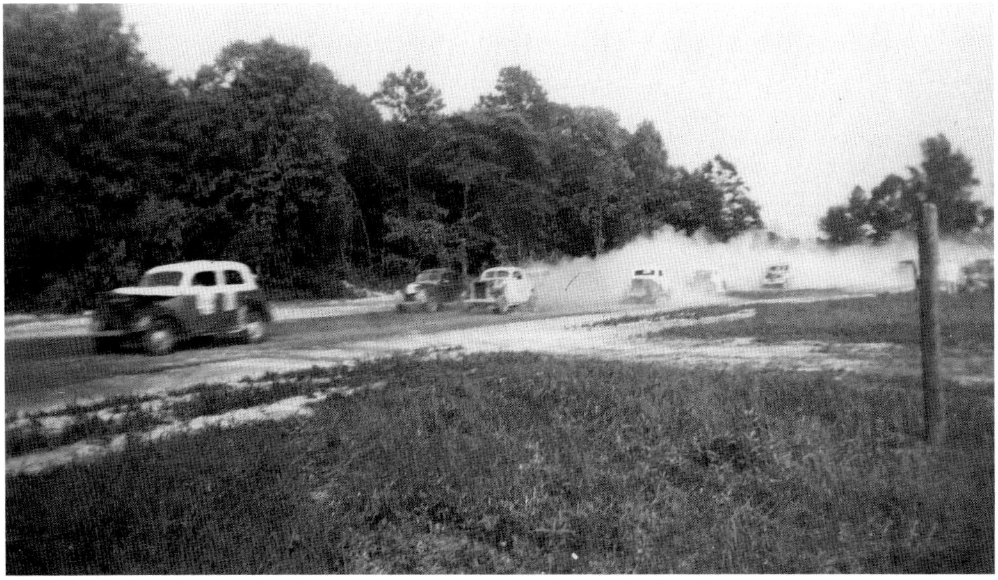

Dust clouds like the one seen here were the bane of both drivers and fans. Dusty tracks made it dangerous for drivers and impossible for fans to witness the action. At Green Tree, drivers could easily drive into the woods, as there were no walls or fences around the track. (Courtesy of Charlie Brown.)

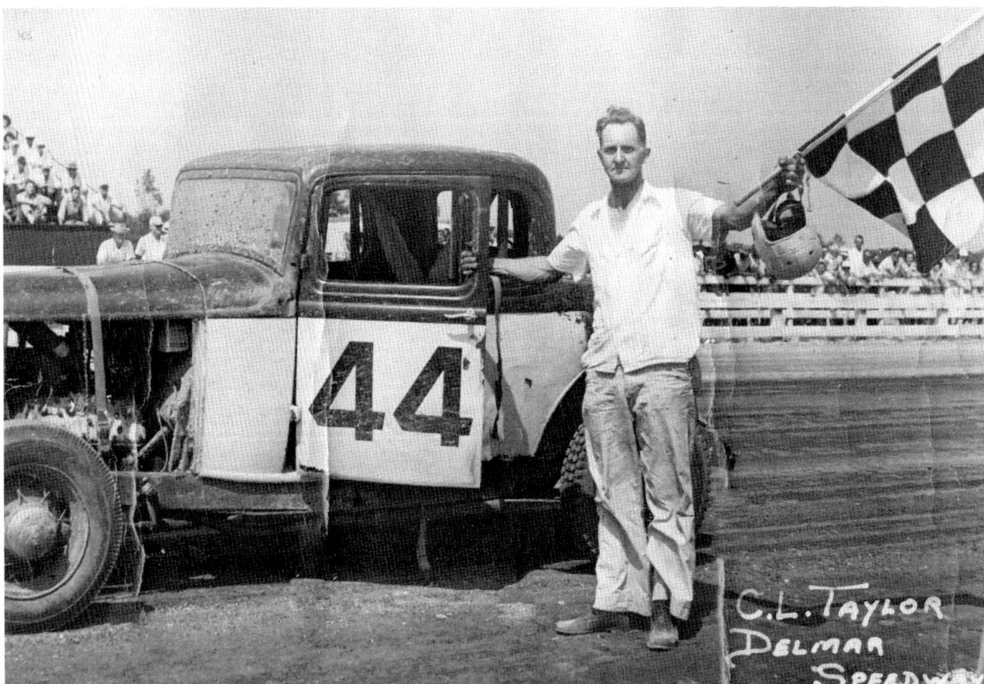

C.L. Taylor is pictured with the checkered flag at Delmar Speedway. "Pop" Taylor, as he was often called, would drive his race car to the track instead of towing it; after the races, he simply drove it home. (Courtesy of Louis O'Neal.)

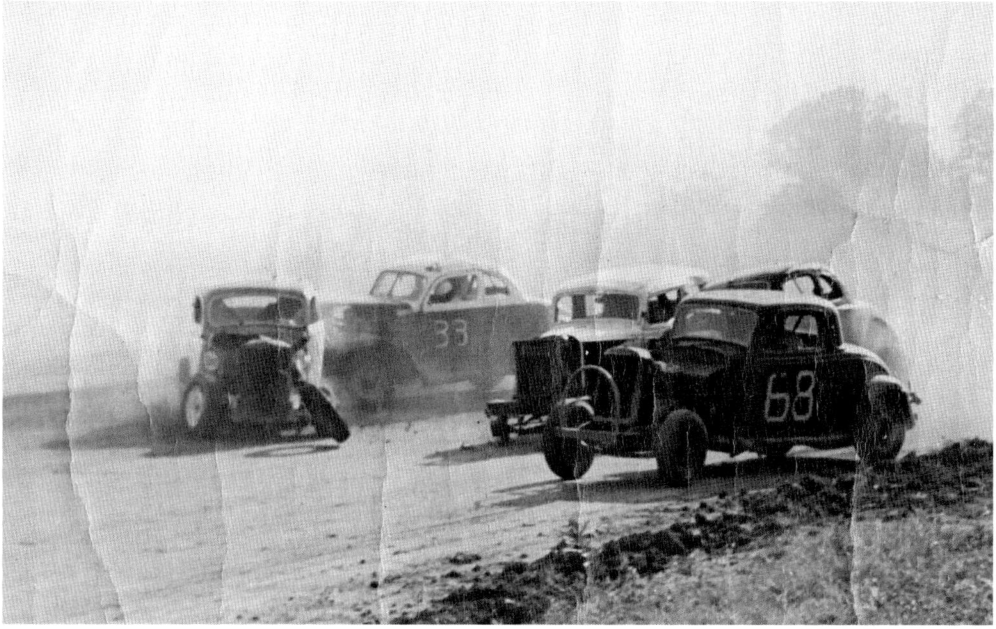

Cars pile up quickly in this photograph of Myers Speedway, and at least two racers have lost their front wheels. Often, dust was so bad that what would have been a one-car spin often became a multicar pileup. (Courtesy of Louis O'Neal.)

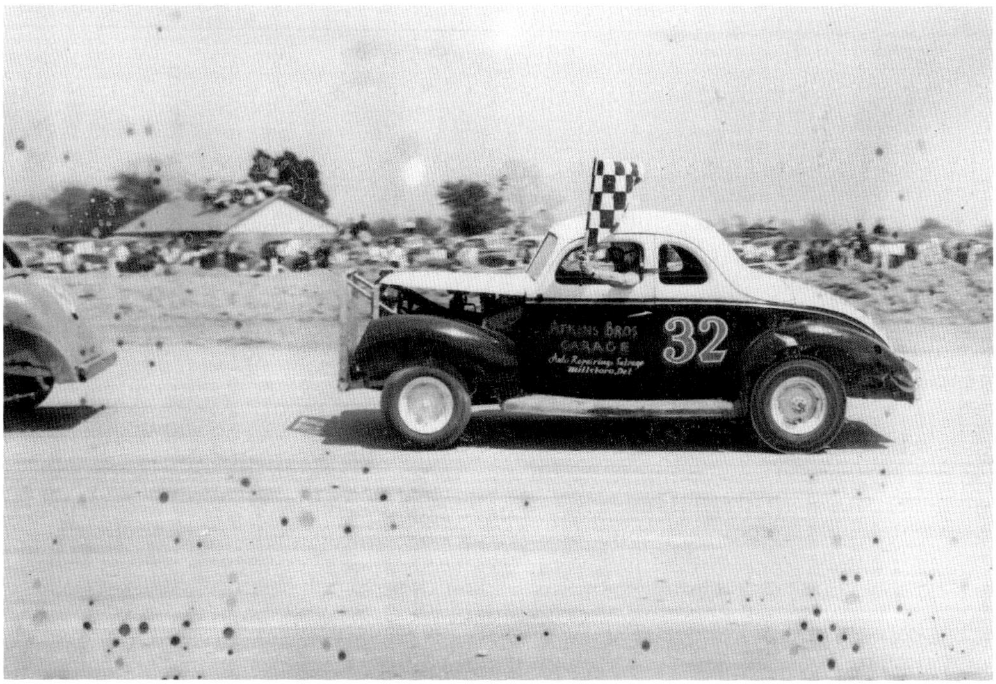

The 1940 Ford has a cultlike following. Legendary for its ability to haul moonshine, the car quickly became the choice of many racers. The No. 32 car driven by Bob Atkins is a great example of an early 1940 Ford Modified. (Courtesy of Louis O'Neal.)

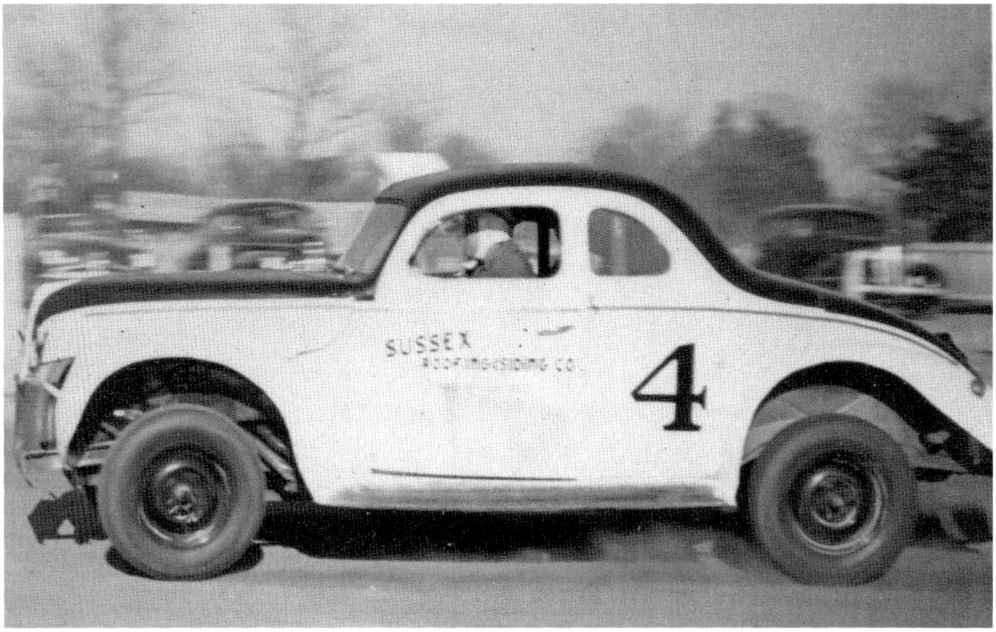

Doc Williamson slides his 1940 Ford through the turn at Myers Speedway. Spectators' cars line the outside of the turn, with little more than a picket fence between the people and the speeding racers. (Courtesy of Louis O'Neal.)

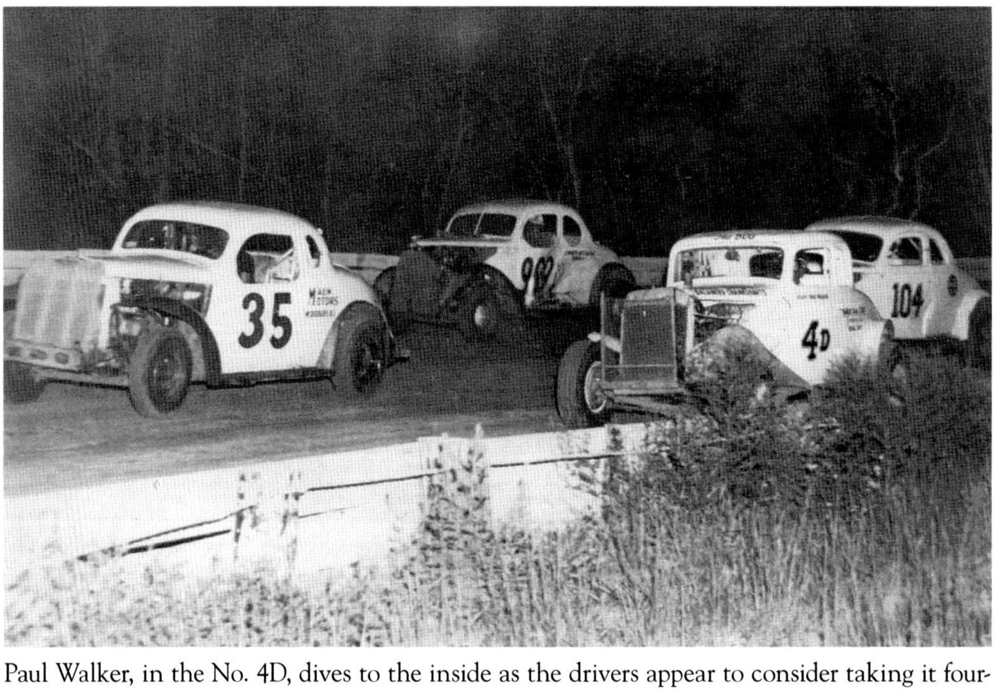

Paul Walker, in the No. 4D, dives to the inside as the drivers appear to consider taking it four-wide in the corner. The styles of the cars may have changed over the years, but the skill and determination it takes to drive a car on the absolute limit remains the same today as when racing first started. (Courtesy of Paul Mills.)

In the photograph below, drivers get the "one to go" signal at the Delaware State Fairgrounds Speedway in Harrington. Flagman Tom Brown wears the jacket of the Delaware Stock Car Racing Association; DSCRA was just one of the sanctioning bodies that hosted stock car races in the area. At right is a program for the day's events that features a listing of the top drivers of the era. The race, held on September 4, 1950 (Labor Day), benefitted the Harrington Fire and Ambulance Fund. (Right, courtesy of Louis O'Neal; below, courtesy of Charlie Brown.)

NO.	DRIVER	OWNER	ADDRESS
47	Bill Walker	Fed. Pest Controll	Milford, Del.
5	Dick Mundorf	Mitchells Hatchery	Millsboro, "
78	Carey Williams	Lane Bros.	Florida
7	Bob Long	Duncan Bros.	Pocomoke, Md.
38	Norris Reed	Henry Bros.	Denton, "
44	C. L. Taylor	C. L. Taylor	Delmar, Del.
75	Jack Jones	Hasting Bros.	Salisbury, Md.
74	Norwood Ellingsworth	N. Ellingsworth	Frankford, Del.
30	Paul Bennington	J. Mills	Milford, Del.
3	Buck Hopkins	W. & D. Motors	" "
11	L. Clendaniel	L. Clendaniel	Frankford, Del.
65	J. Mundorf	J. Mundorf	Millsboro, "
81	E. Short	J. Hastings	Georgetown, "
21	P. Walker	Moore Chev. Ser.	Lewes, "
19	Bob Tice	R. Wallace	Baltimore, Md.
77	G. Betts	G. Betts	Stokely, Del.
41	H. Williams	Joe Komorowski	Milford, "
1	Bill Scott	Geo. Bowers	Salisbury, Md.
2	Slim Christinsen	Cannons Garage	Milford, Del.
9	H. Kohland	H.Kohland	Harrington, Del.
24	R. Sammons	R. Sammons	Seaford, "
11x	Jim Hayes	E. Calhoun	Seaford, "
18	P. Fowler	B. Parker	Georgetown, Del.
45	A. Adkins	Adkins Bros.	Millsboro, "
32	J. Matin	B. Adkins	" "
22	Henry Short	H. Short	Lincoln, "
15	D. Carey	D. Carey	Stokely, "
13	Bob Burkhart	Bob Burkhart	Wilmington, "
66	R. Sherman	Mathews Motors	Pocomoke, Md
8	C. Mulholland	J. Bowers	Milford, Del.
29	Oliver West	E. Clark	Pittsville, Md.
49	J. Stulfus	M. Joseph	Georgetown, Del.
6	Howard Krouse	Brown & Gray	Harrington, "

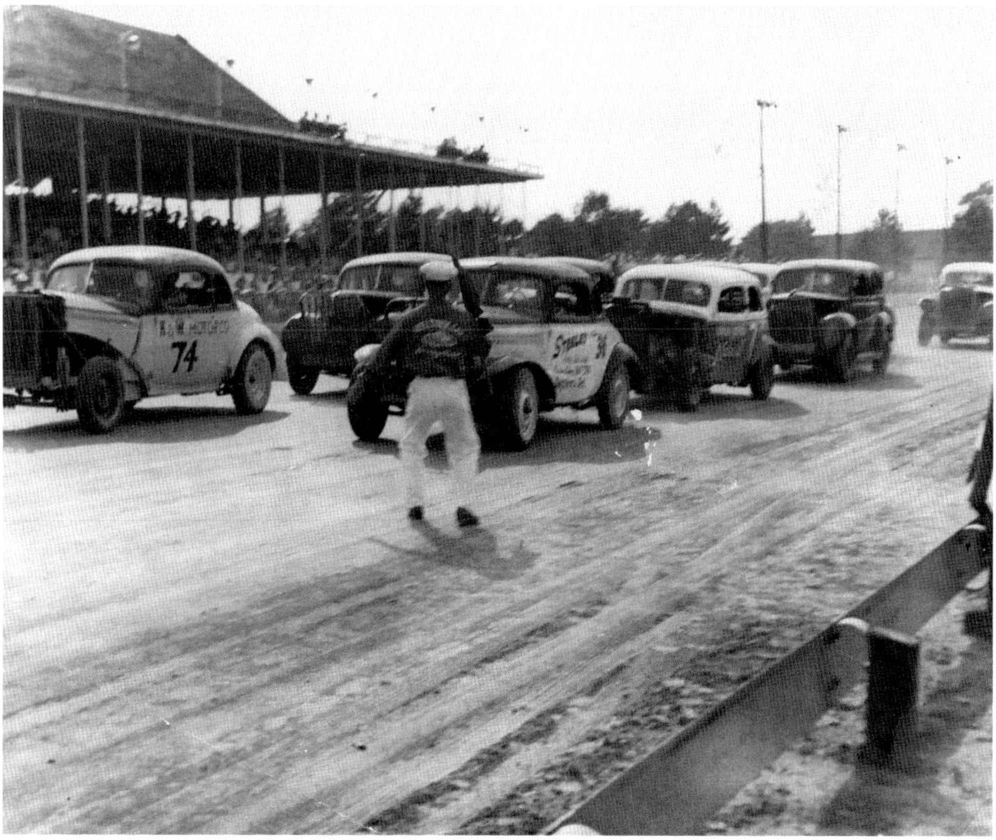

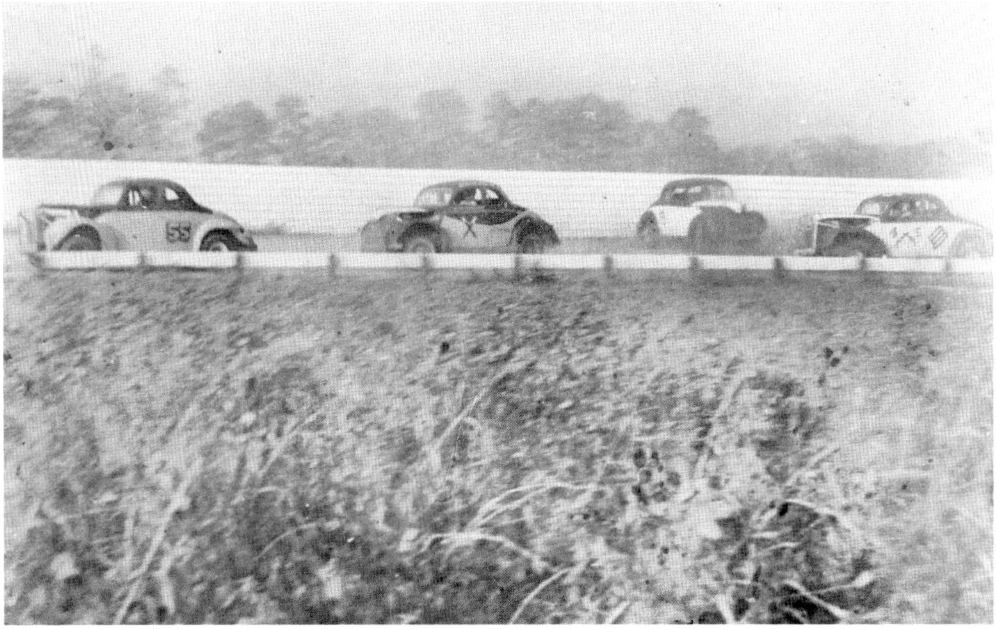

In this image, four 1940 Ford Modifieds travel around the Delaware State Fairgrounds racetrack. Many race cars have crashed through the backstretch wall and onto Fairground Road, which is located directly behind the wall. (Courtesy of David Grey.)

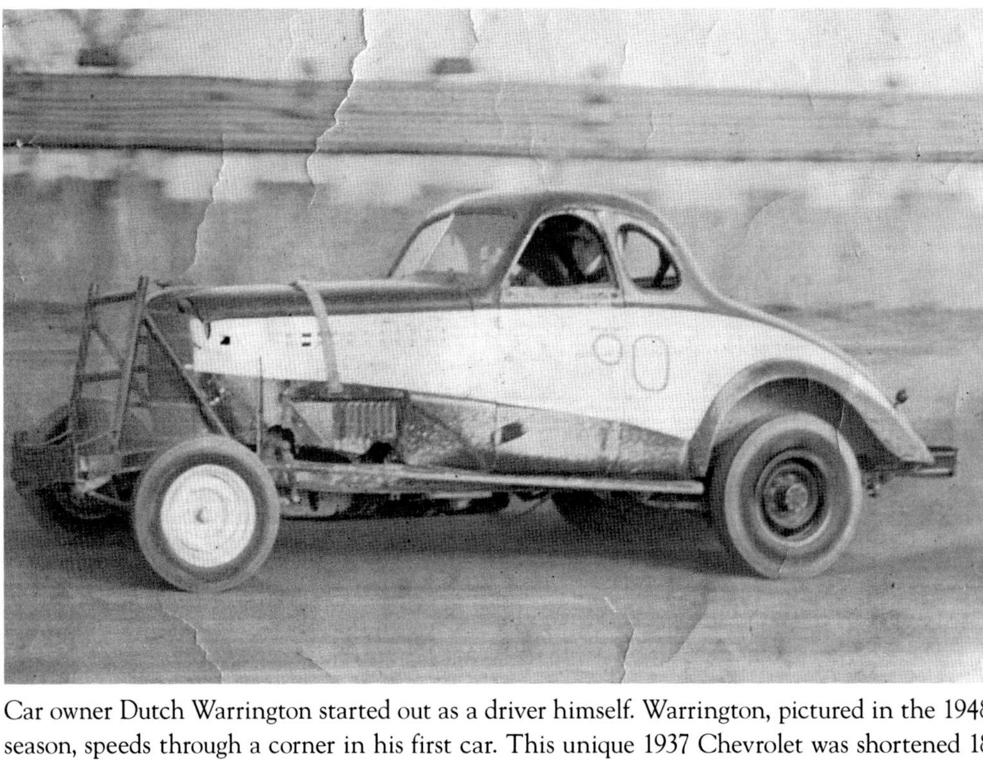

Car owner Dutch Warrington started out as a driver himself. Warrington, pictured in the 1948 season, speeds through a corner in his first car. This unique 1937 Chevrolet was shortened 18 inches in length to improve its handling. (Courtesy of Butch Warrington.)

Many Delawareans remember Parker Bohn of New Jersey and his famous No. 659 Modified race car. Powered by a 302-cubic-inch straight-six engine, this unique car won many races in Delaware. Stories have been told of the huge flames that shot from the exhaust when Bohn let off the throttle to enter corners. (Courtesy of Louis O'Neal.)

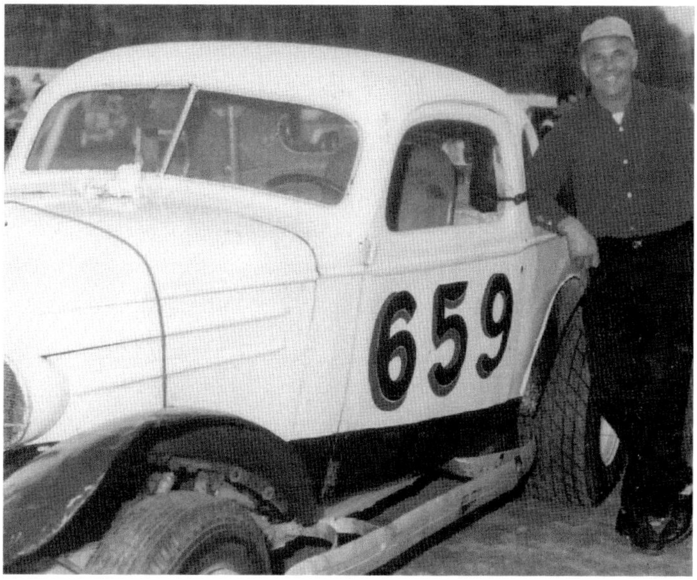

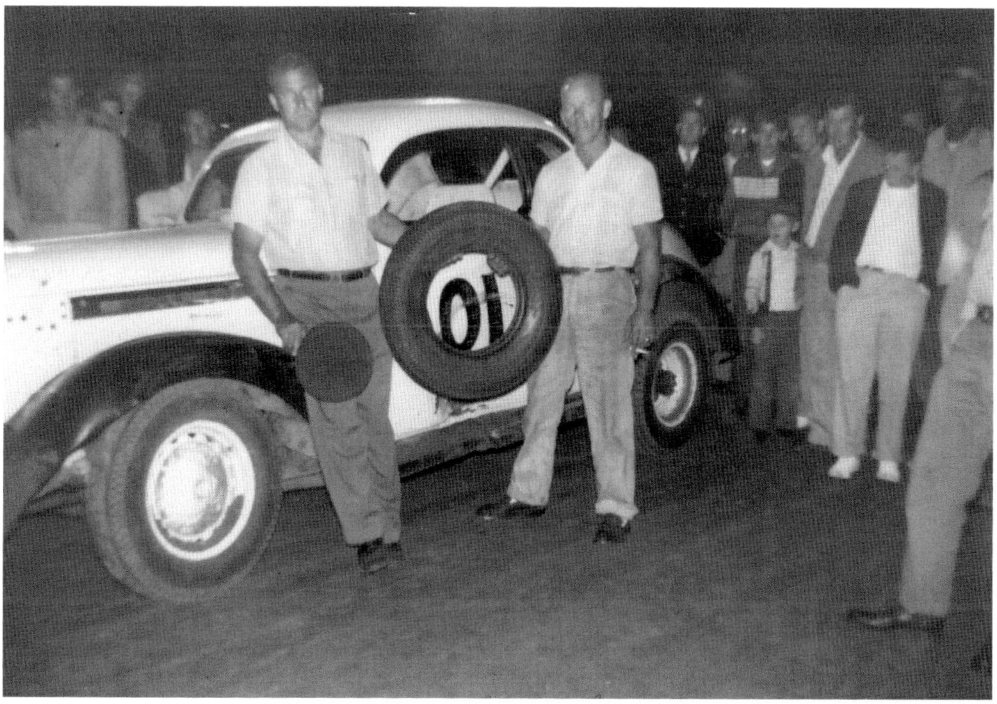

Walt Messick (left) and race winner Lou Johnson hold a new tire—a bonus for winning the night's feature. Messick was a great friend of racing, and his business, Taylor & Messick, which was founded in 1951, has sponsored several cars and many races over the years. (Courtesy of Charlie Brown.)

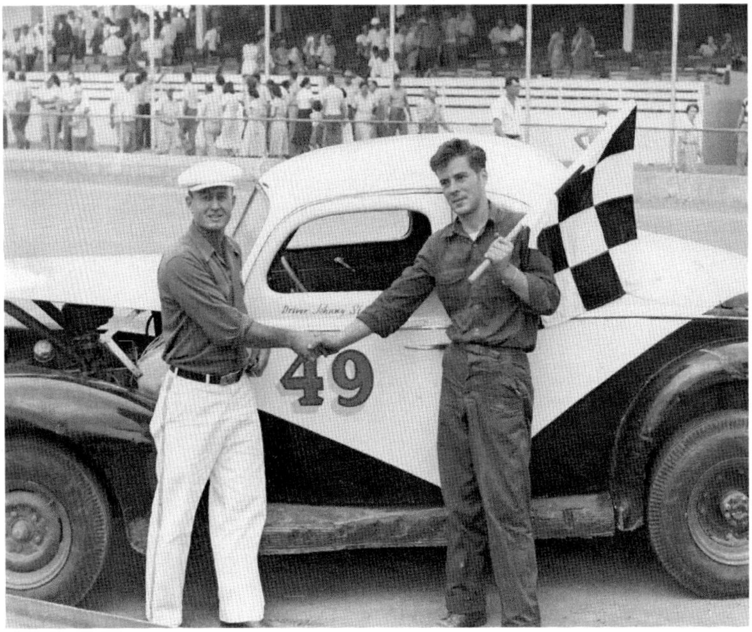

As the crowd disperses to enjoy the fair at Harrington, Tom Brown (left) shakes the hand of Johnny Stoltzfus after his victory in the Melvin Joseph–owned No. 49. (Courtesy of Charlie Brown.)

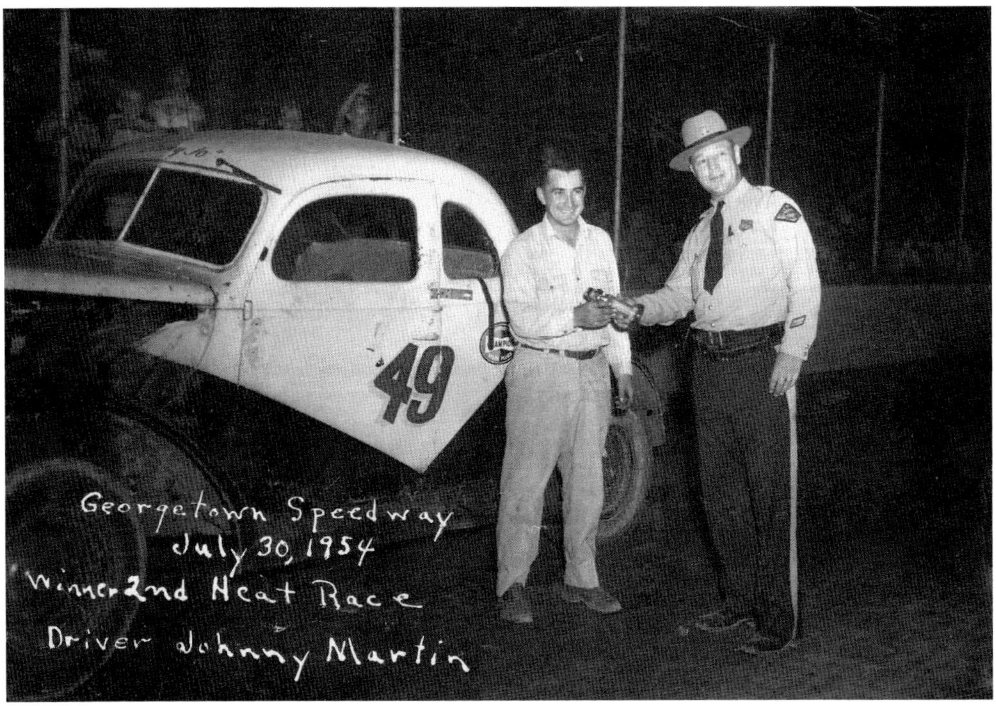

An unidentified Delaware state trooper presents Johnny Martin with a trophy for a Modified heat win. Martin was driving the No. 49 Modified owned by Melvin Joseph. One wonders how many of the children looking through the fence went on to become race car drivers themselves. (Courtesy of Melvin Joseph Jr.)

Horace Williams Sr. wears the helmet of the famous Niblett Brothers–sponsored No. 3D Modified, which was owned by Howard Davis of Seaford, Delaware. Williams was a popular local racer from Bridgeville. (Courtesy of Horace Williams Jr.)

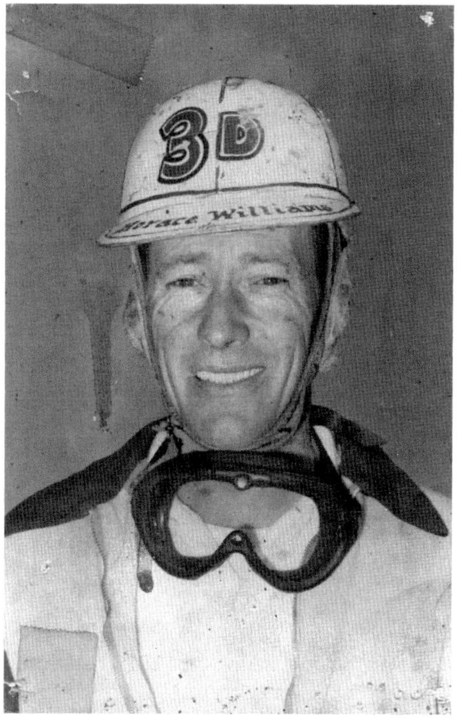

Dutch Warrington (left) fielded cars for some of the best drivers in the Mid-Atlantic area. Vince Conrad, Bill Raughley, Johnny Martin, and Harold Bunting all drove for Warrington at some point in their careers. (Courtesy of Butch Warrington.)

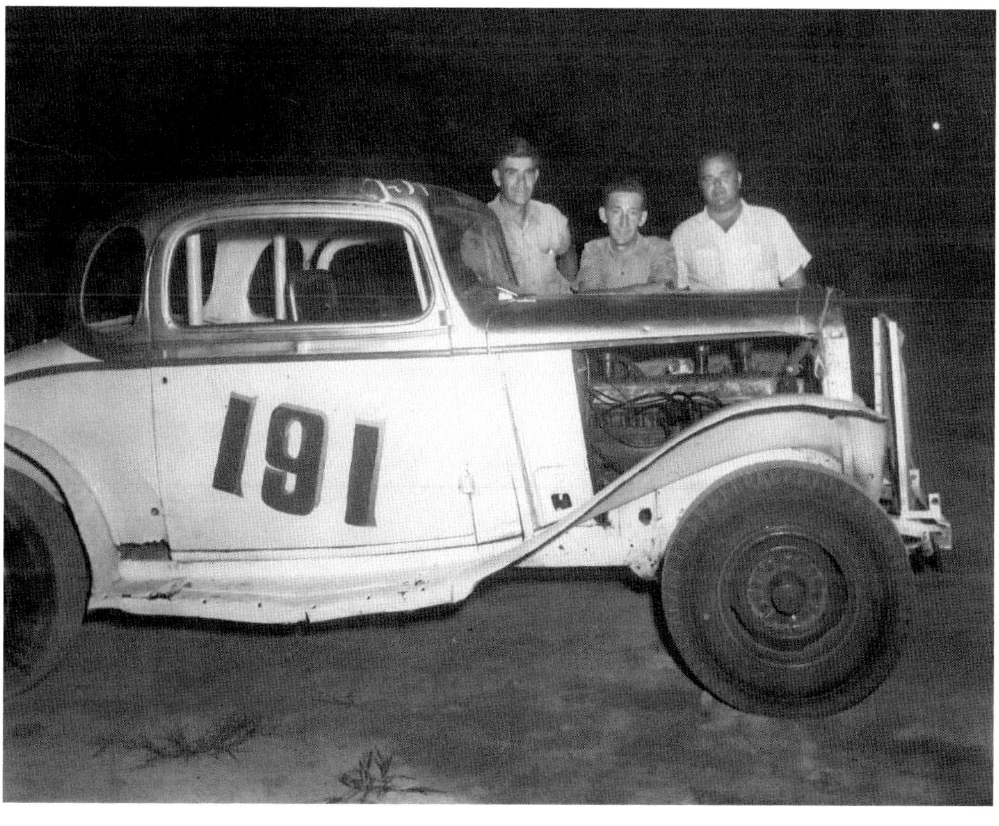

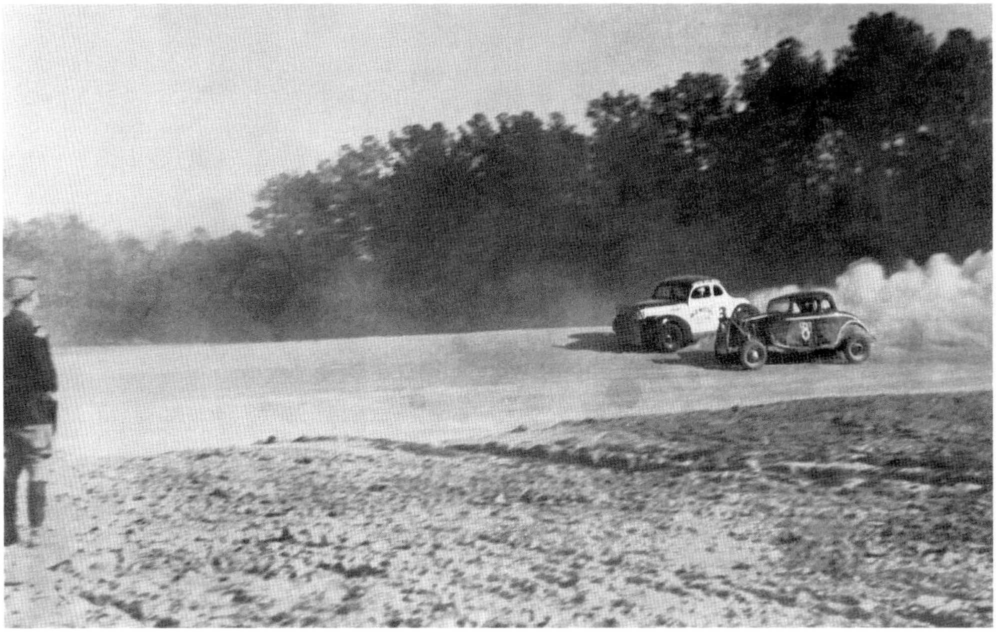

Auto racing in the 1950s was one of the most exciting events a spectator could witness in person. One can only imagine what must be going through this young boy's head as he watches these racers blast by at unheard-of speeds at Georgetown. (Courtesy of David Grey.)

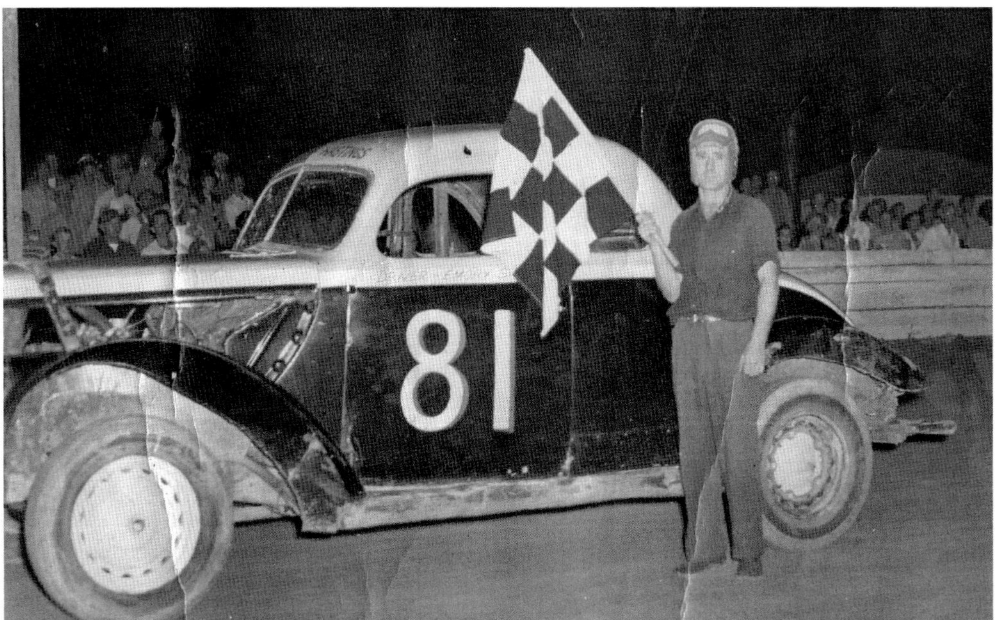

Emory Short sports a helmet and goggles in this victory photograph. Both the passenger door and hood of the car are lashed shut with leather belts—a far cry from today's Modifieds, which require that the driver slide through an opening in the side and sit in the center of the car. (Courtesy of Louis O'Neal.)

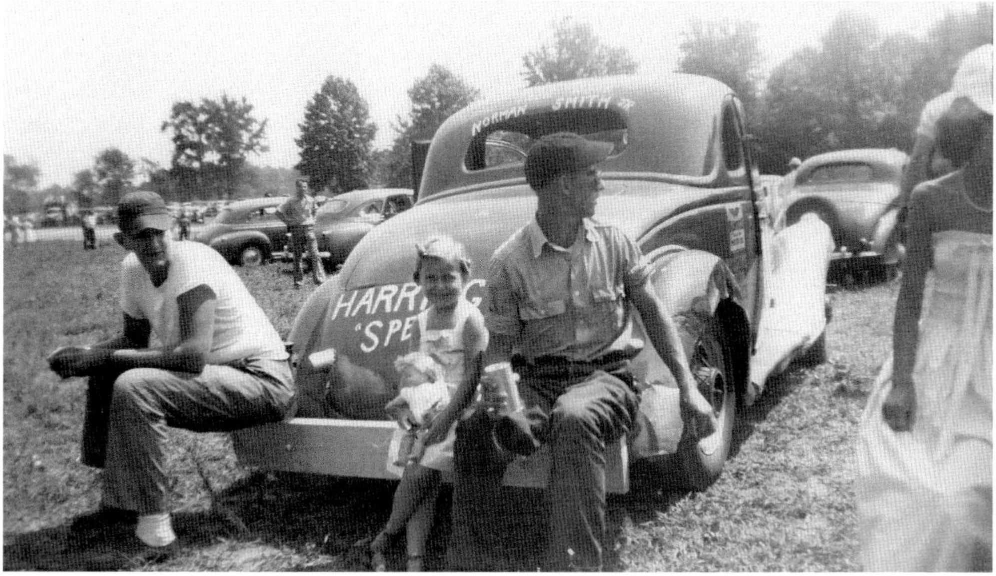

Members and fans relax on the infield of Green Tree Raceway. Back then, going to the races was a special event. While those working on the cars donned everyday clothes, spectators often wore their best outfits to the track—such as the little girl on the bumper and the woman at right. (Courtesy of Charlie Brown.)

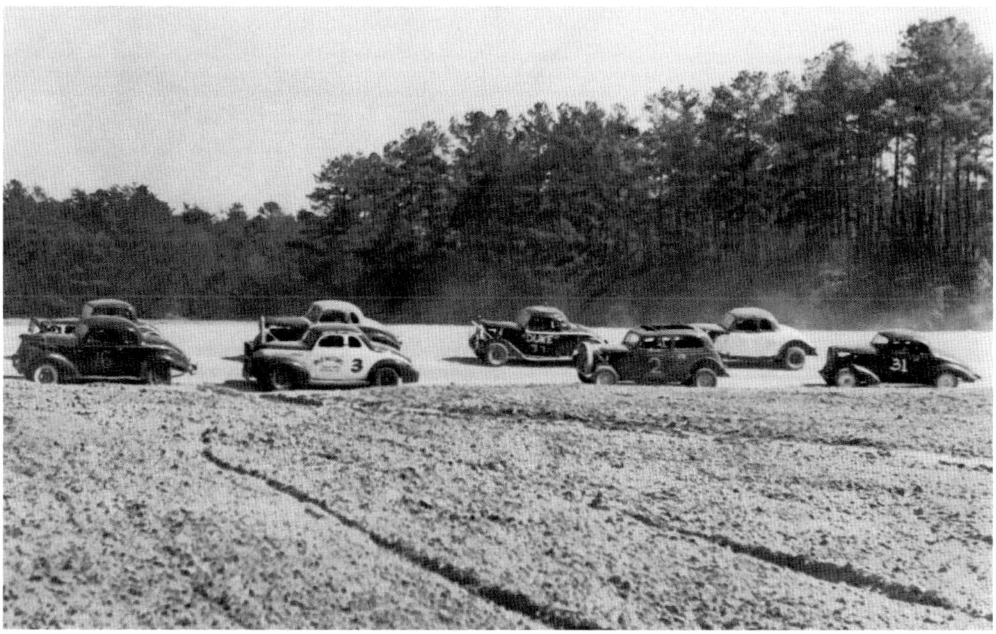

In what is thought to be an extremely early photograph from Georgetown Speedway, cars line up to take the green flag. Georgetown Speedway was NASCAR-sanctioned in its early days; however, this photograph was likely taken before that endorsement. Note that the No. 2 car has a hole in the metal roof. Early NASCAR rules required a complete steel roof over the driver's head. (Courtesy of David Grey.)

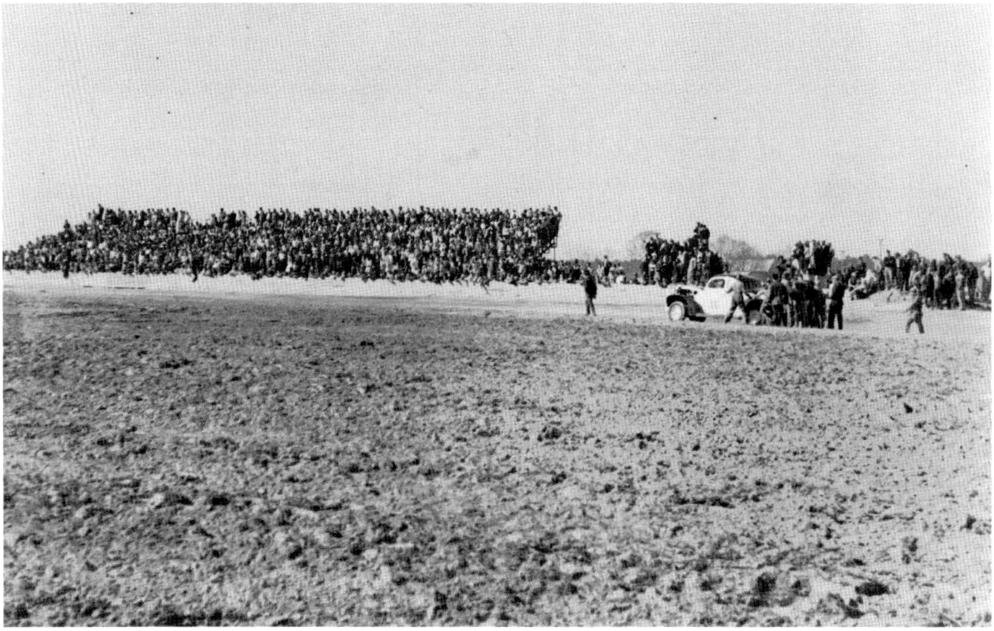

A packed house prepares to watch the action at the new Georgetown Speedway. In this photograph, plow marks are still visible on the infield of the speedway. As at most early dirt tracks, people gathered dangerously close to the track to get the best view. Here, many stand next to the track with little or no protection. (Courtesy of David Grey.)

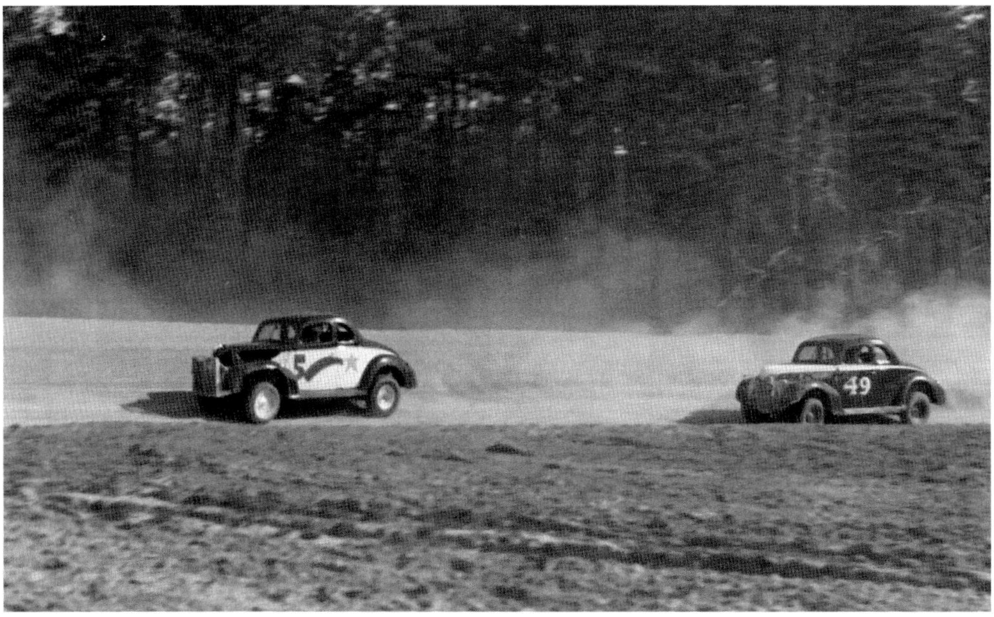

In this photograph, Johnny Martin's No. 5 leads the way, with the Melvin Joseph–owned No. 49 close behind. Sunday races at Georgetown could draw crowds of over 3,000 people in the 1950s. Cars often averaged 65 miles per hour on the half-mile track and hit over 100 miles per hour on the straightaways. (Courtesy of David Grey.)

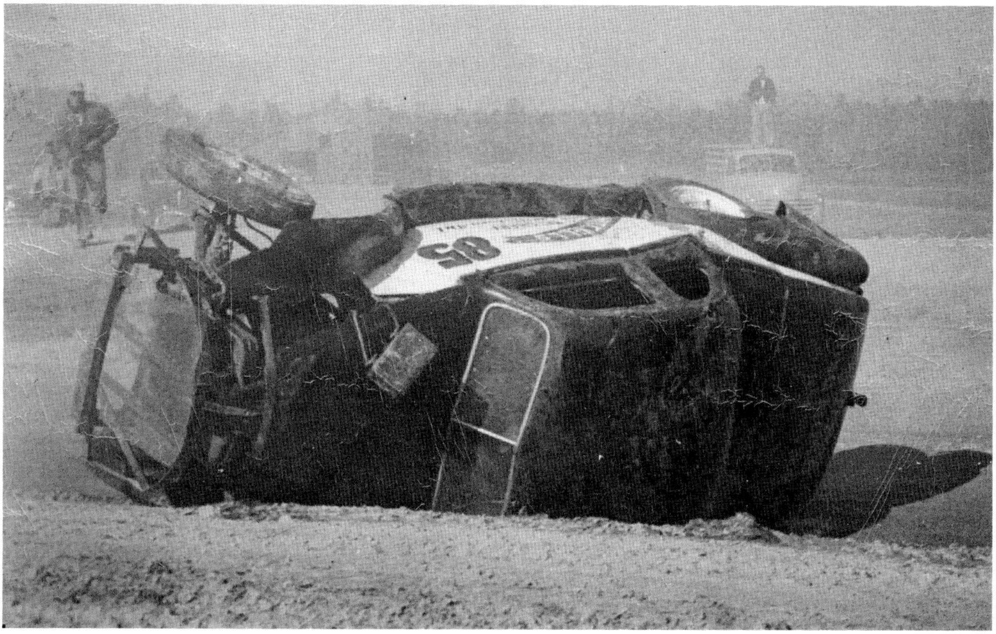

The Mitchell's Hatchery–sponsored car driven by Dick Mundorf takes a spill at Myers Speedway in Bridgeville. At left, a concerned crew member runs to the car. In the early days of stock car racing, when there was an accident, the crew—if not all of the crews in the pits—ran out to provide assistance. (Courtesy of Louis O'Neal.)

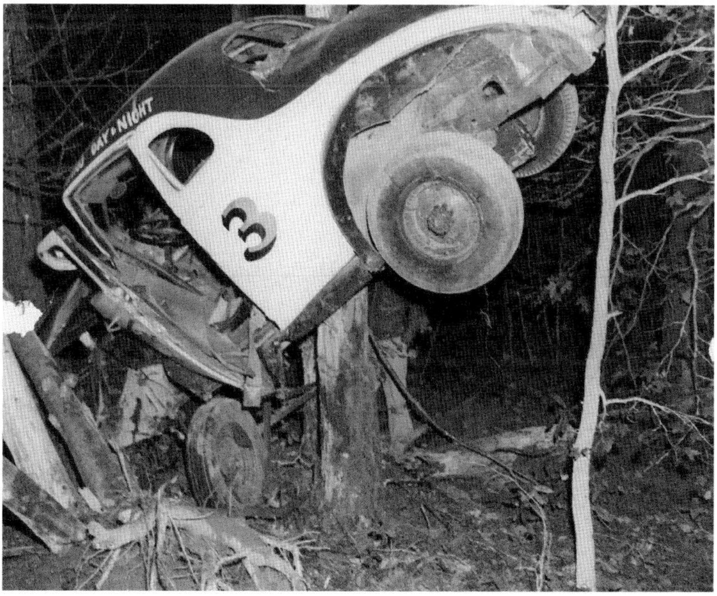

Pushing the limits of these machines sometimes ended in disaster, as shown in this image from Georgetown Speedway. Driver "Buck" Hopkins was fortunate to walk away from this horrible wreck with just a broken arm. Inside the car, an early roll cage is visible, along with a seat belt hanging from the car. (Courtesy of Louis O'Neal.)

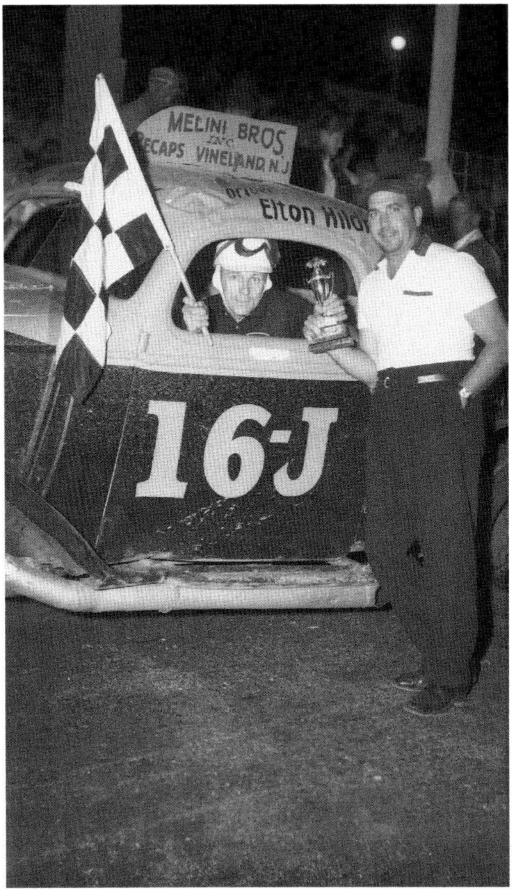

Elton Hildreth, with his car in Victory Lane, accepts the trophy from promoter Bill Nocco at Wilmington Speedway in 1958. (Courtesy of the Walt Chernokal Collection, Racemaker Archive.)

Dutch Warrington's No. 191 was one of the few local cars to make the trip to the Daytona Beach races. Here, Warrington (far left) and the crew take a break from preparing the car before the big event. (Courtesy of Butch Warrington.)

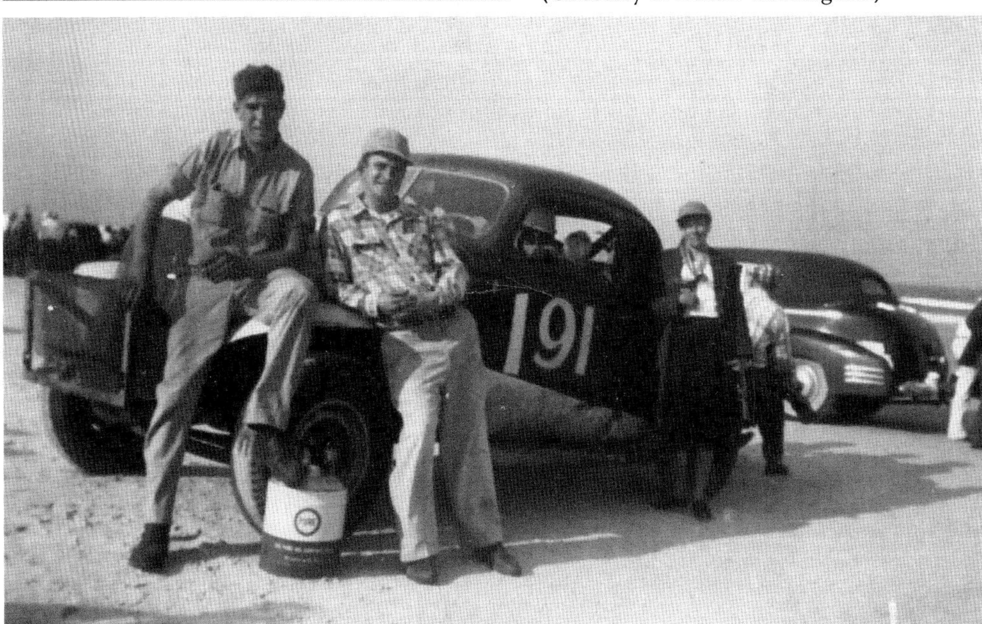

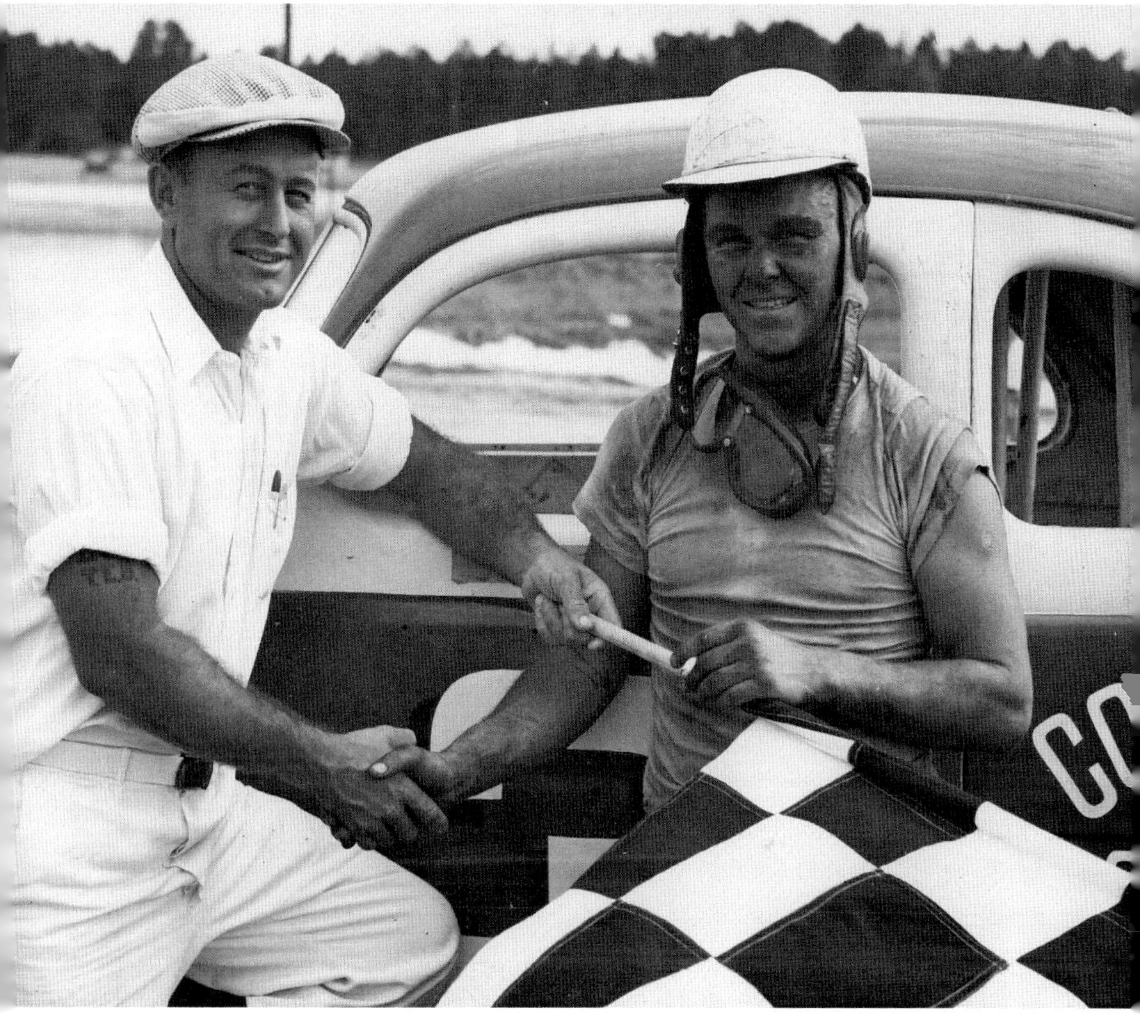

In this 1953 image, Frankie Schneider (right) accepts the checkered flag from flagman Tom Brown at Delmar Speedway. Schneider was from Sergeantsville, New Jersey, and often made the trip to the lower Delaware race tracks. He earned his nickname, "The Old Master," because of his ability to "master" anything with wheels. (Courtesy of Charlie Brown.)

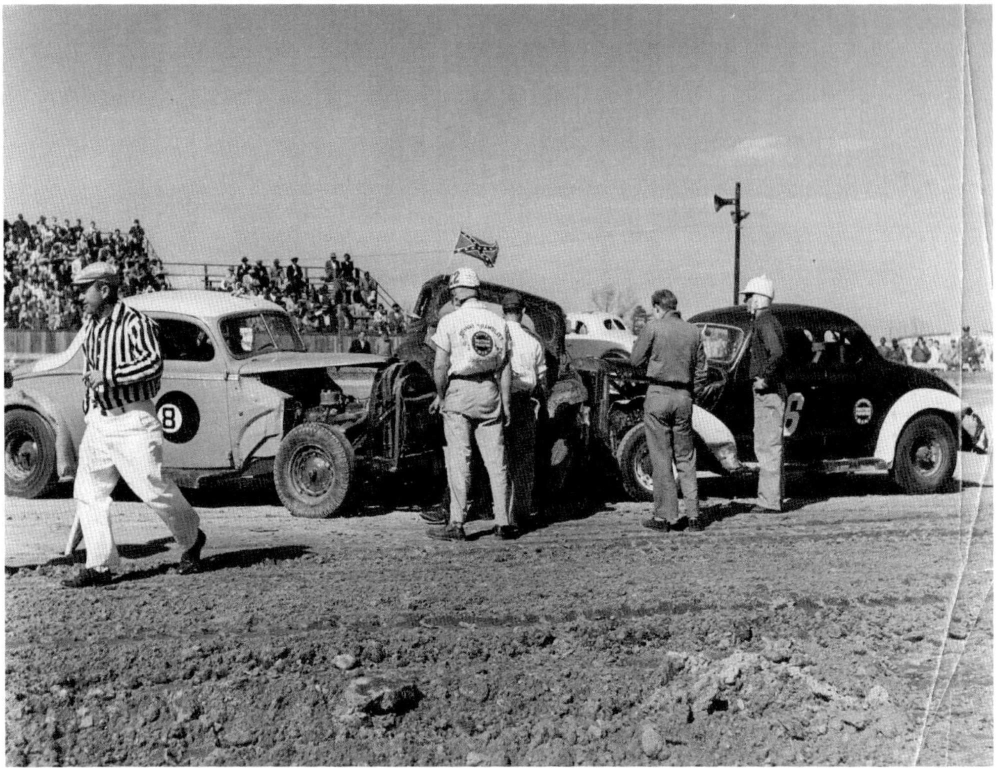

Drivers assess the damage to their cars after a wreck at Delmar in the early 1950s. Johnny Cramblitt's No. 22 car, sandwiched between the other two, appears to have sustained the most damage. (Courtesy of Charlie Brown.)

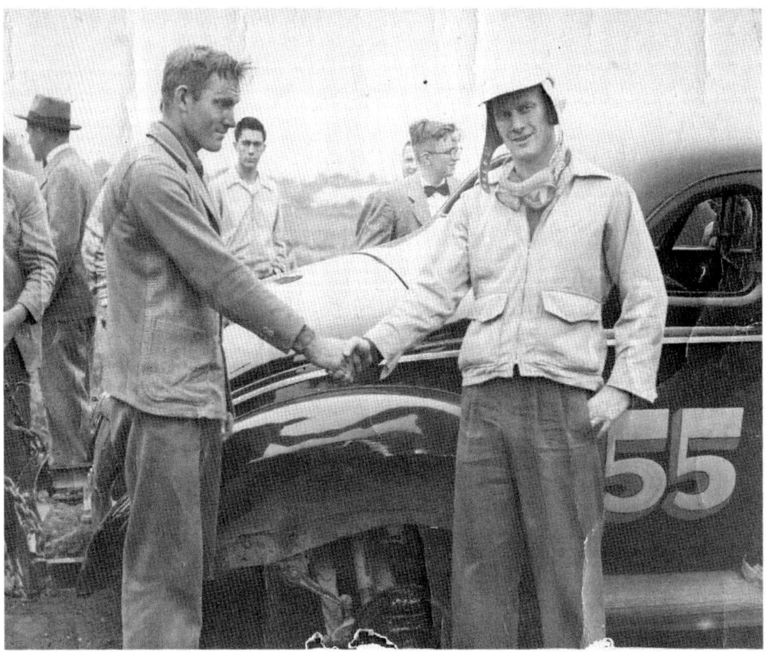

Racers have always had a mutual respect for one another. The right rear of the No. 55 car, visible below the men's hands, seems to be in bad shape. Since tow chains are hooked to the car, one could assume that these two are making amends for a racing incident. (Courtesy of Louis O'Neal.)

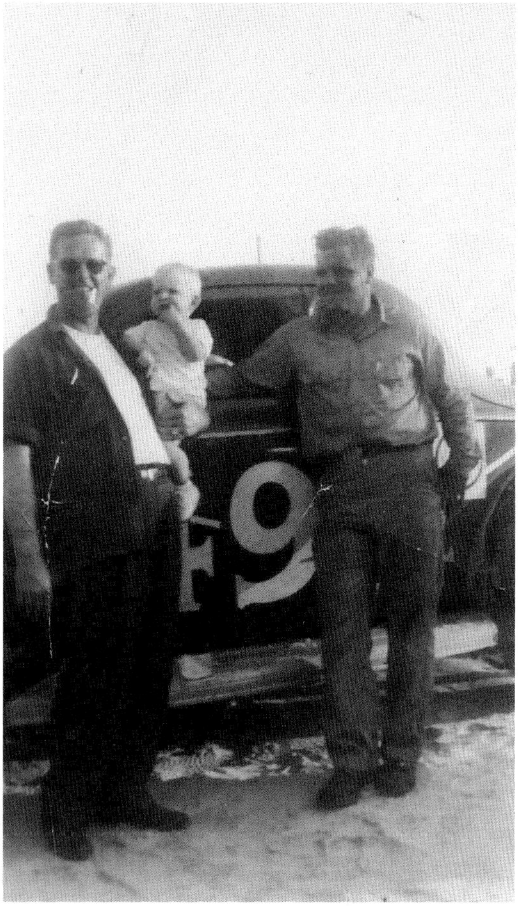

Car owner Melvin Joseph (left), Melvin Joseph Jr. (center), and driver Banjo Matthews are next to the 1955 Modified Race–winning car at Daytona Beach. The car was named "Mel Jr."—the moniker was painted over the top of the windshield. The team won $900 for averaging 98.04 miles per hour on the 4.2-mile road-and-beach course. (Courtesy of Joe Ann Adams, representing the Melvin Joseph family.)

A selected few Delaware racers and owners made the trip to race the hallowed sand of Daytona Beach, Florida. The 4.2-mile course went down Highway A1A to the south turn and returned on the sands of the beach. Here, the Melvin Joseph–owned No. 49 races towards the north turn. (Courtesy of Joe Ann Adams, representing the Melvin Joseph family.)

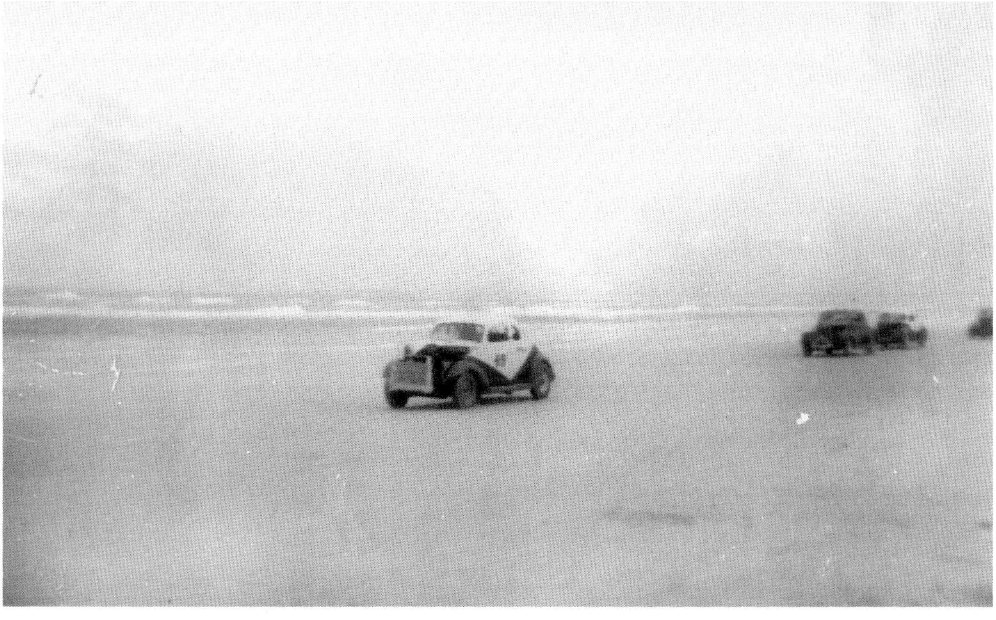

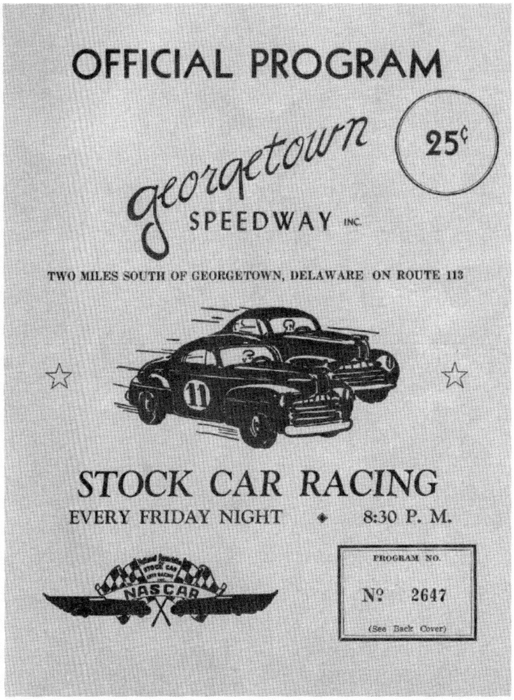

This program from Georgetown Speedway advertises NASCAR-sanctioned racing every Friday night. For just 25¢, fans got a program that contained a driver's list, some driver biographies, a timing sheet, and advertisements for local racing supporters. Many got the programs autographed by their favorite driver to keep as a souvenir. (Courtesy of Louis O'Neal.)

Ken Marriott accepts the winner's trophy at the 1953 Camp Barnes Benefit Stock Car race at Georgetown Speedway. The Delaware State Police started Camp Barnes in 1947 as a summer youth camp. Today, the race is held at Delaware International Speedway and attracts large crowds and the best drivers from up and down the East Coast. (Courtesy of Charlie Brown.)

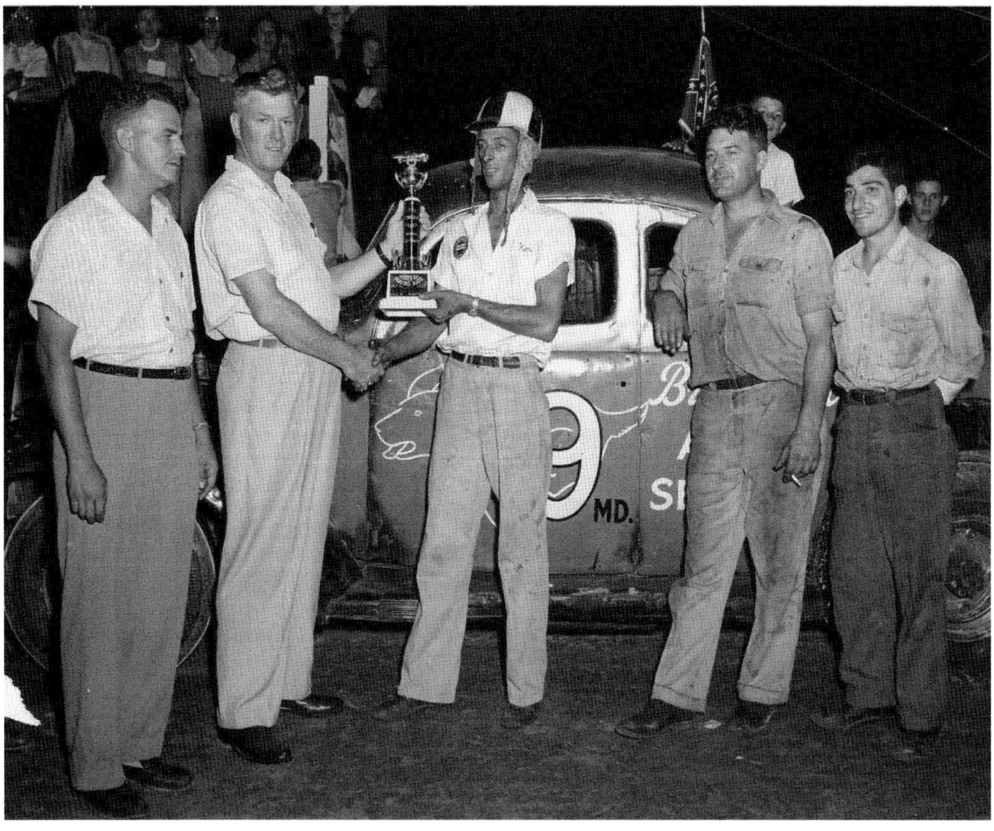

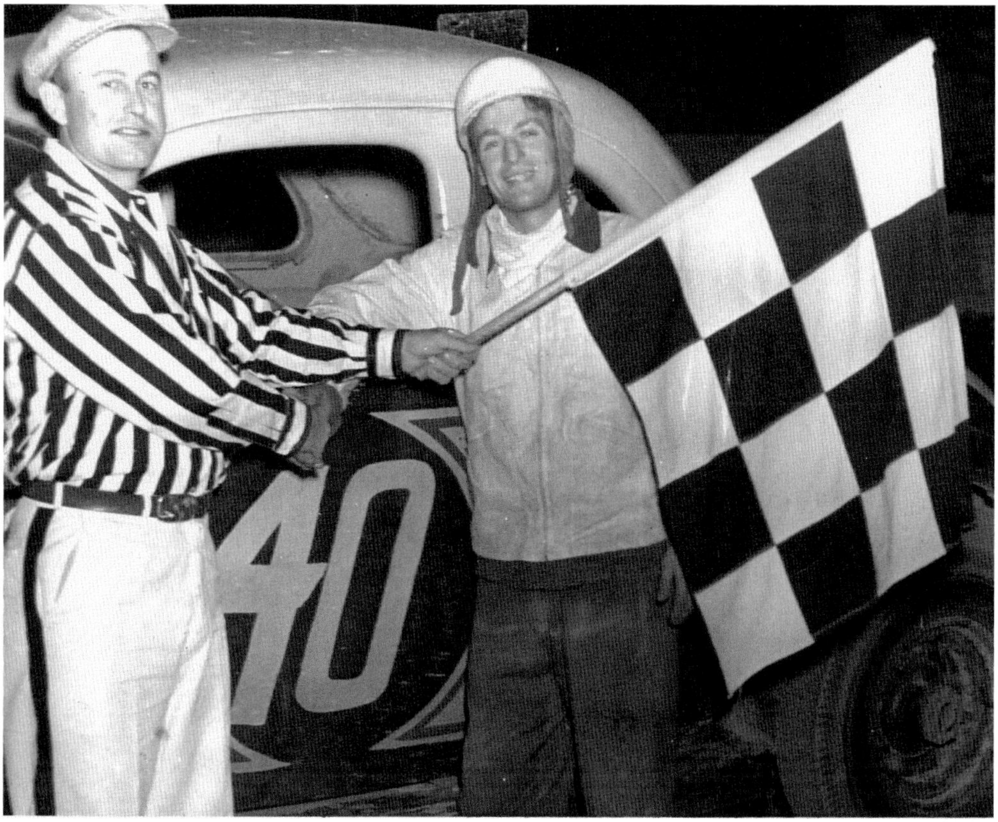

Driver Wally Campbell accepts the checkered flag from Tom Brown. Campbell was one of the most talented drivers to sit behind the wheel of a race car. This victory came at Georgetown Speedway in 1951. He won the 10-mile race with a time of 9 minutes and 26 seconds. Tragically, Campbell's career was cut short when he was killed in a Sprint Car wreck during practice in Salem, Indiana, on July 17, 1954, just one day after his 28th birthday. (Courtesy of Charlie Brown.)

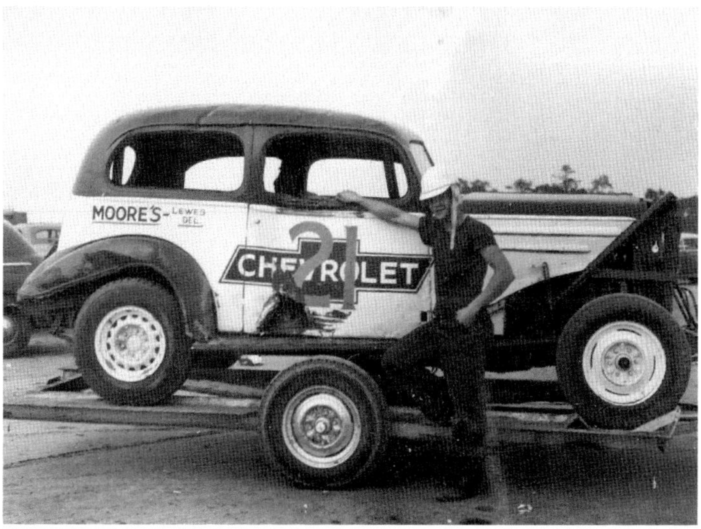

Paul Walker, of Lewes, Delaware, scored 274 National Modified points in 1953. He is pictured in the victory lane at Georgetown Speedway next to the No. 21 Modified. Walker went on to much success at other tracks—such as Little Lincoln at Lincoln, Delaware—in the No. 4. (Courtesy of Louis O'Neal.)

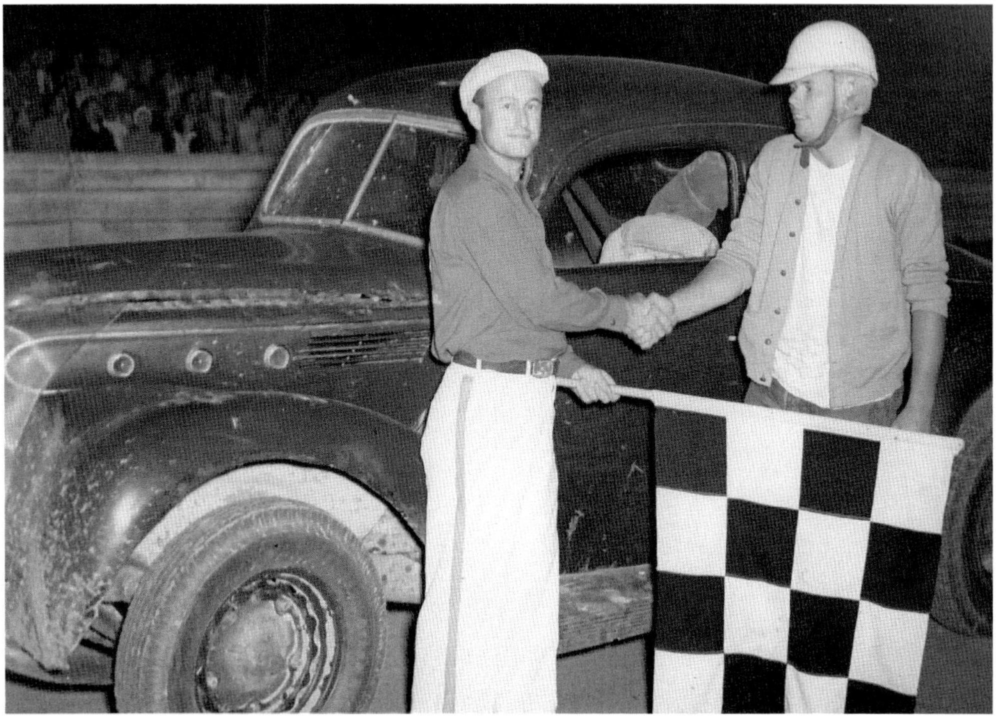

Carey Williams (right) shakes the hand of flagman Tom Brown after a victory at Georgetown Speedway. Williams wears standard attire of the era, when jeans, a T-shirt, a jacket, and a racing helmet were all that "protected" a driver. This was quite different from the Nomex fire suits and full-face helmets of today. (Courtesy of Charlie Brown.)

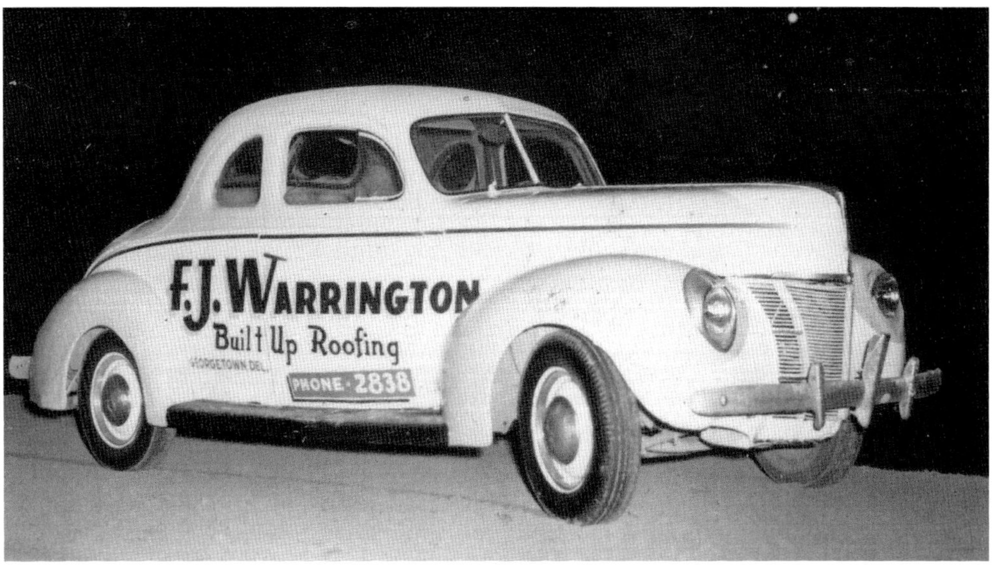

Frank Warrington, owner of car No. 16W, traveled to the races in his 1940 Ford that advertised his roofing company. The 1940 Ford was one of the most popular vehicles to use as a race car, as well as for "moonshine running." (Courtesy of Louis O'Neal.)

Standing beside the No. 191 Modified named "Cindy" are, from left to right, Bo Dodd, Paynter Lynch, Raymond Elliott, Kenny Steel, Dutch Warrington, and Cliff Wilkes. Cindy had a distinctive straight-six-cylinder Chevrolet engine with a Wayne head to increase horsepower; the heavily modified engine often beat the larger V-8 engines. (Courtesy of Butch Warrington.)

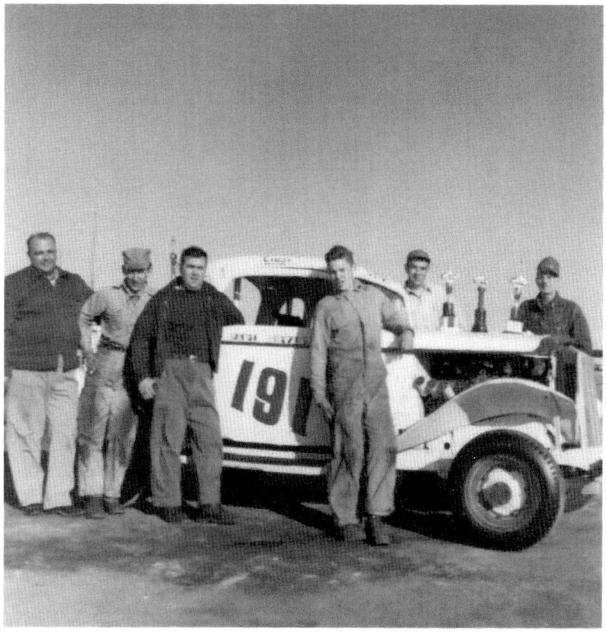

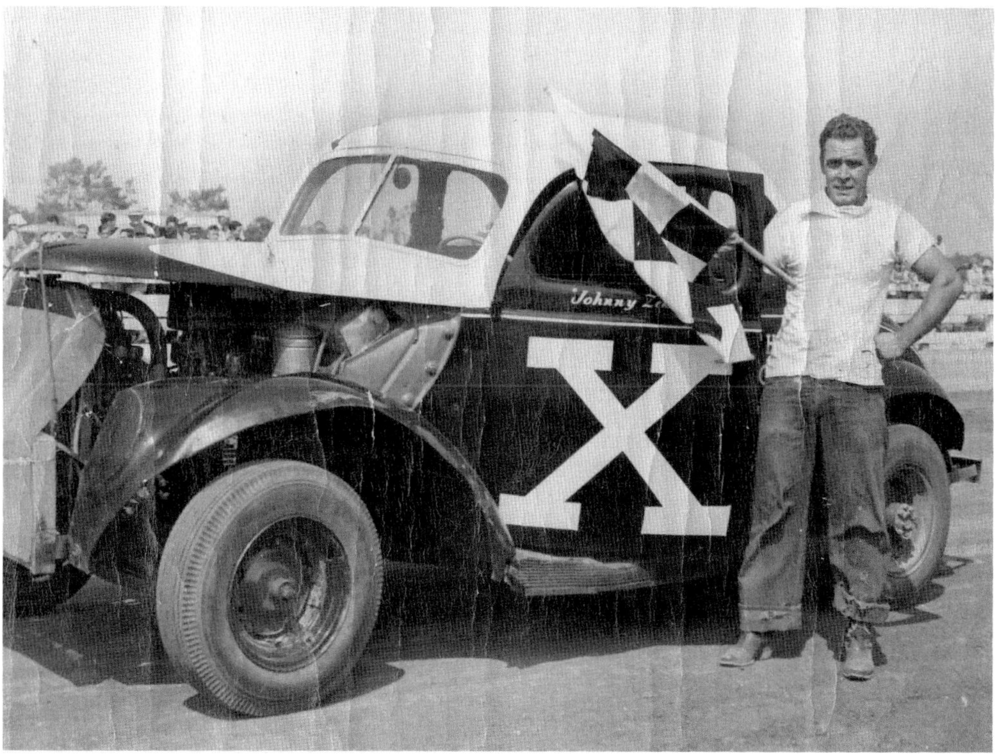

By the looks of Johnny Zeek and his car, he must have won this race from the pole. This victory shot from Delmar Speedway shows Zeek's car in "like new" condition. It was rare for a race car to look like this for long. On the small dirt tracks, racing was a contact sport, and racers would use the "chrome horn" to move a competitor whenever necessary. (Courtesy of Louis O'Neal.)

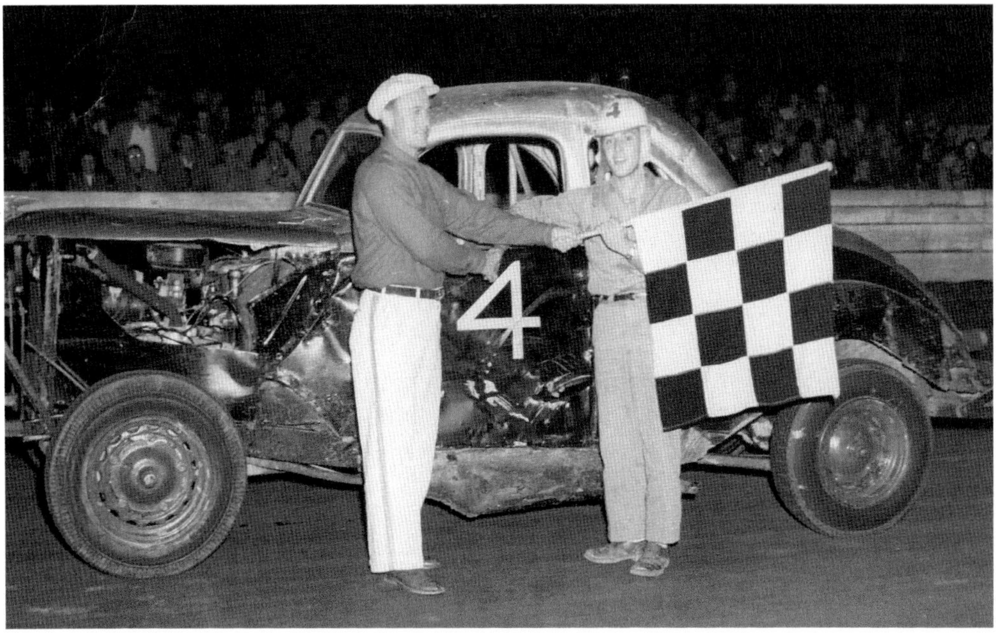

The No. 4 car of JR Collins appears well worn in this victory photograph taken at Georgetown Speedway in 1951. The expression on Collins's face says all the hard work was worth it. For many racers, there is no better feeling in the world than winning. (Courtesy of Charlie Brown.)

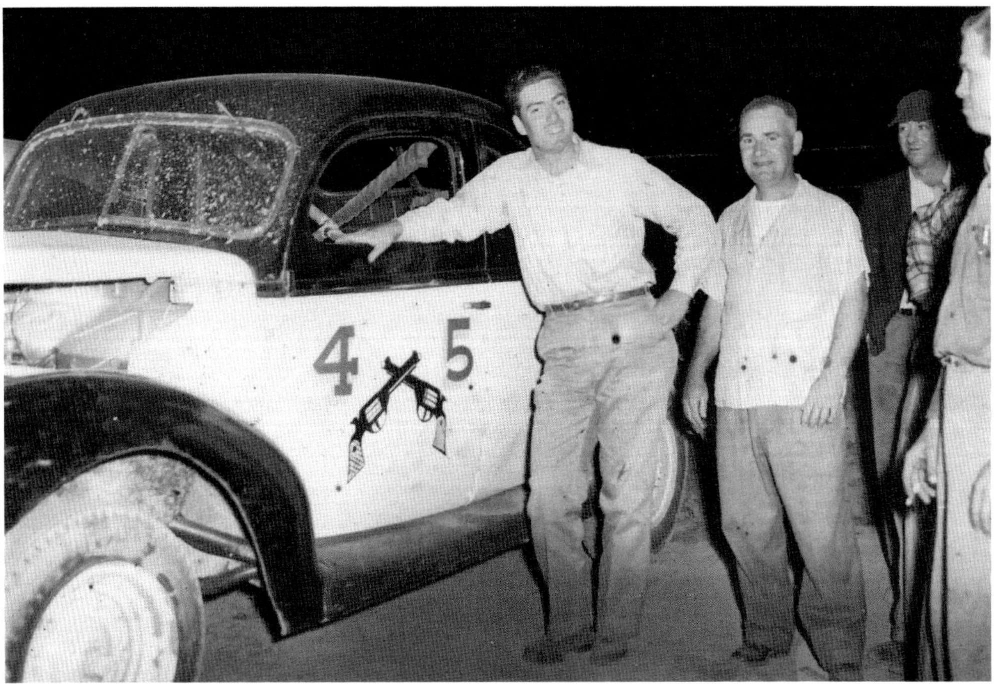

The Adkins brothers' No. 45 had an interesting paint scheme. In this image, everyone is all smiles after a hard-fought night at the races. Sometimes, even if a driver did not come home with a win, bringing the car back in one piece could be just as satisfying. (Courtesy of Louis O'Neal.)

Owner has High Praise for

LEE TIRES

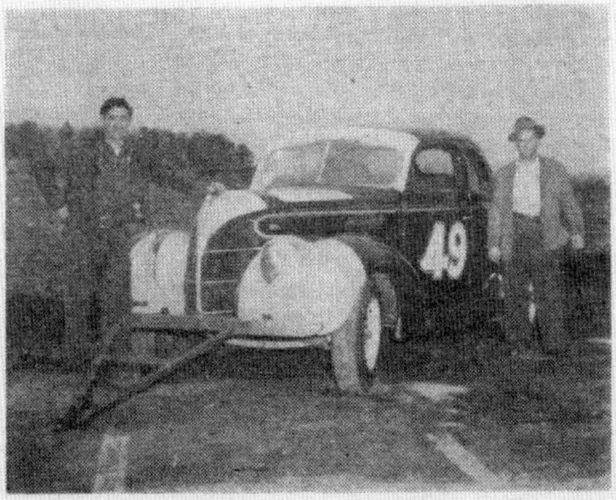

Second in 100 Mile Race at Daytona Beach

LEE TIRES

Clifton O. Brittingham, local LEE TIRE dealer (left) and Melvin L. Joseph (right) stand beside Stock Car No. 49, which placed second in the recent 100-mile race at Daytona Beach, Florida.

Mr. Joseph, well-known in the Eastern part of the country stock racing field and operator of the local Raceway, gave credit this week to Lee Tires as being the prime factor for the success of his car in the Florida grueling event in which No. 49 lead the field of more than one hundred starters for 18 laps and only fell to second place due to mechanical difficulties. Mr. Joseph also said that in all his experience in the racing field, Lee Tires were in his opinion the most practical for the job. These tires were regular Lee Tires and were not especially made for racing cars.

Clifton Birmingham (left), a local Lee tire dealer, and car owner Melvin Joseph pose next to the No. 49 car that finished second at the 100-mile stock car race on Daytona Beach. Companies often used racing as a marketing tool—if it could survive the rigors of racing, then it was most likely good enough for the daily driver. Joseph fielded cars at the Daytona Beach races for years. Throughout his time as a car owner, Joseph's cars were always marked No. 49, which signified the many good things that happened in his life in 1949. (Courtesy of Melvin Joseph Jr.)

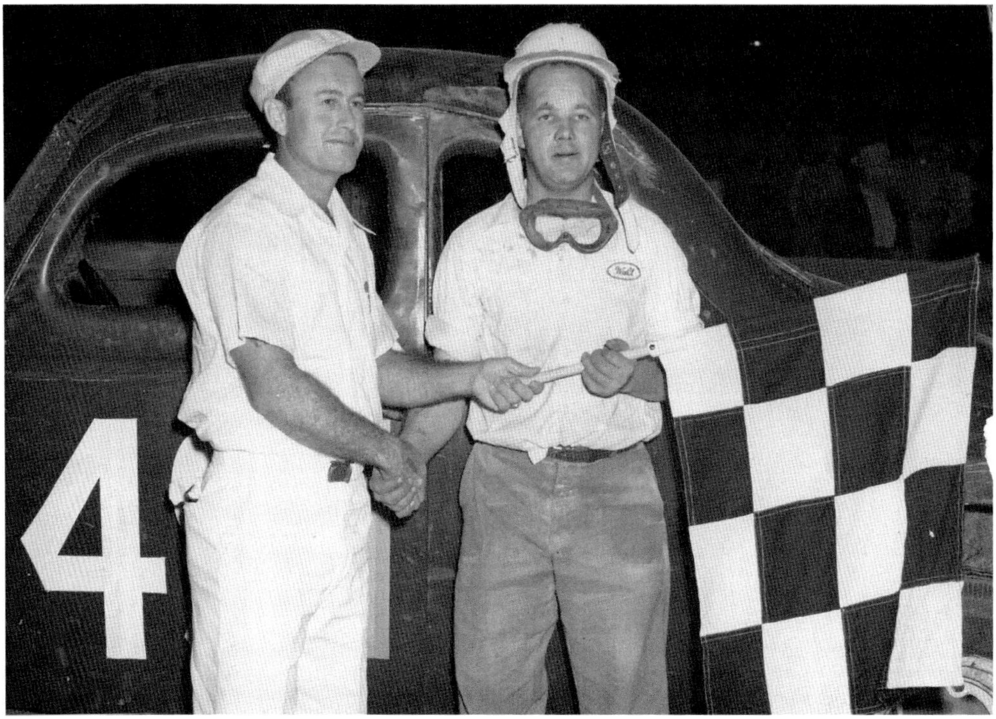

In this 1953 photograph, Walt Riggon (right) shakes flagman Tom Brown's hand at Georgetown Speedway. Brown's love of racing was passed down to his son, Charlie Brown. Charlie is the longtime announcer at Delaware International Speedway, as well as being a respected motorsports columnist. (Courtesy of Charlie Brown.)

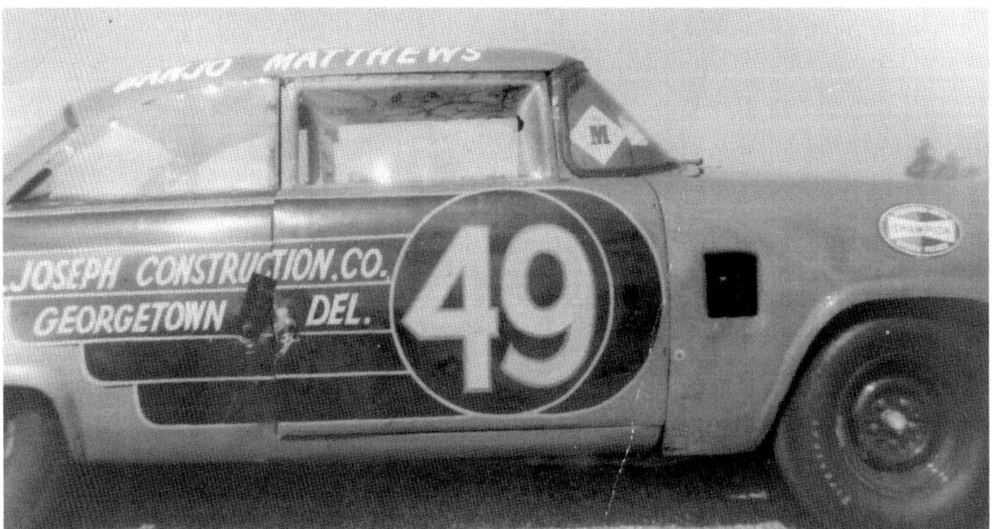

Banjo Matthews drove the No. 49 Melvin Joseph–owned Modified to victory in the first Modified race, held at the new Daytona International Speedway in 1959. Note the plate on the side of the car to keep the door shut. (Courtesy of Melvin Joseph Jr.)

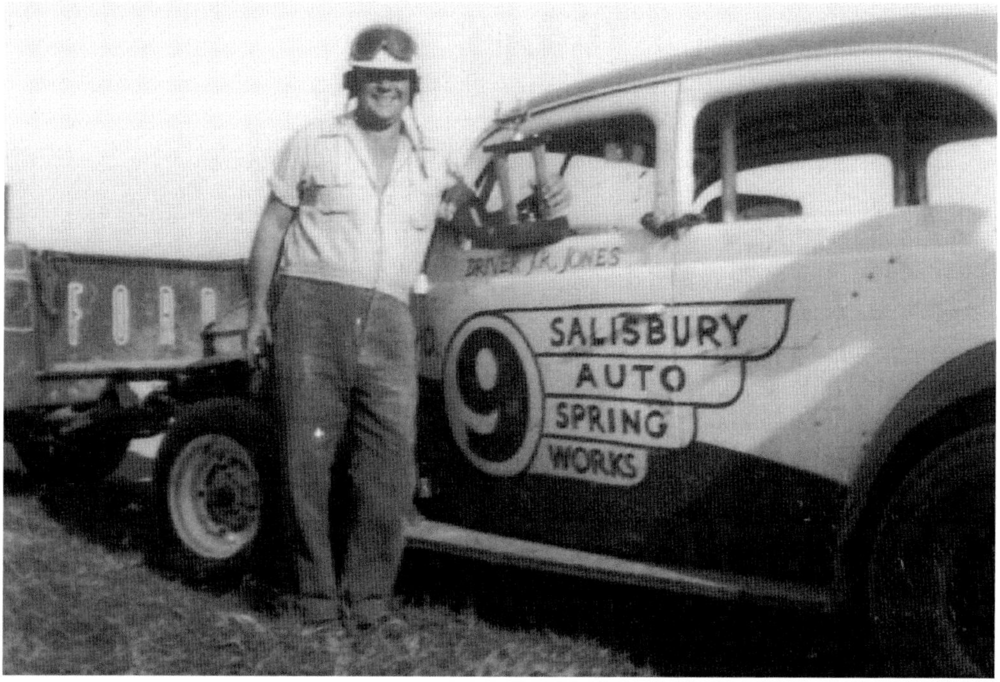

J.R. Jones poses next to the Salisbury Auto Spring Works car No. 9. Note that the race car is towed with a tow bar behind the Ford truck (visible at left). Instead of buying a trailer, drivers and owners would simply rig up brake lights and attach them to the back of the race car before heading to the track. (Courtesy of Louis O'Neal.)

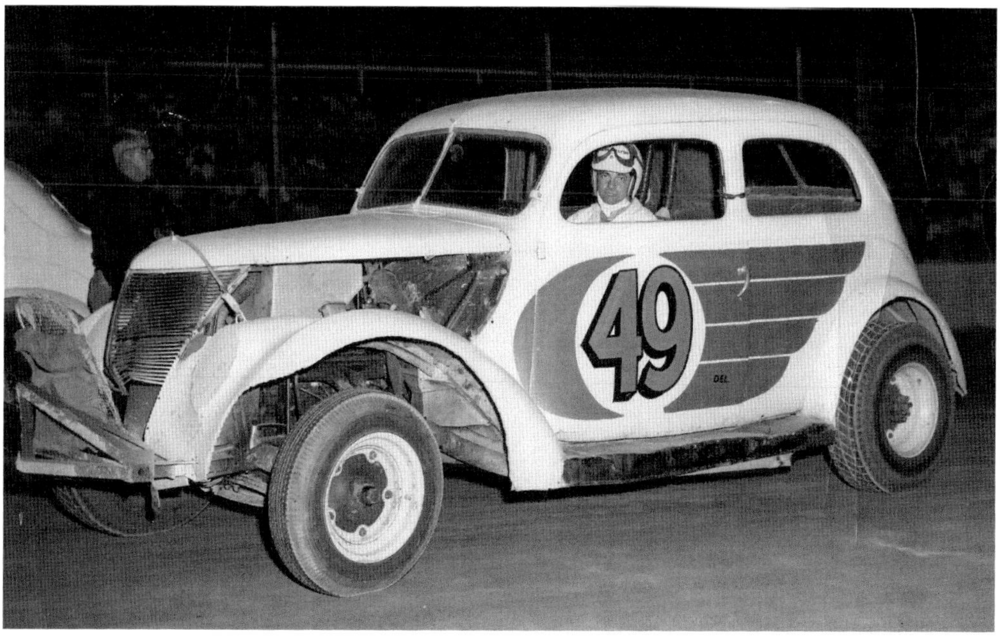

This beautiful Modified, owned by Melvin Joseph, is driven by Dean Pelton of Takoma Park, Maryland. (Courtesy of Melvin Joseph Jr.)

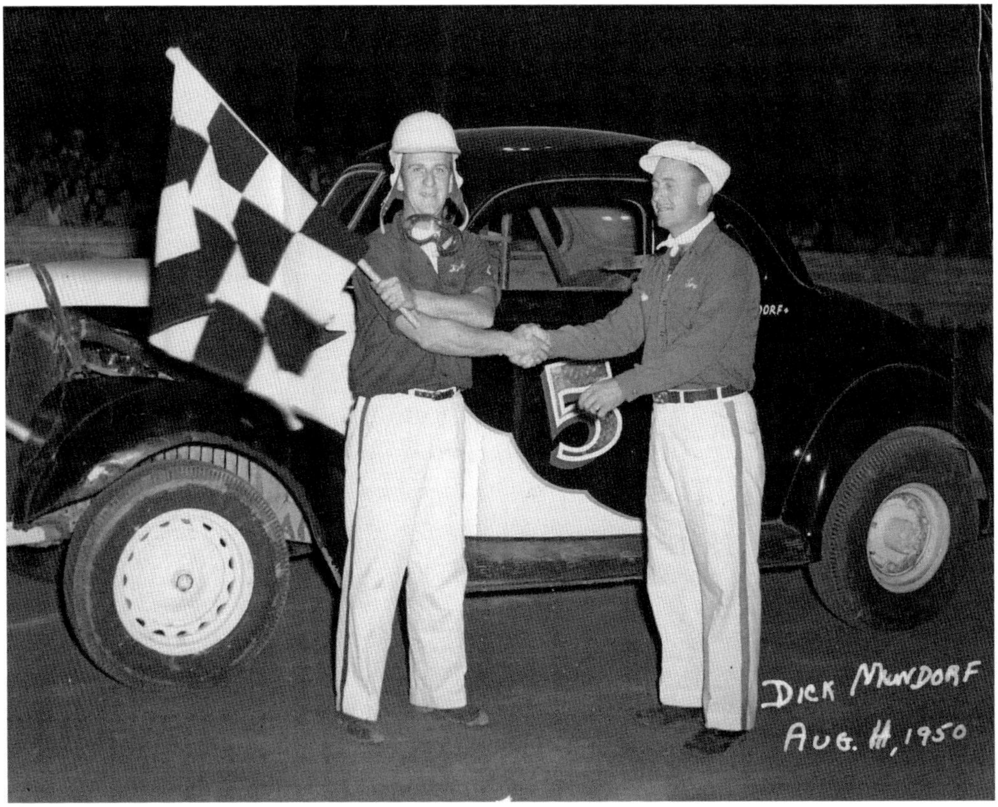

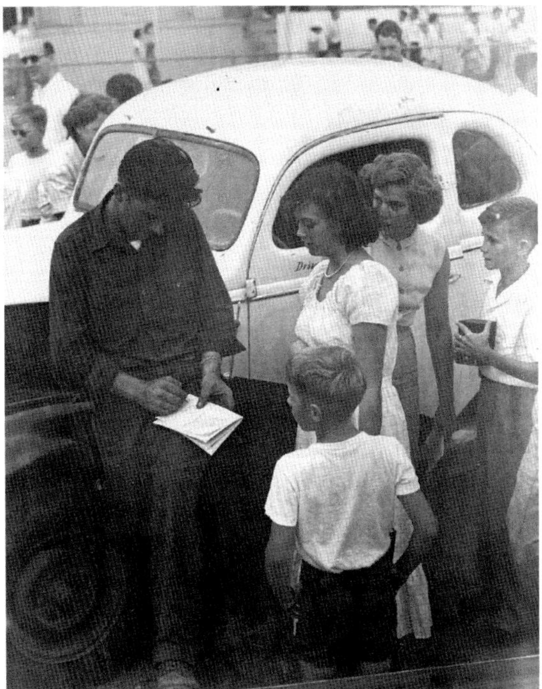

Flagman Tom Brown congratulates driver in Victory Lane. Dick Mundorf (left) was a winning driver at Georgetown Speedway in the 1950s. He was also an excellent painter and artist. Mundorf lettered numerous cars around Delaware. As sponsors started to appear on the sides of cars, vehicles began to have more elaborate paint schemes and lettering. (Courtesy of Charlie Brown.)

As long as there have been cars and drivers, there have been race fans. Here, Johnny Stoltzfus takes time after a victory to sign an autograph for a young fan. The cars may have changed, but the scene at the local dirt track is much the same today; drivers always have time to talk to fans and sign autographs for the racers of tomorrow. (Courtesy of Charlie Brown.)

Johnny Martin was an immensely talented and popular driver in the Mid-Atlantic area. Martin was from Lewes, Delaware, and in 1953, he competed in both the Sportsman and Modified classes. Martin drove for many of the top owners in the area and earned wins in almost every car he drove. (Courtesy of Louis O'Neal.)

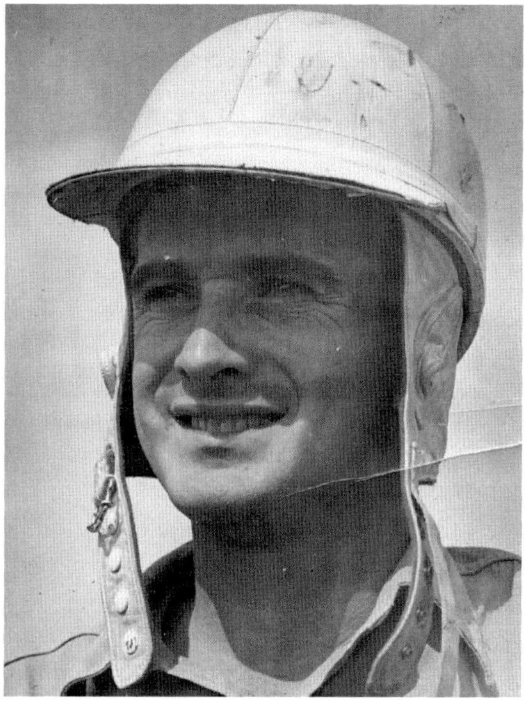

Johnny Martin (left) accepts a winning trophy from Cliff Lawson. Lawson was president of the Delaware Auto Racing Association from 1951 to 1956. (Courtesy of Charlie Brown.)

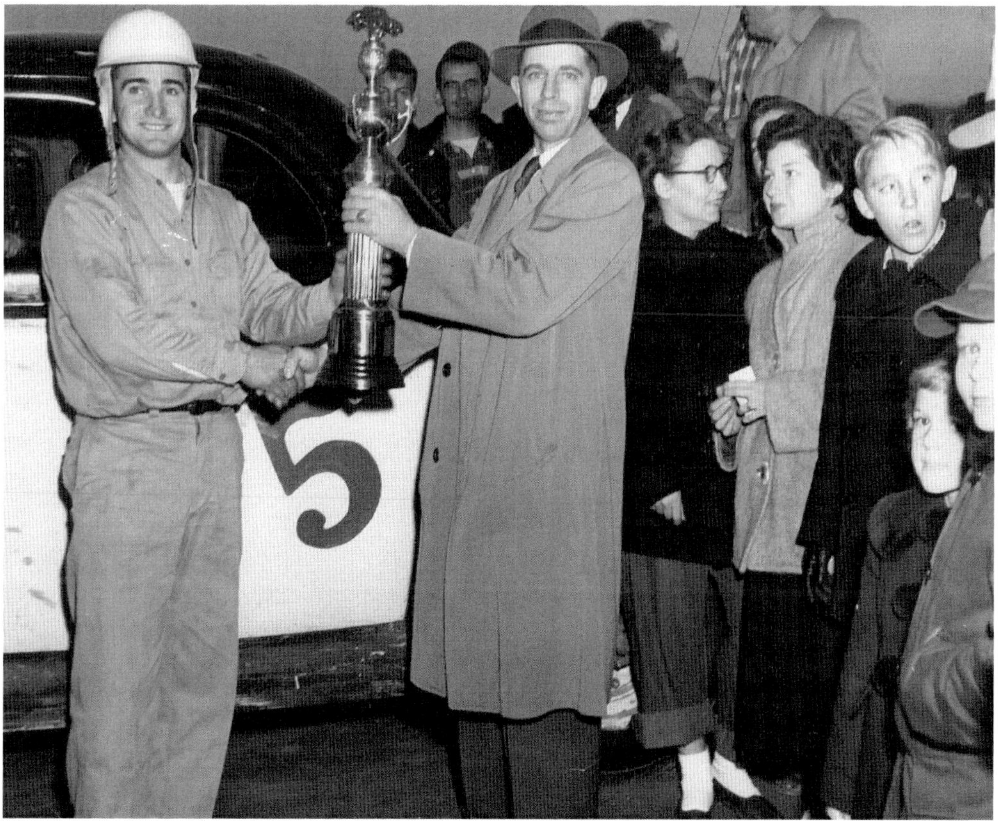

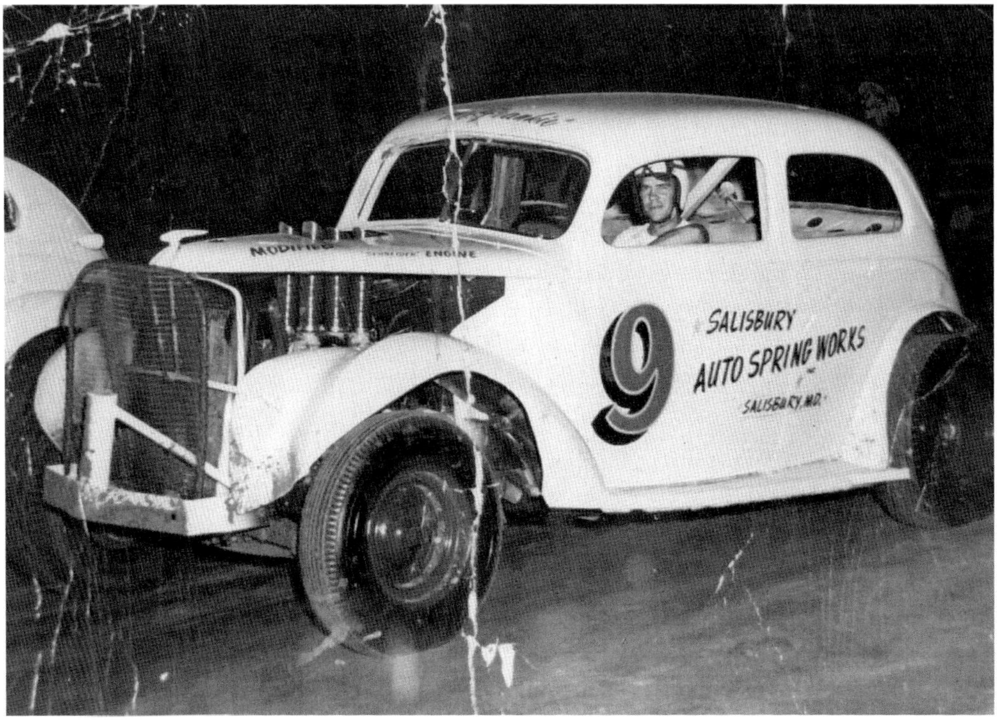

Paul Walker had the privilege of driving this legendary race car. The No. 9 Salisbury Spring Works–sponsored car was powered by a Frankie Schneider–built engine. The huge screen on the front was to protect the radiator from rocks and debris. (Courtesy of Snookie Vent.)

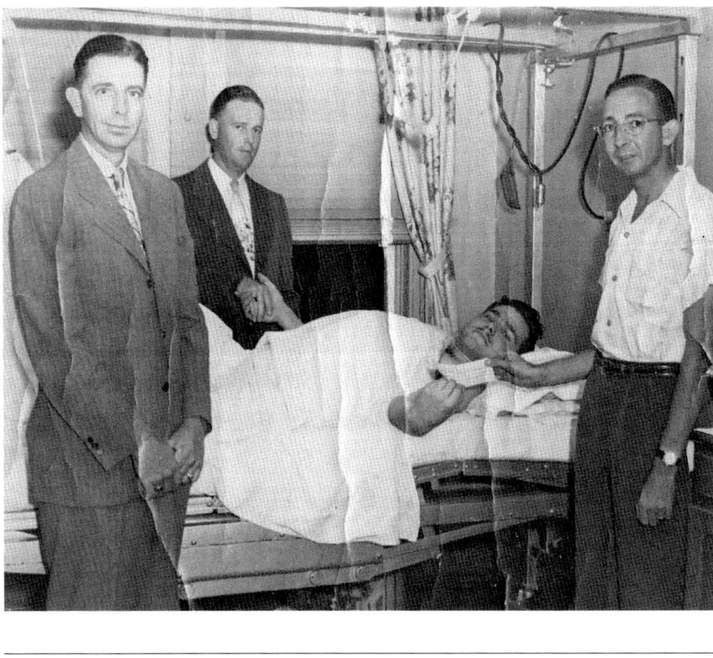

Pictured here are, from left to right, Cliff Lawson, Melvin Joseph, George Hudick, and "Stinky" Davis. Despite the enormous competition and will to win, racers can be a close-knit bunch. Here, a check is being handed to Hudick after a hat was passed in the pits to help with injuries he sustained while racing. (Courtesy of Louis O'Neal.)

1957 NASCAR Modified Champion Ken Marriott (right) ran 72 races in his championship year, winning 14 and finishing second 11 times. In this 1953 photograph, Marriott poses with Tom Brown after a hard-fought victory at Delmar Speedway. (Courtesy of Charlie Brown.)

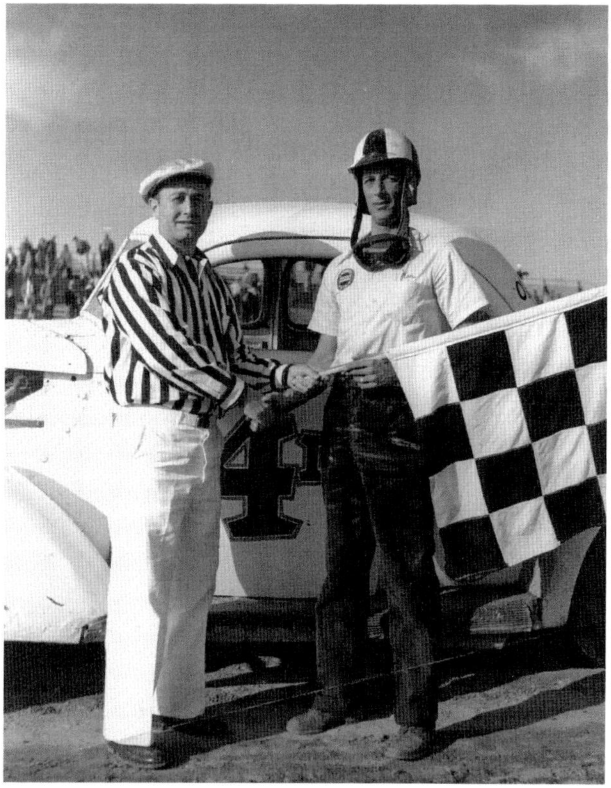

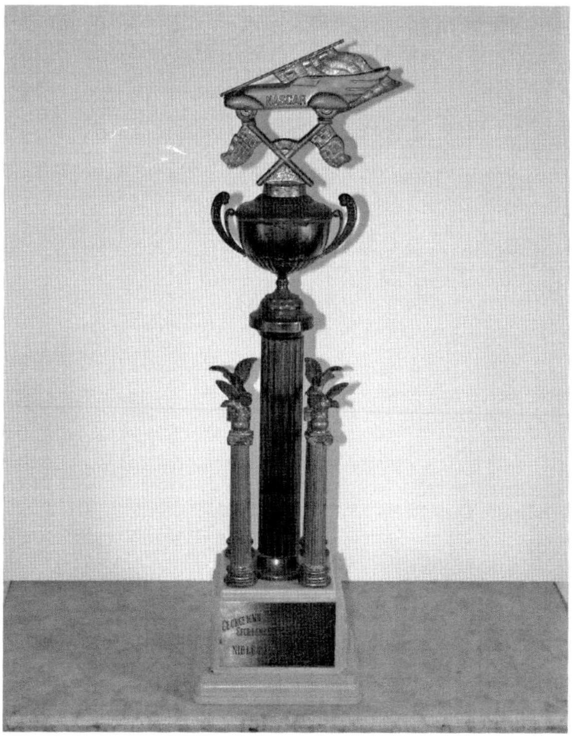

This early NASCAR trophy, owned by Keith Short, was given to the Niblett brothers, the winning 1955 Sportsman Car owners for the season at Georgetown Speedway. The NASCAR logo on top, with the winged car, is one of the earliest versions of the organization's logo. (Photograph by Don Allen.)

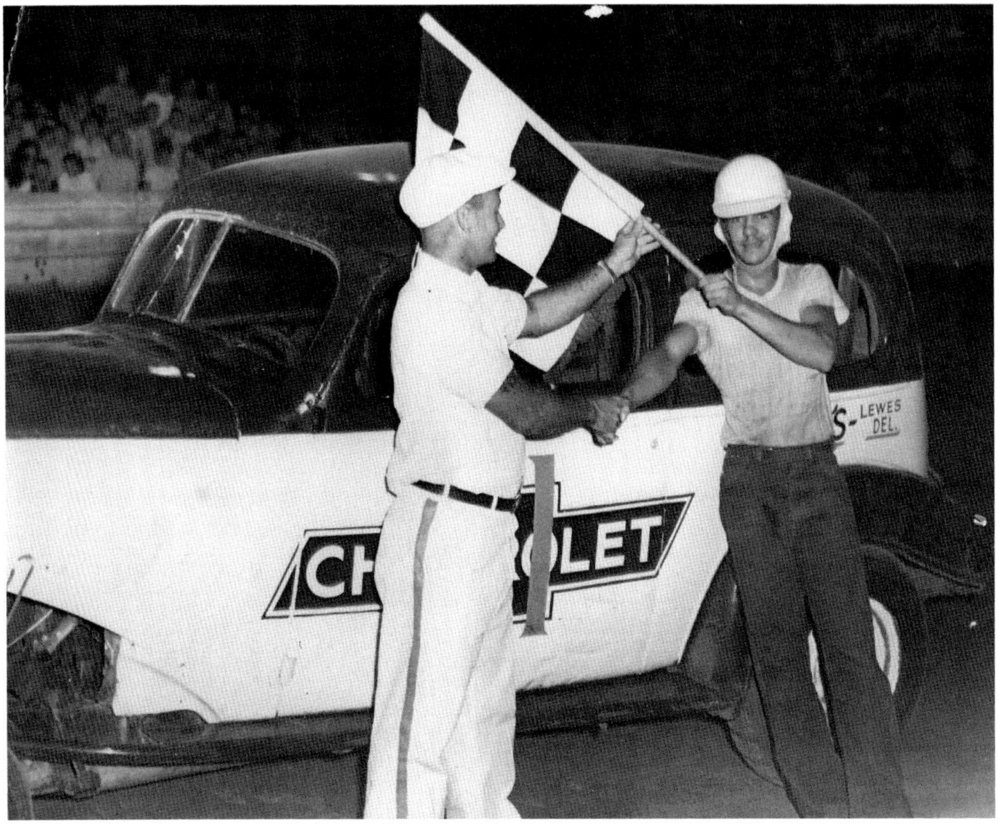

The smiles on these drivers' faces show that the hard work they put into their cars and all the risk-taking on the track was worth it. Racers know that there is no feeling in the world that compares to winning any given race. In the above photograph, Delaware local Paul Walker gladly accepts the checkered flag from Tom Brown at Georgetown Speedway. In the below photograph, Wally Campbell smiles for the camera after winning at Georgetown in 1953. (Both, courtesy of Charlie Brown.)

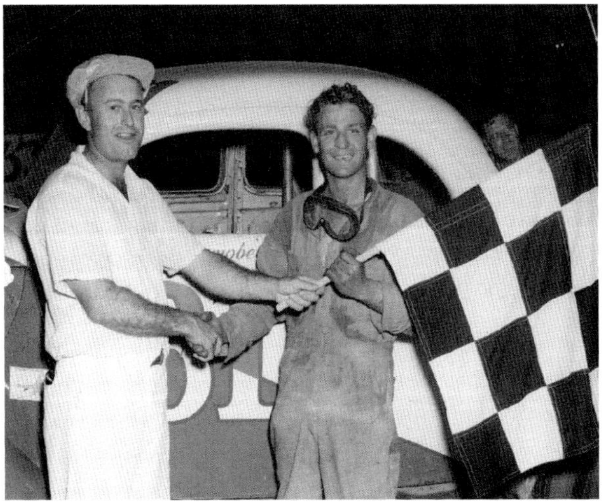

3

Changing Times

As racing began to gain traction throughout the state of Delaware during the 1960s, 1970s, and 1980s, many new tracks were created. Little Lincoln Speedway opened in 1967; fans would arrive early to back their vehicles up to the fence to get the best view of the action. Racetracks like Blackbird. Willow Grove. along with Little Lincoln all closed their doors in the 1970s, leaving only Delaware International Speedway (US 13) and Georgetown running on a weekly basis.

Times were changing, and so were the cars. During the 1960s and early 1970s, almost all cars were hand-built from parts found in any junkyard. As early coupe and coach bodies became harder for Modified racers to find, the newer Gremlin, Mustang, and Pinto bodies became popular because of their availability. Later, Modifieds would use no production bodies, and custom sheet-metal bodies would be constructed to take maximum advantage of aerodynamics. Chassis became more specialized also, as racers could purchase purpose-built racing chassis instead of using frames from the junkyard. Tobias, Profile, Weld, Olsen, and Bandit were just a few well-known chassis manufacturers.

In the 1970s, as open-wheel Modifieds changed, they were joined by the mighty Sprint Cars. These open wheel cars began to show up with large wings and could circle the track at unheard-of speeds. The closed wheel cars also changed as stock bodies gave way to custom sheet-metal bodies. With new chassis, new bodies, better race-specific parts, and very large engines, drivers turned mind-numbing laps at breakneck speeds around tracks up to a half-mile in length. Huge crowds witnessed large car turnouts during this time, as racing's popularity was growing at a record pace. Perhaps more change and evolution took place during this period in racing than any other.

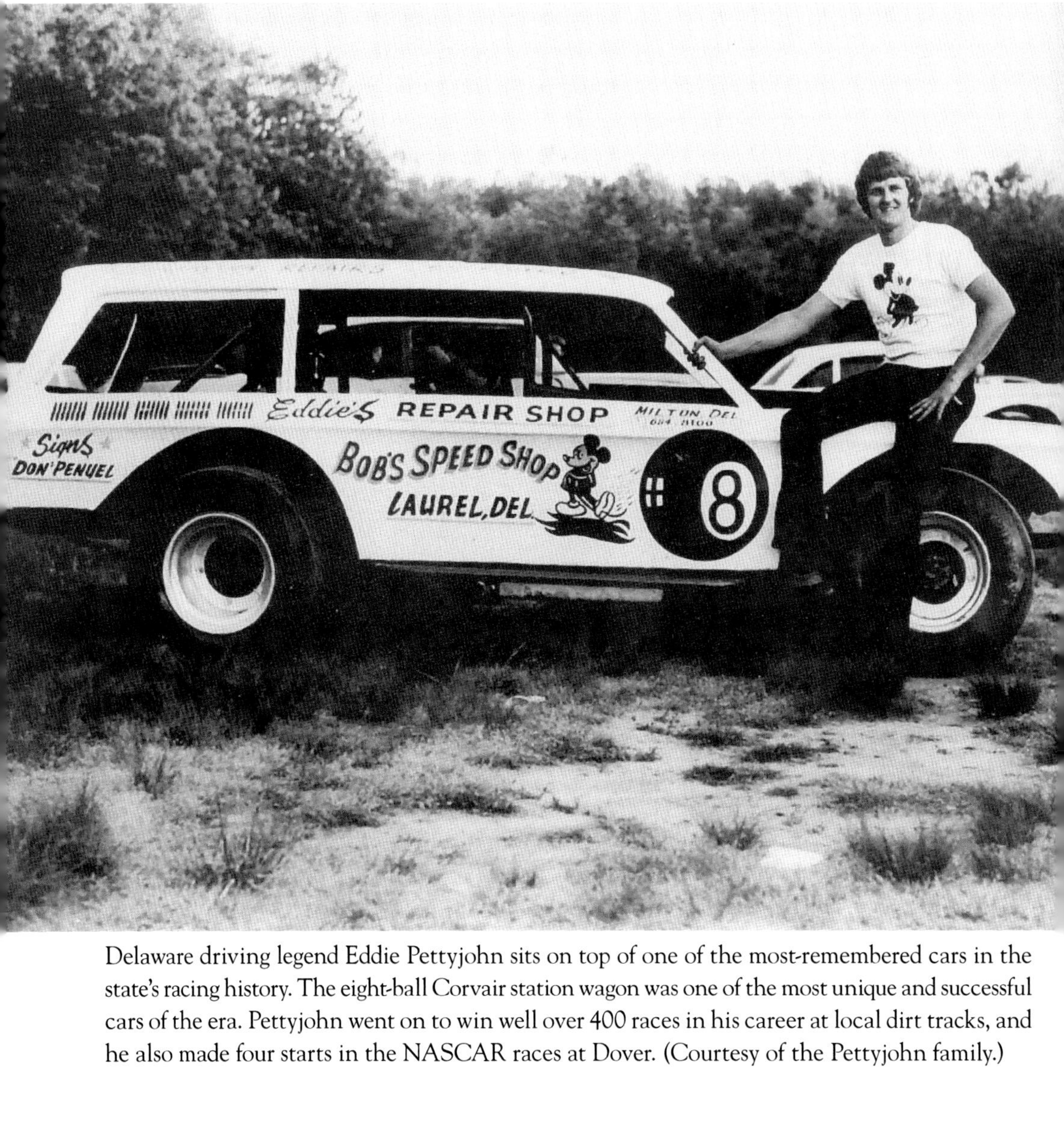

Delaware driving legend Eddie Pettyjohn sits on top of one of the most-remembered cars in the state's racing history. The eight-ball Corvair station wagon was one of the most unique and successful cars of the era. Pettyjohn went on to win well over 400 races in his career at local dirt tracks, and he also made four starts in the NASCAR races at Dover. (Courtesy of the Pettyjohn family.)

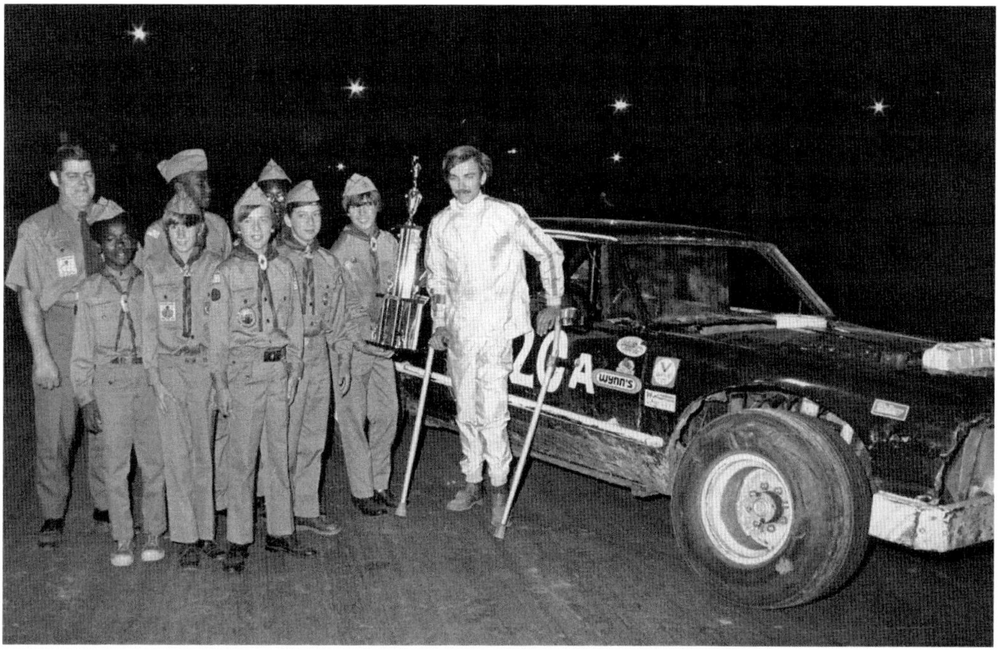

Losing both legs in the Vietnam War did not stop Ron Slade from driving a race car. Here, Slade, an inspiration to all, accepts a trophy from a local troop of Boy Scouts. Slade's car, No. 20A, appeared on the Camp Barnes Benefit Stock Car Race patch for years. (Photograph by Fred Boyer, courtesy of Don and Linda Allen.)

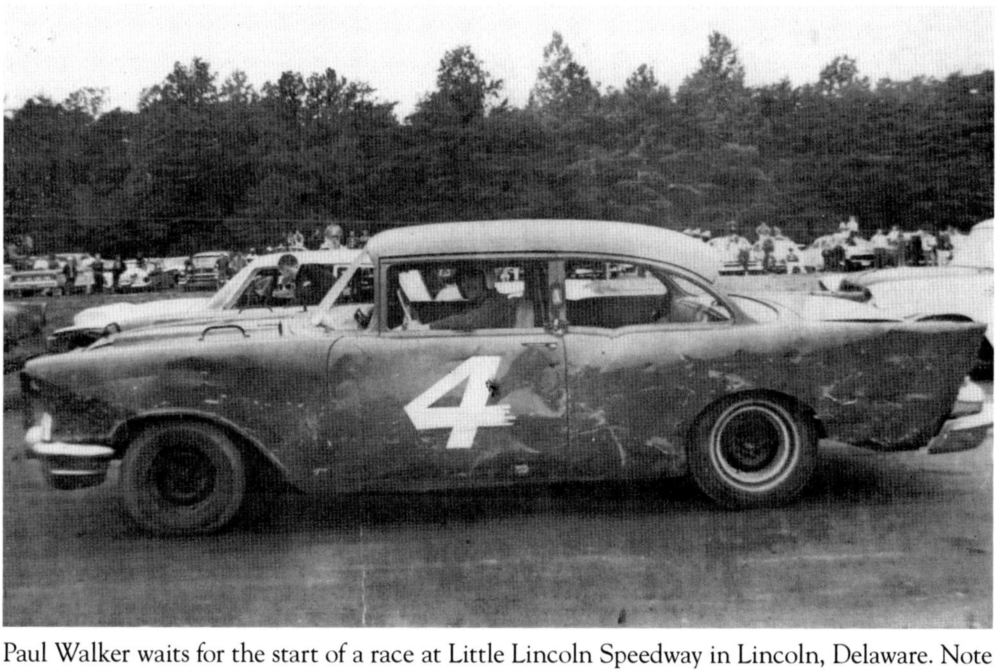

Paul Walker waits for the start of a race at Little Lincoln Speedway in Lincoln, Delaware. Note the line of cars backed up to the fence to view the action. Fans would arrive hours early to ensure a prime viewing spot. (Courtesy of Paul Mills.)

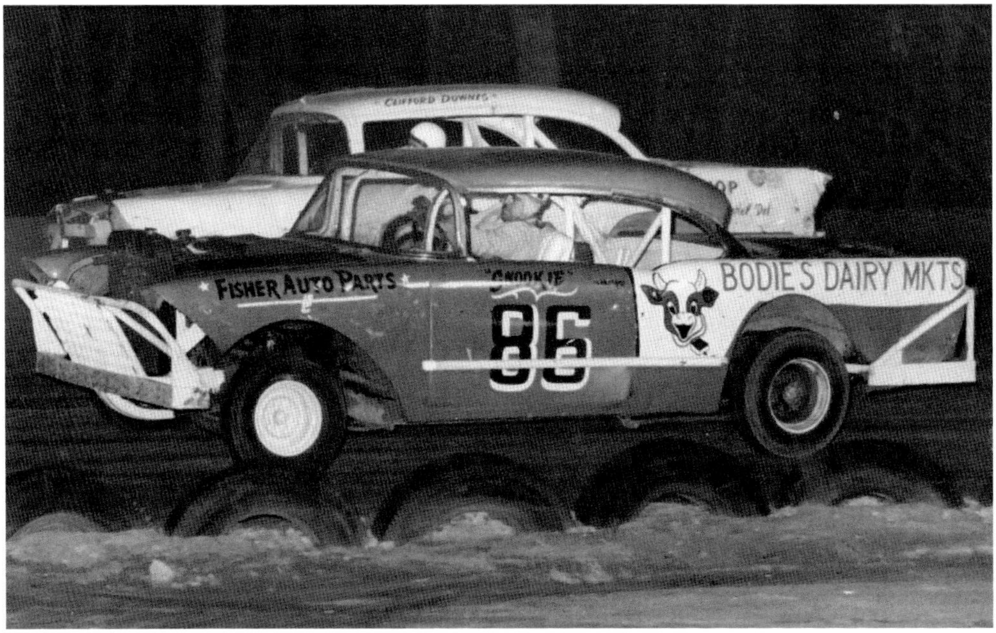

Snookie Vent grabs a handful of steering wheel at Little Lincoln Speedway. Vent, a successful racer, went on to start Snookie's Speed Parts in Milton, Delaware. The speed shop has provided parts and services for racers for over 35 years. (Courtesy of Snookie Vent.)

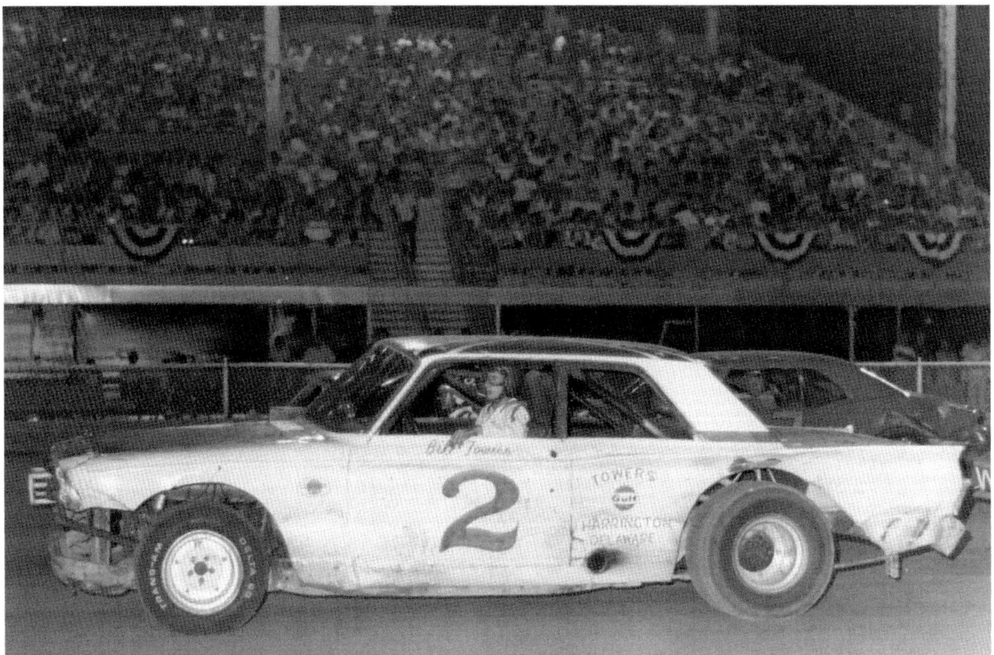

Bill Towers races before a standing-room-only crowd at the 1973 Delaware State Fair. Although the loose dirt surface made it difficult to pass at Harrington, both fans and racers always looked forward to this special event. (Courtesy of Charlie Brown.)

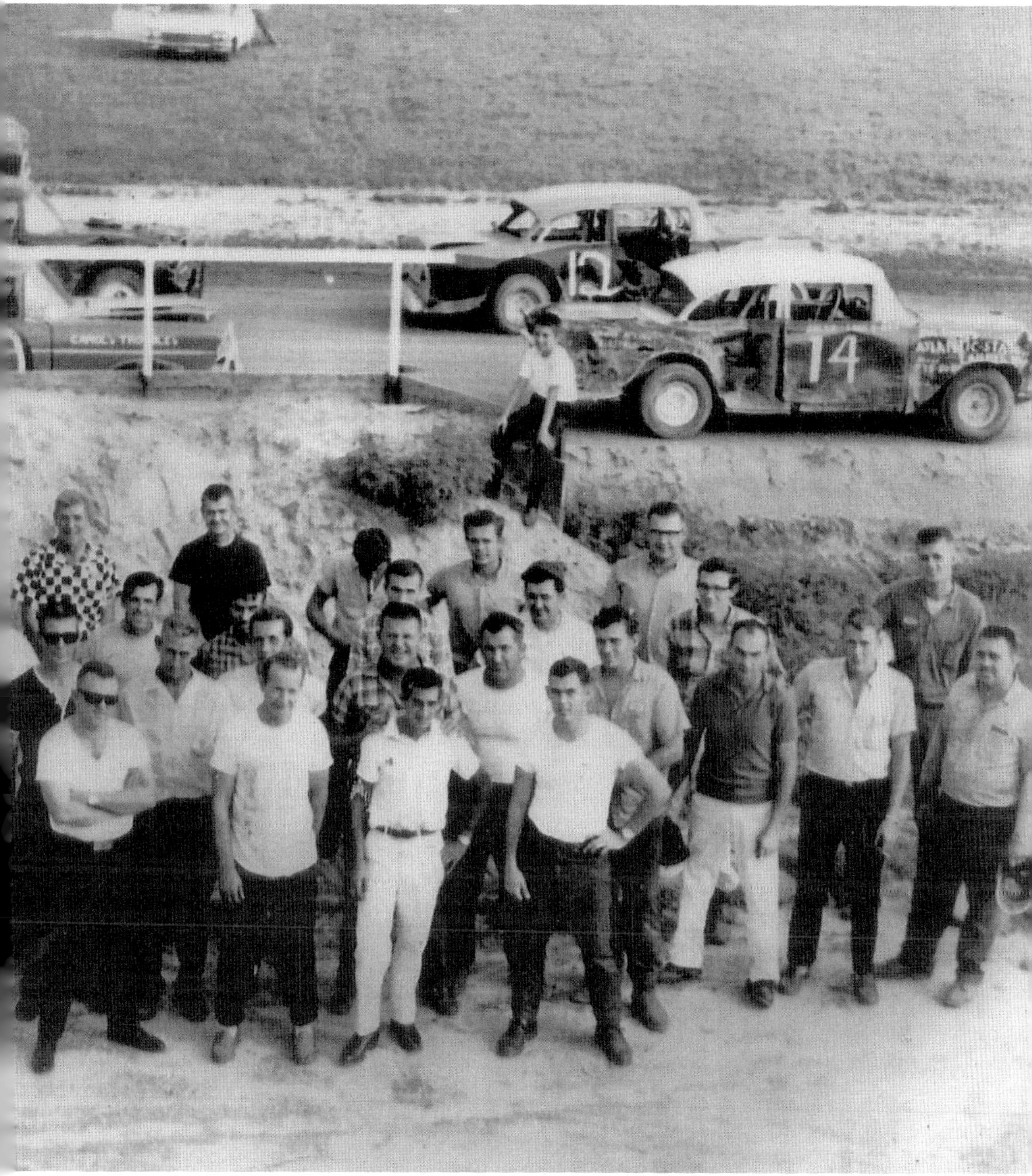

Pictured in this early Little Lincoln photograph are, from left to right, (first row) Jerry West, Harold Warrington, Dave White, and Vaughn Morgan; (second row) Abby Mitchell, George Smith, Calin Hammond, Sonny Brittingham, Billy Pressley, Buddy Messeck, Les Nailor, Hershel Moore, and Snookie Vent; (third row) Russell Bradley, Dave Schamp, unidentified, Harold Bunting, Jack Sapp, Bill Richards, and Eddie Pettyjohn; (fourth row) Harry Dutton, Chet Harrison, Paul Walker, Fred Workman, Charlie Moore, and Jack Fitzgerald. The kid on the bank is Donnie Dutton. (Courtesy of Snookie Vent.)

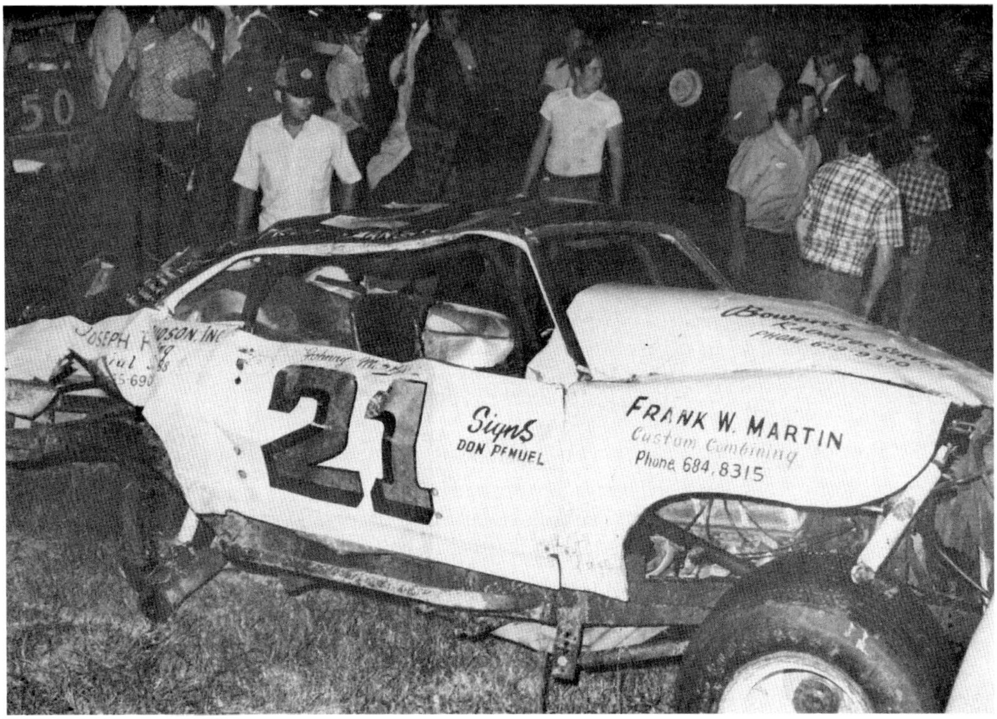

This photograph shows the last ride of Johnny Martin. This mangled wreck of a car was all that was left after an accident. Though the effects of the wreck led to Martin's retirement from racing, he will always be remembered as one of Delaware's first superstar racers. (Courtesy of Charlie Brown.)

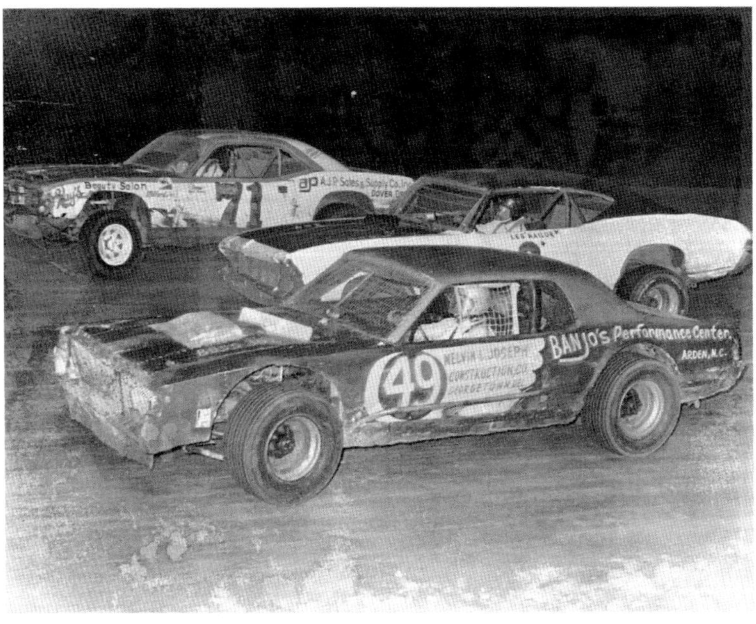

Melvin Joseph Jr. (No. 49), Les Nailor (No. 9), and Ron Lavere (No. 71) go three-wide during feature action. A wide range of body styles is represented in this photograph, which was taken during an era when drivers built their cars from scratch. (Courtesy of Melvin Joseph Jr.)

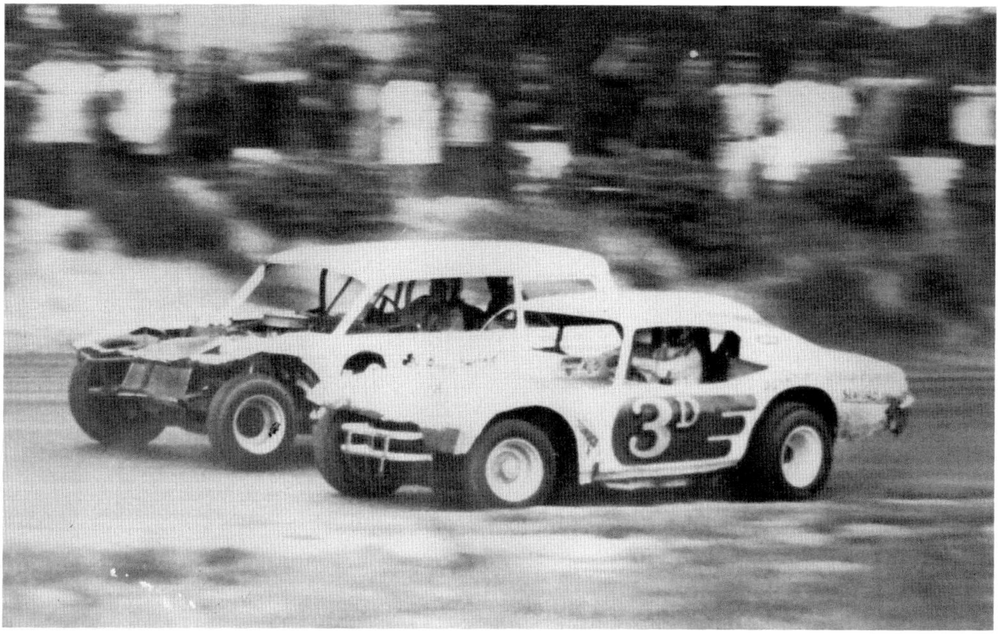

Two Delaware racing icons go door-to-door at full speed. Haines Tull, in the No. 3D, has the inside lane as Eddie Pettyjohn does his best to go around the outside. Drivers could race like this for laps and never touch or spin out a car—a testament to their skill and determination. (Courtesy of Paul Mills.)

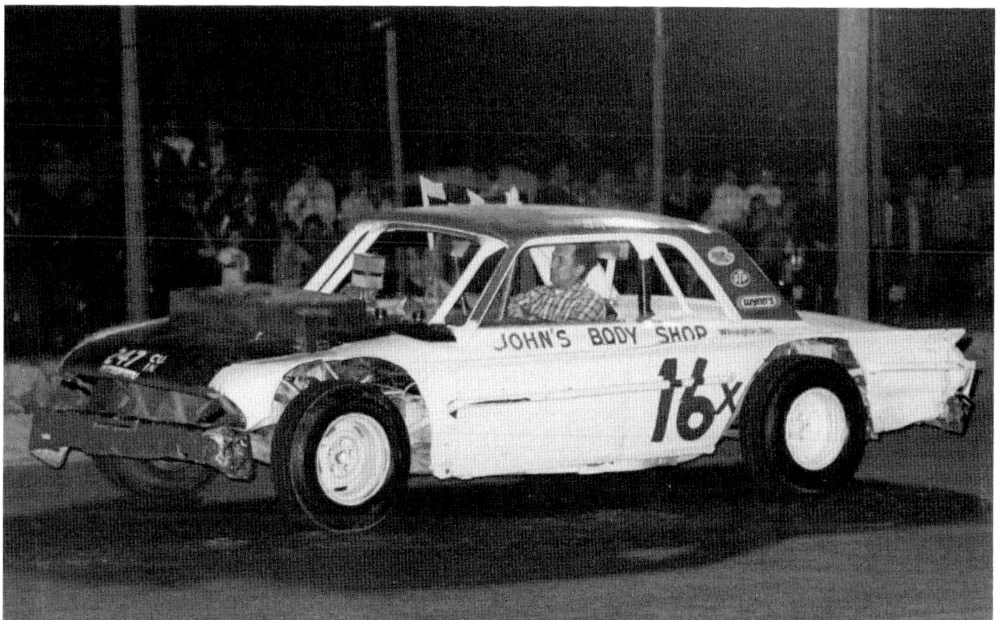

The six-cylinder class provided just as much action as the faster eight-cylinder class at Little Lincoln Speedway. Here, Lloyd Sawyer takes a victory lap with the checkered flag in hand. (Photograph by Walter T. Chernokal, courtesy of Keith Short.)

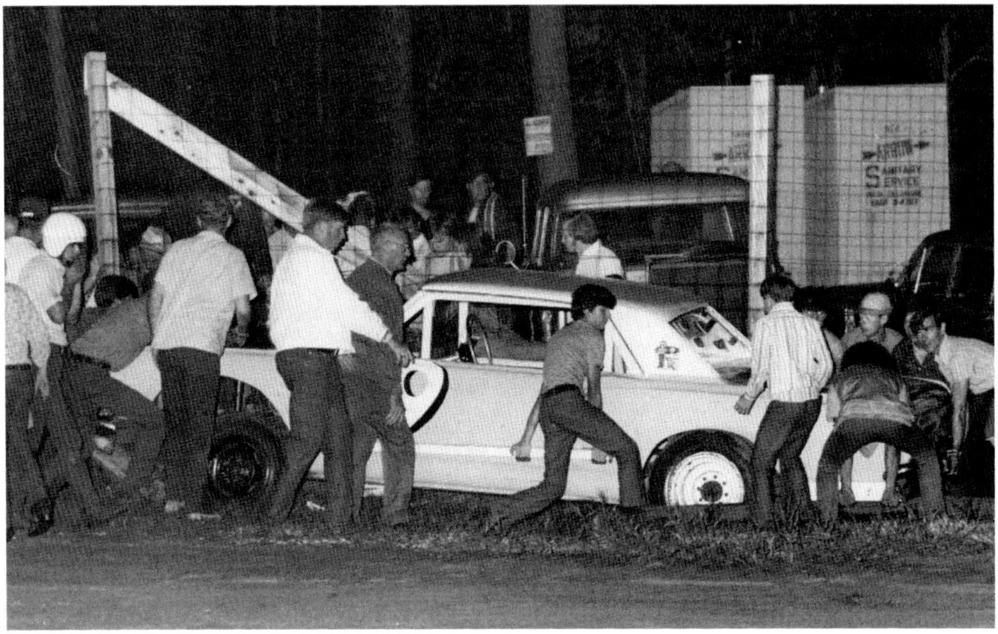

Driver Richard Dix gets a little help removing his car from a ditch. In the early days of racing, long before promoters were concerned about insurance liability, fans and crews often entered the track to assist drivers when needed. (Courtesy of Betty Wyatt-Dix.)

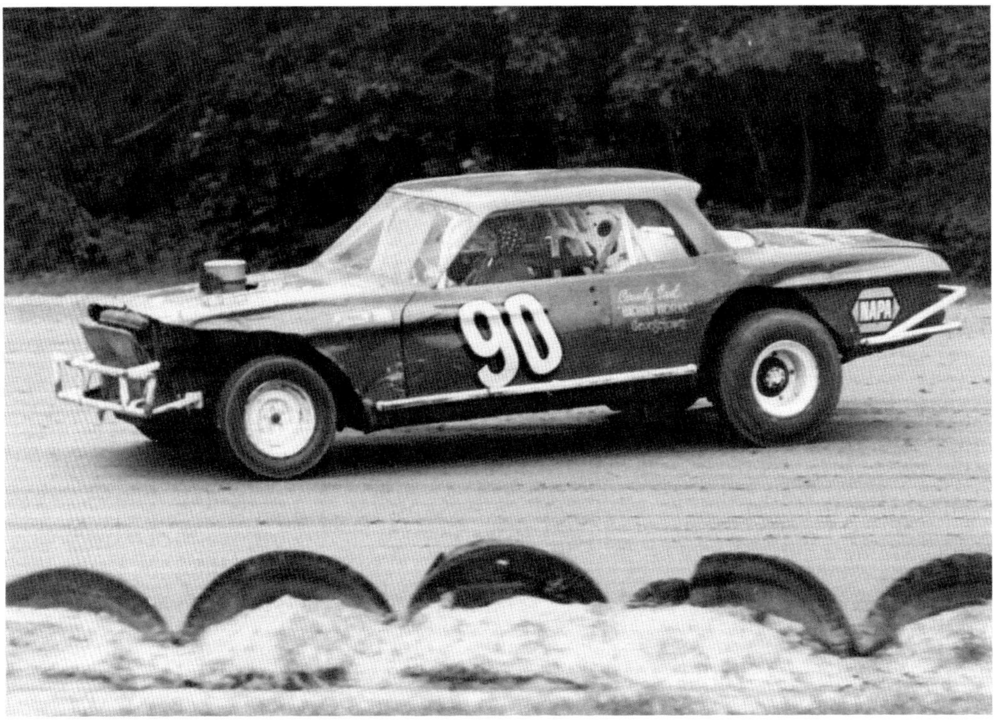

Jack Sapp sports his famous polka-dot helmet while pushing his Plymouth Valiant to the limit at Little Lincoln Speedway. (Photograph by Walter T. Chernokal, courtesy of Keith Short.)

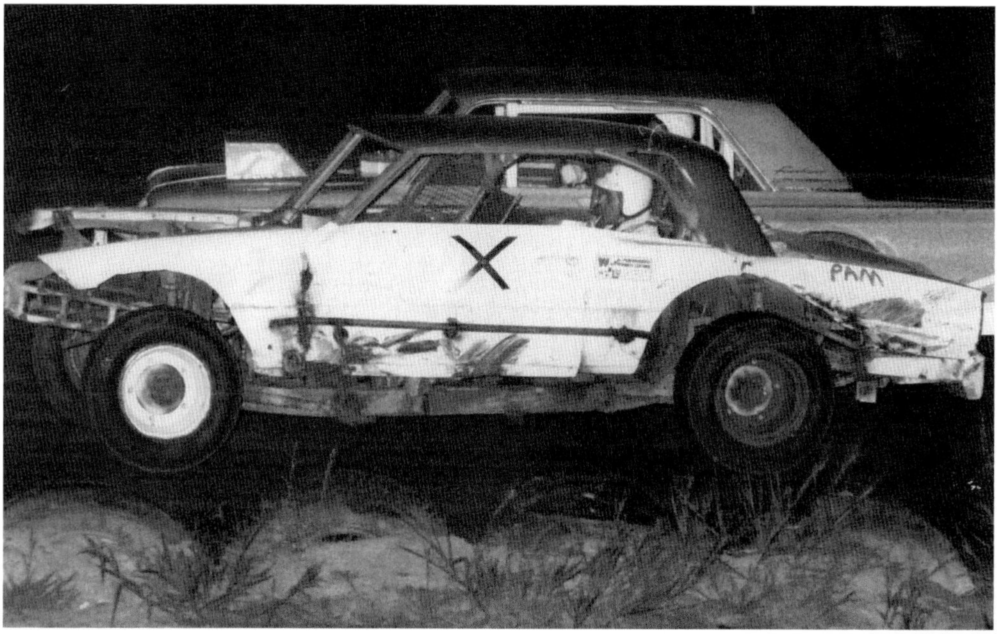

George Harrison, in the No. X car, appears to be a backseat driver in this photograph. Drivers would move the engine toward the back of the car for ideal weight distribution, which increased handling. Drivers often had little comfort in the cockpit, as early race cars were all about speed and function. (Photograph by Walter T. Chernokal, courtesy of Keith Short.)

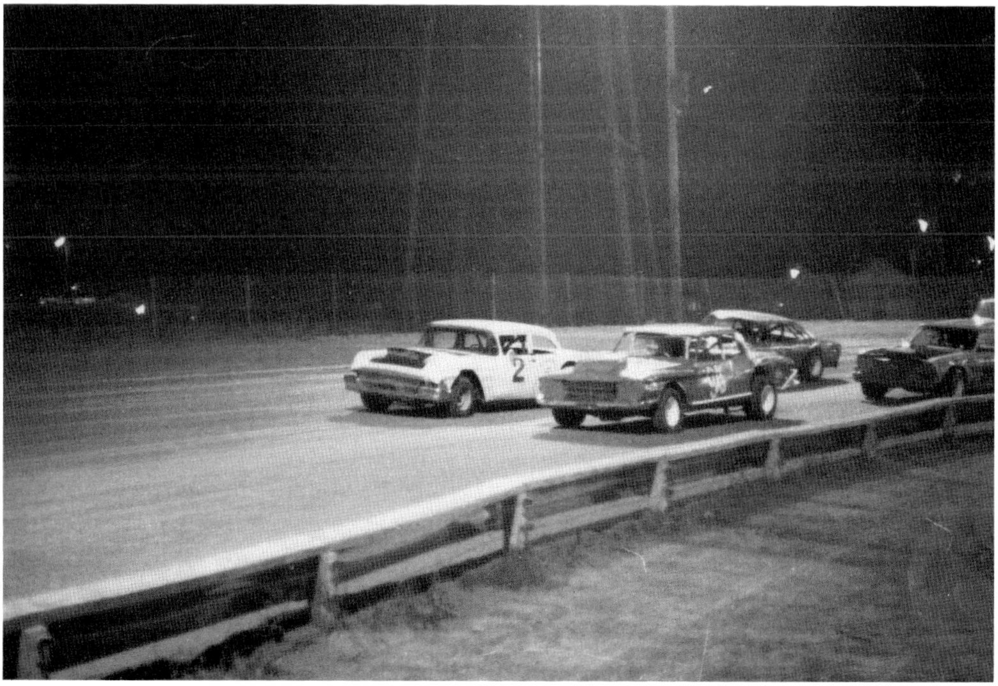

Coming down to the green flag at the Delaware State Fair are Jack Sapp (No. 90), Bill Towers (No. 2), Stan Busby (No. 76), and Harold Bunting (No. 80). (Courtesy of Charlie Brown.)

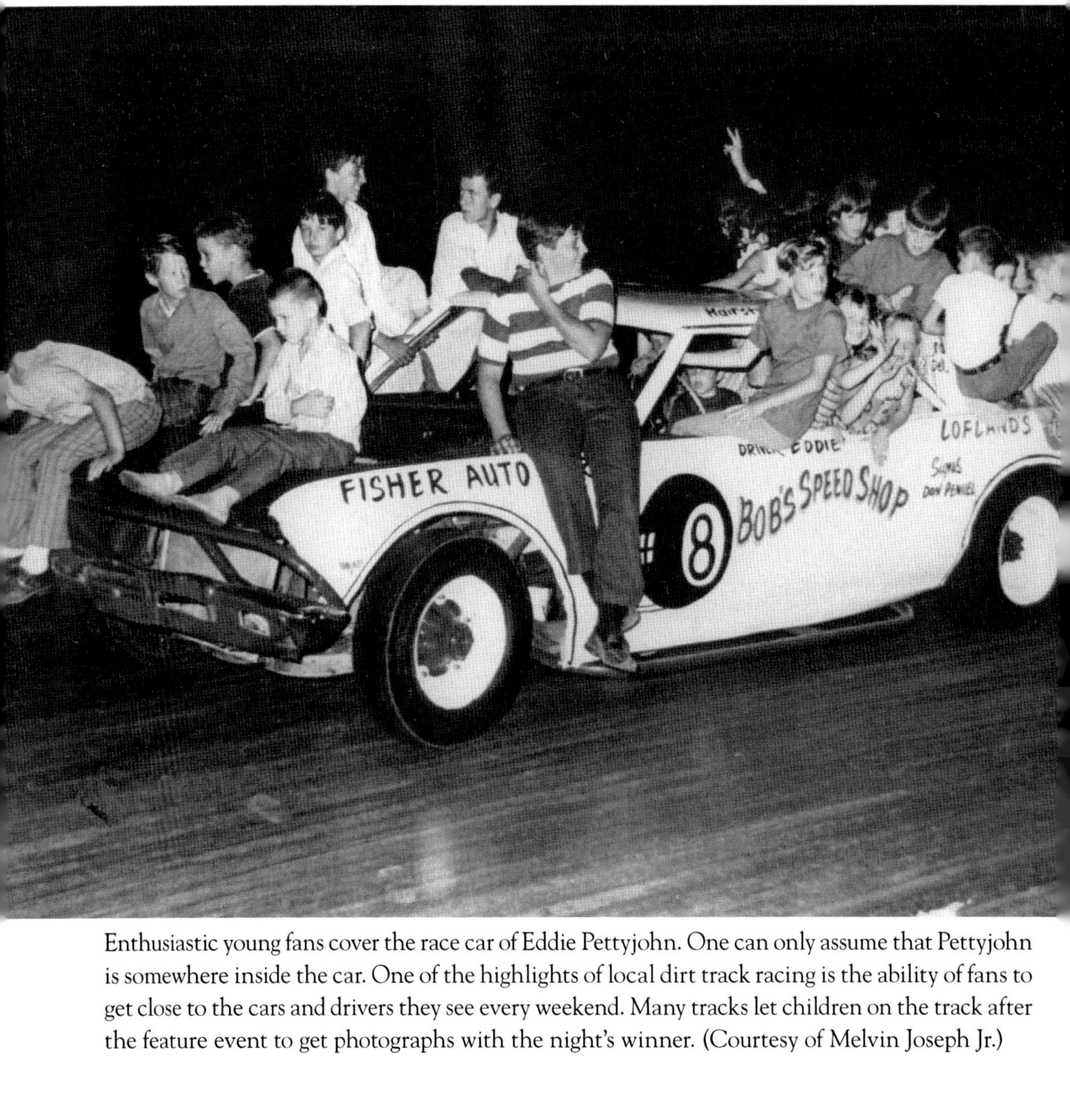

Enthusiastic young fans cover the race car of Eddie Pettyjohn. One can only assume that Pettyjohn is somewhere inside the car. One of the highlights of local dirt track racing is the ability of fans to get close to the cars and drivers they see every weekend. Many tracks let children on the track after the feature event to get photographs with the night's winner. (Courtesy of Melvin Joseph Jr.)

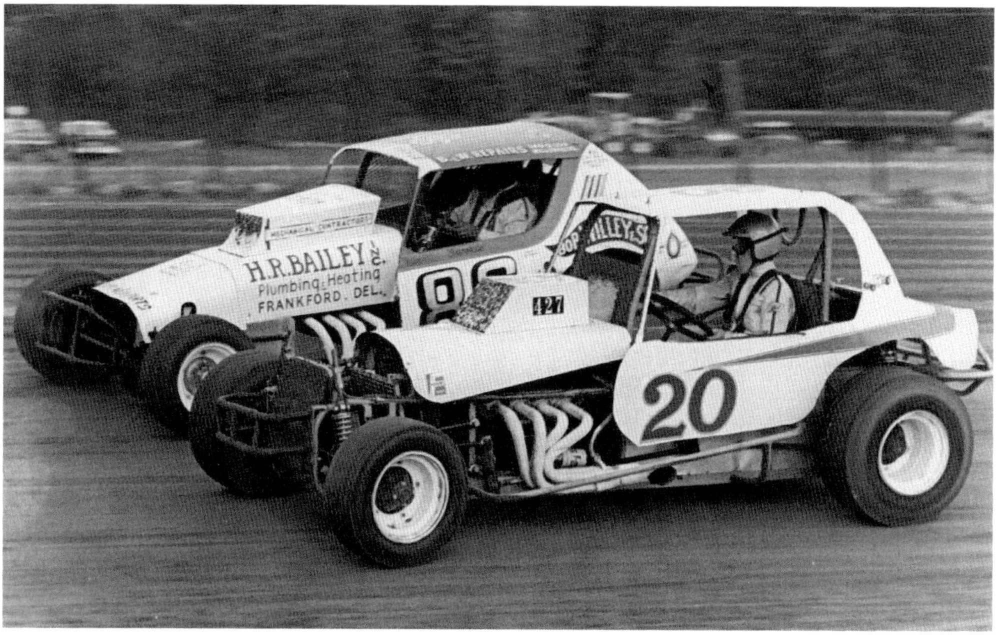

Paul Walker Jr. (No. 20) and Snookie Vent (No. 86) race around Georgetown Speedway just inches from each other. This view of the No. 20 car shows how little side protection drivers had in these evolving Modifieds. (Courtesy of David Grey.)

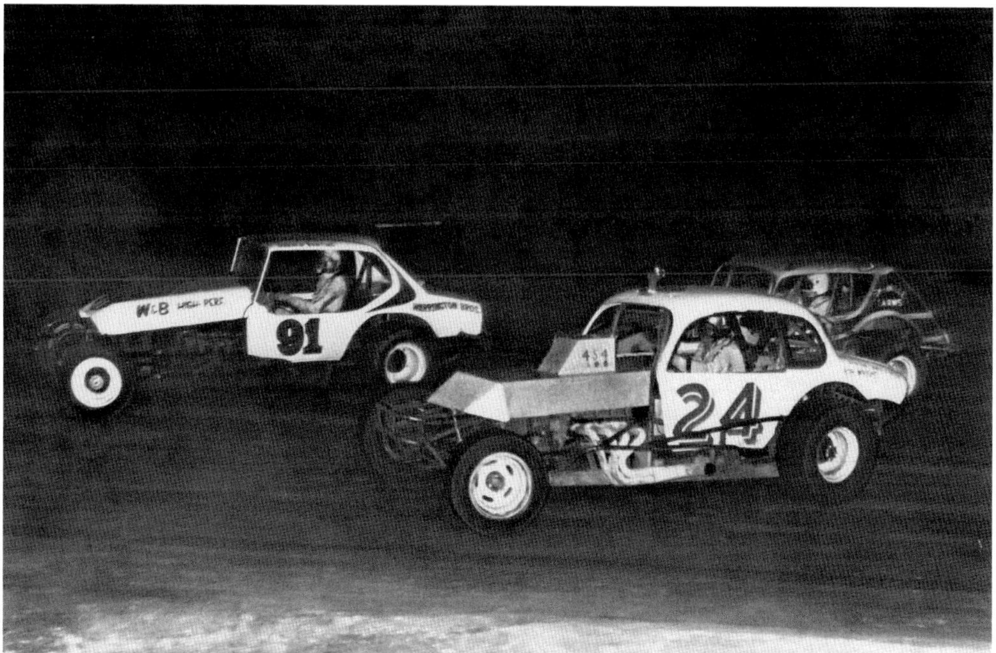

This photograph shows three distinct body styles of early-1970s Modifieds. Harold Bunting, in the No. 91, leads the No. 24, driven by either Ray Riggins or Joe Massey, who shared driving duties during the race season, and the No. 1 driven by Walter Breeding. (Courtesy of Charlie Brown.)

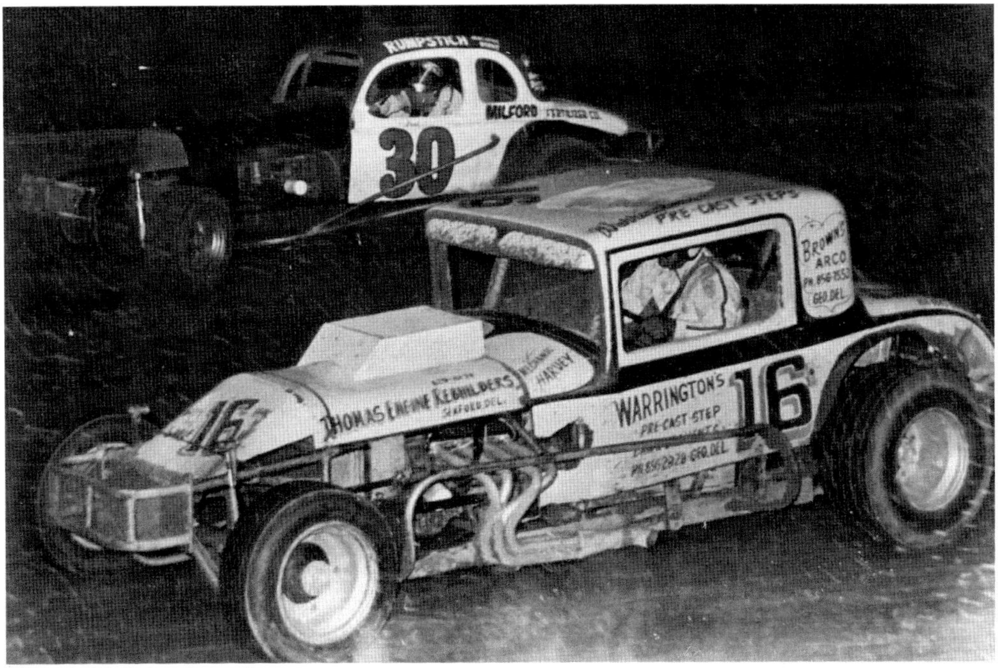

Cordia Warrington (No. 16) and Fred Workman (No. 30) take two distinctive racing lines as they power though the corners. One of the best things in this era of racing was the ability to see the driver fighting the steering wheel in the corners. Today's cars are much safer, and the driver is barely visible. (Courtesy of Paul Mills.)

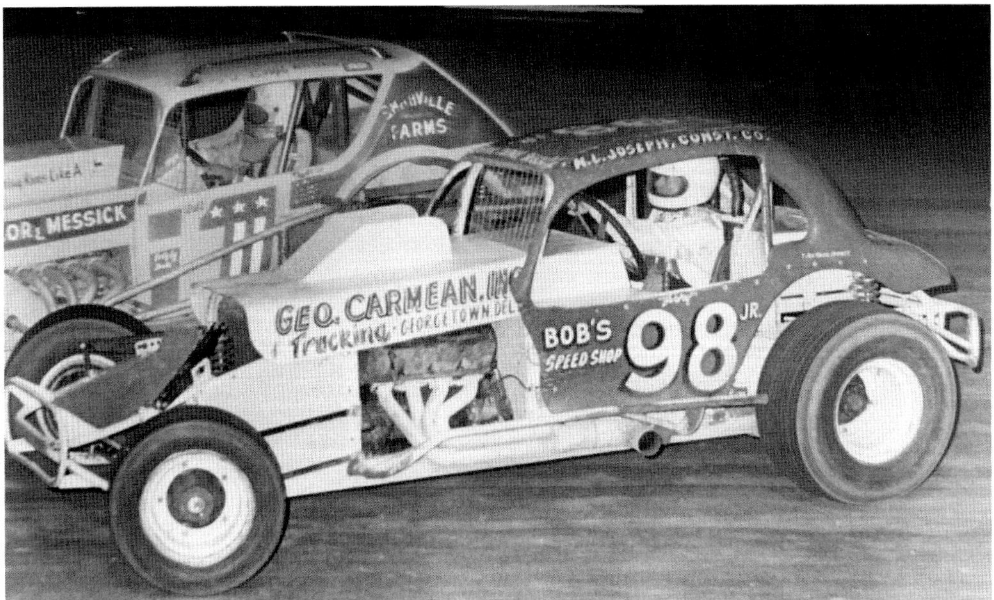

Jerry West (No. 98) broad-slides his car to try to get under Walt Breeding (No. 1). Both drivers are wearing new, safer full-face helmets. Note the cantilever suspension system on the front of West's car. (Courtesy of the Don Allen Collection.)

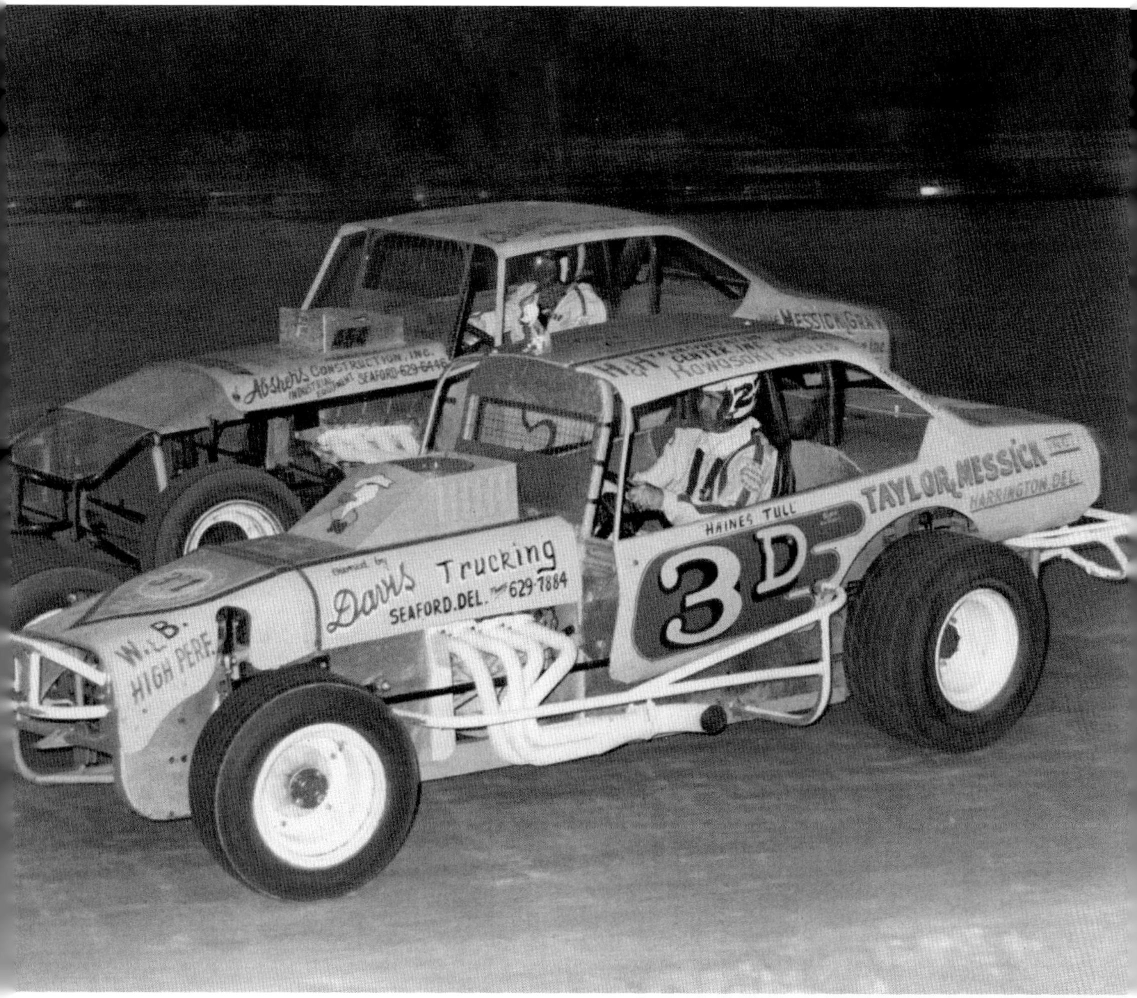

The popular Haines Tull (No. 3D) and Jack Sapp (No. 56) race door-to-door at Georgetown Speedway. The open-face helmets and lack of driving gloves are clearly visible, along with the Donald Duck attached to the top of Tull's car. (Courtesy of David Grey.)

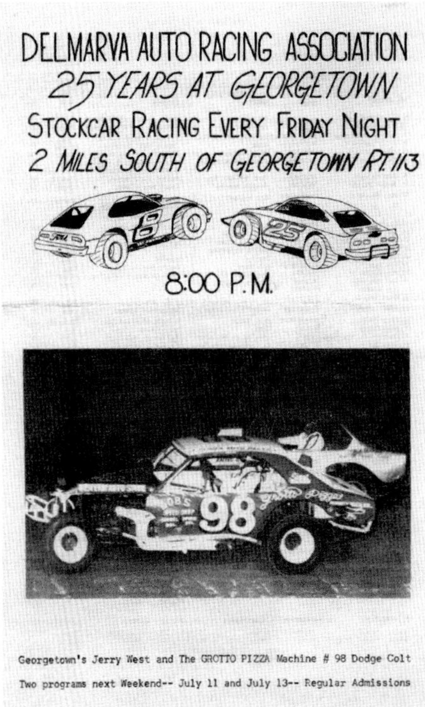

This Georgetown racing program advertises Friday-night racing starting at 8:00 p.m. sharp. For years, Georgetown ran on Friday nights, and Delaware International ran on Saturday nights. Many hotel parking lots looked like pits at a track as racers prepared their cars for the next night. (Courtesy of the Don Allen Collection.)

Snookie Vent assesses the damage to his No. 86 Modified after a tangle with Harold Bunting (No. 91). The racing action sometimes got too close, as drivers pushing their machines to the limit were not likely to back down or give an inch. (Courtesy of Snookie Vent.)

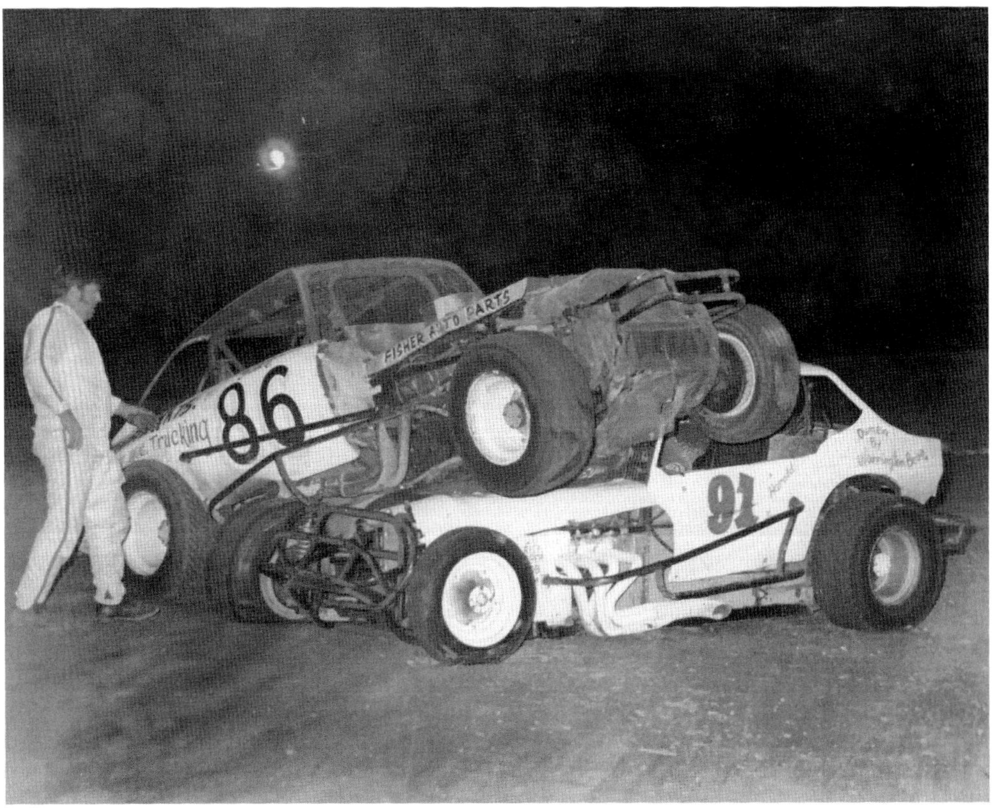

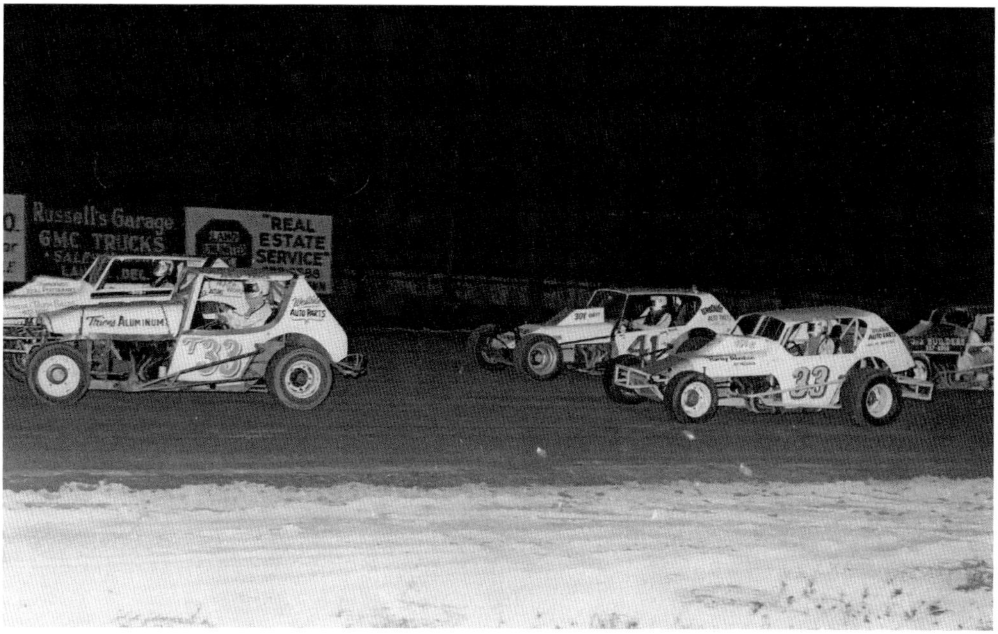

The No. T33 of David Trice and the No. 30 of Bobby Reed lead a pack that includes the No. 41 of Calvin Musser, the No. 33 of Gary Trice, and the No. 24 of Donnie Joseph Jr. (Courtesy of Calvin Musser.)

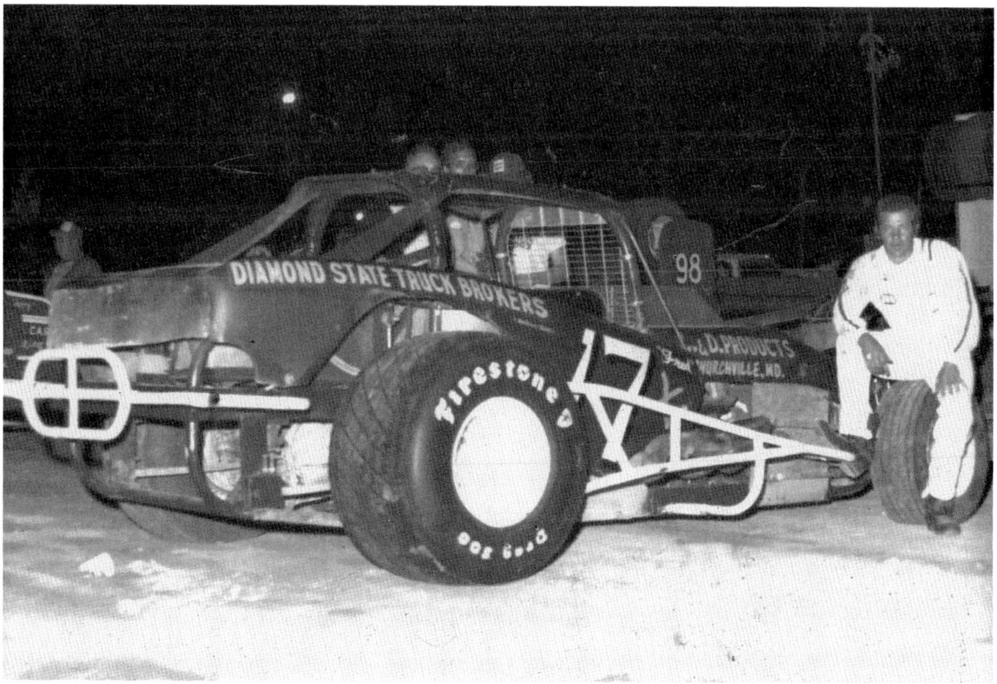

Fred Workman sits on the front tire of his Modified. Note the Firestone Drag 500 tire on the back of the car. Drivers would hand-groove the massive drag tires for use on their Modifieds. (Courtesy of Paul Mills.)

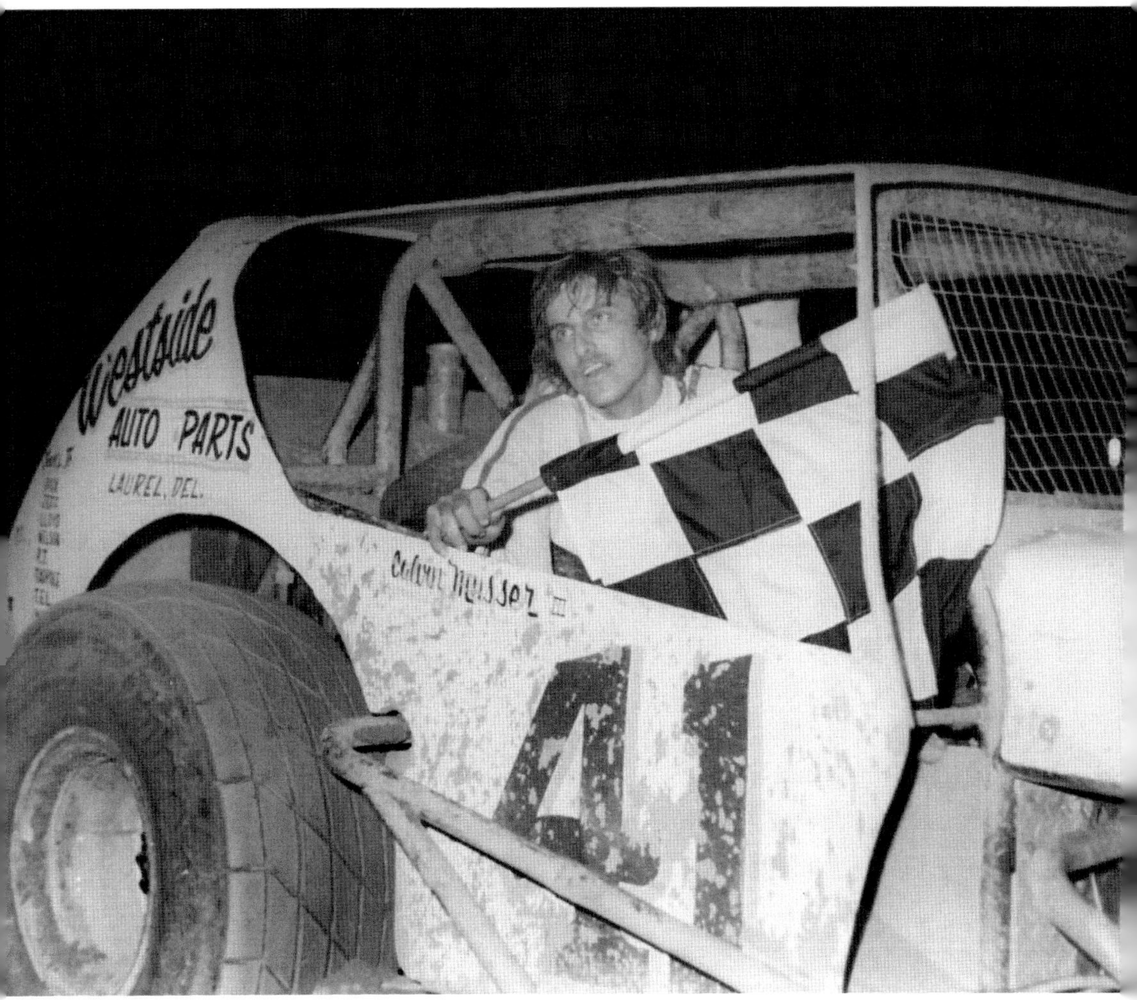

In Victory Lane, Calvin Musser's No. 41 Modified shows the wear and tear of battle on a local dirt track. Musser, of Laurel, Delaware, went on to win the July 27, 1977, race at the Delaware State Fair in Harrington. (Courtesy of Calvin Musser.)

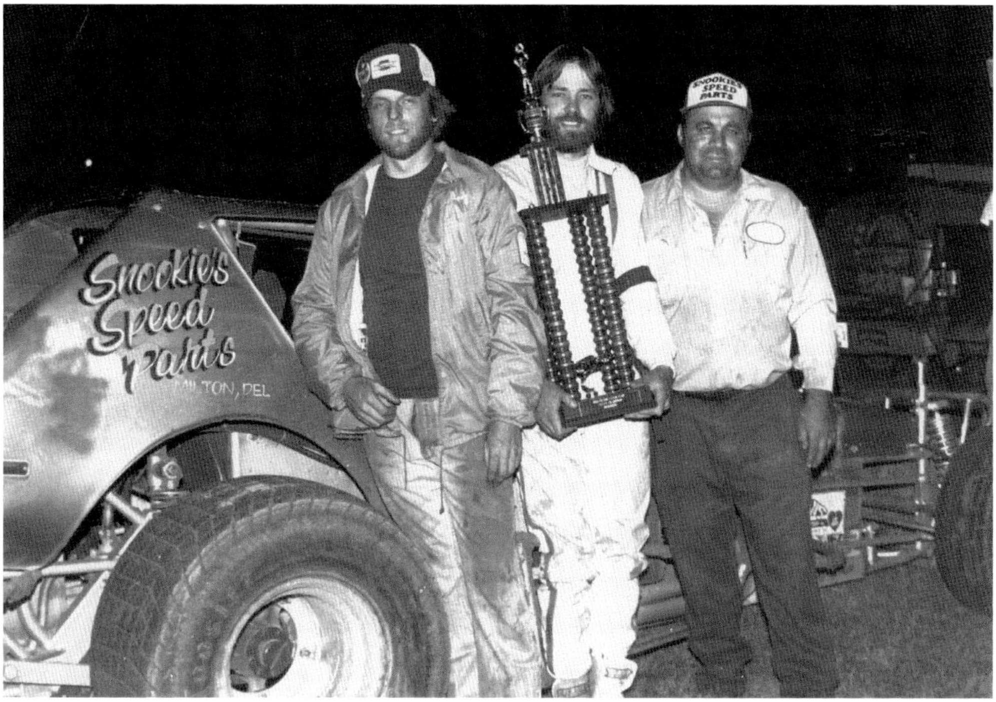

To be a champion takes a team effort. Here, Andy Anderson (left), Bobby Wilkins (center), and Snookie Vent celebrate the 1981 Delaware State Fair Modified Championship. (Courtesy of Snookie Vent.)

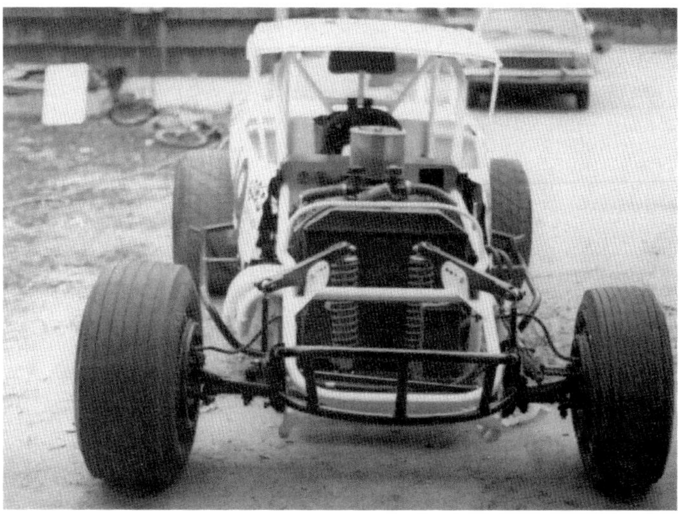

This head-on shot of a Modified shows the large amount of stagger in the tires. Stagger is the difference in tire circumference from left to right. Larger tires are fitted on the right side of a car to help it turn left. Many racers keep this ratio a well-guarded secret at the track. (Photograph by Bob Isaacs, courtesy of the Don Allen Collection.)

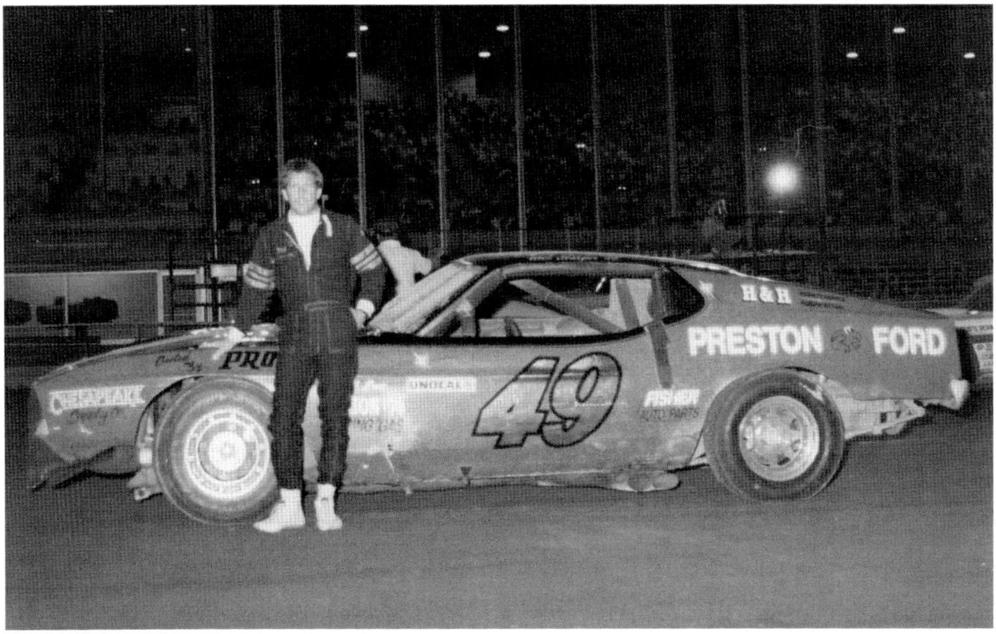

Melvin Joseph Jr. continued the winning ways of the No. 49. Joseph, a fan favorite, was always a threat to win in the Street Modified category. Joseph's bright-orange-and-black Ford Mustangs won many races throughout the state. (Courtesy of Melvin Joseph Jr.)

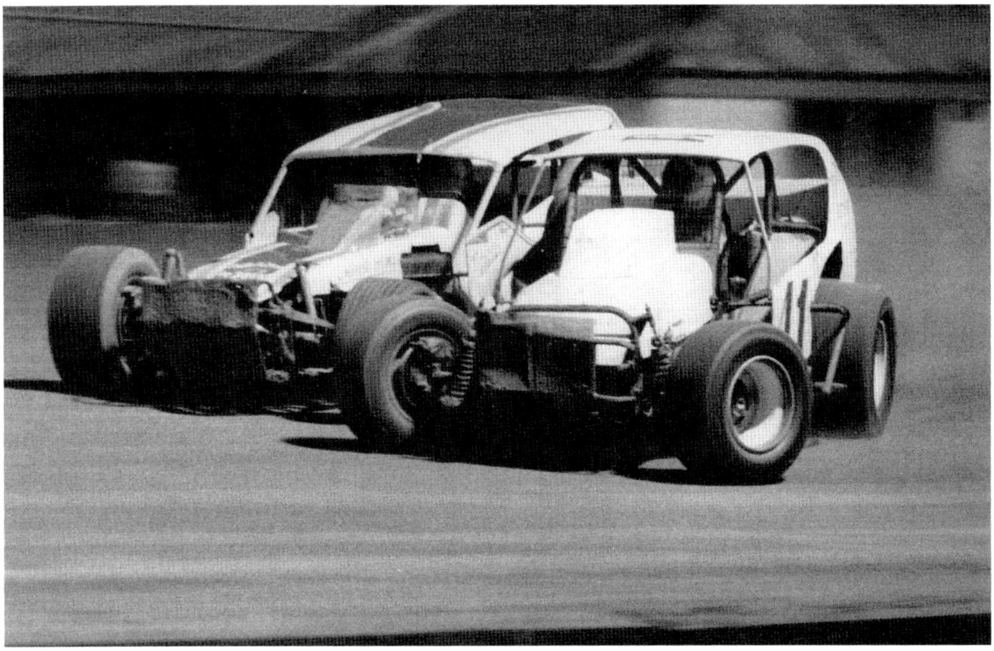

Walt Breeding (left) and Calvin Musser broad-slide through turn two at the Delaware State Fair. While Musser's car was typical of a late 1970s Modified, Breeding's had a radical design, built by Kenny Weld. The "Sidewinder" featured an offset engine, with the driver sitting to the right of the cockpit. (Courtesy of Calvin Musser.)

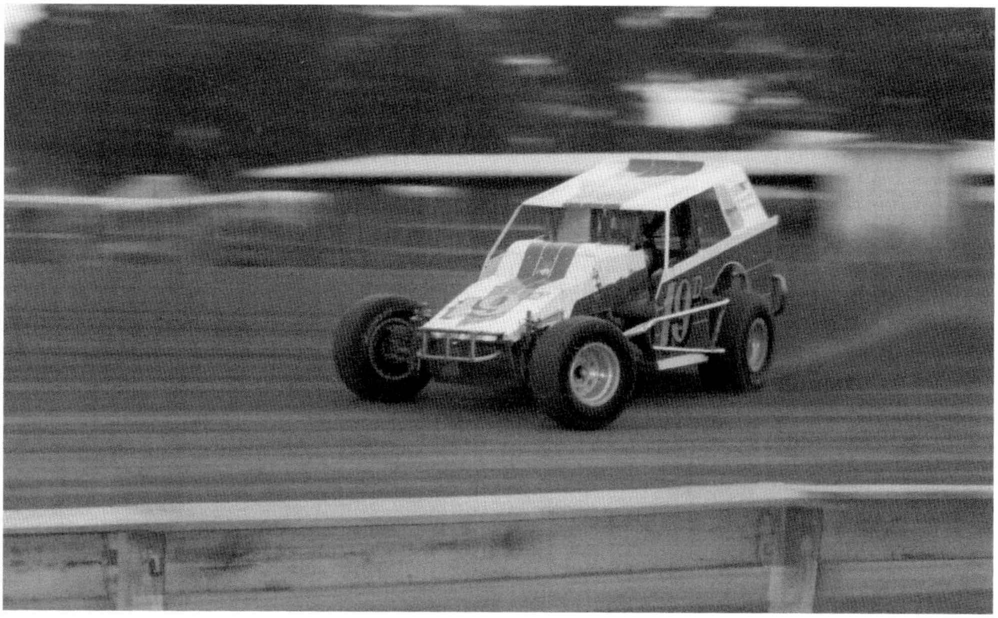

In 1986—his final season—Modified legend Harold Bunting went out a winner at the Delaware State Fair. Bunting swept both races in his No. 19D Modified. His performance earned him the Kent County Motor Sports Driver of the Year Award. (Courtesy of D&L Photos.)

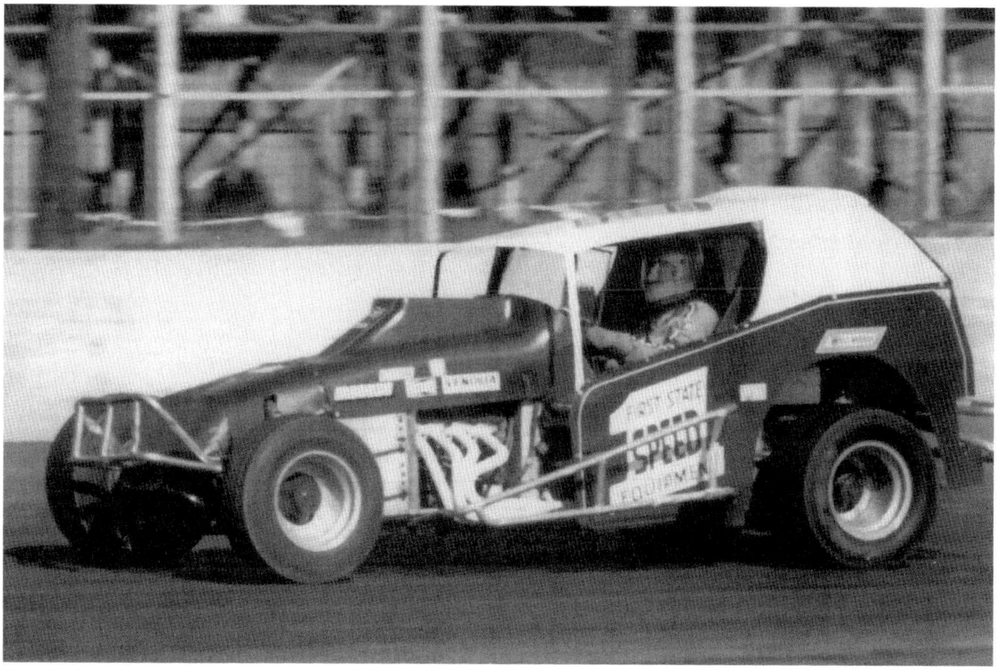

Don Twilley of Dover, Delaware, races past the grandstands at Georgetown Speedway in the fall of 1982. Twilley, who raced in the 1960s, 1970s, and 1980s, was one of just a few racers to have feature wins at Georgetown Speedway, Delaware International Speedway, and Little Lincoln Speedway. (Courtesy of the Twilley family.)

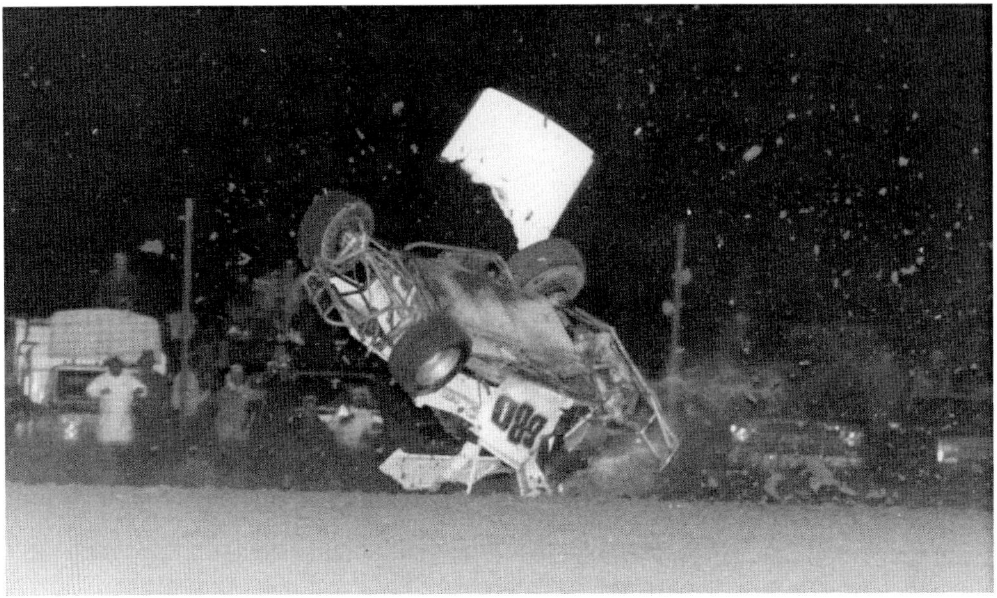

Richard Jarvis goes upside down in his No. 680 Modified. Cars have become much safer, and many innovations have been made. However, racing is still a dangerous sport, and both drivers and promoters do all they can to make sure the driver's safety is the number one priority. (Photograph by Don Marks, courtesy of the Don Allen Collection.)

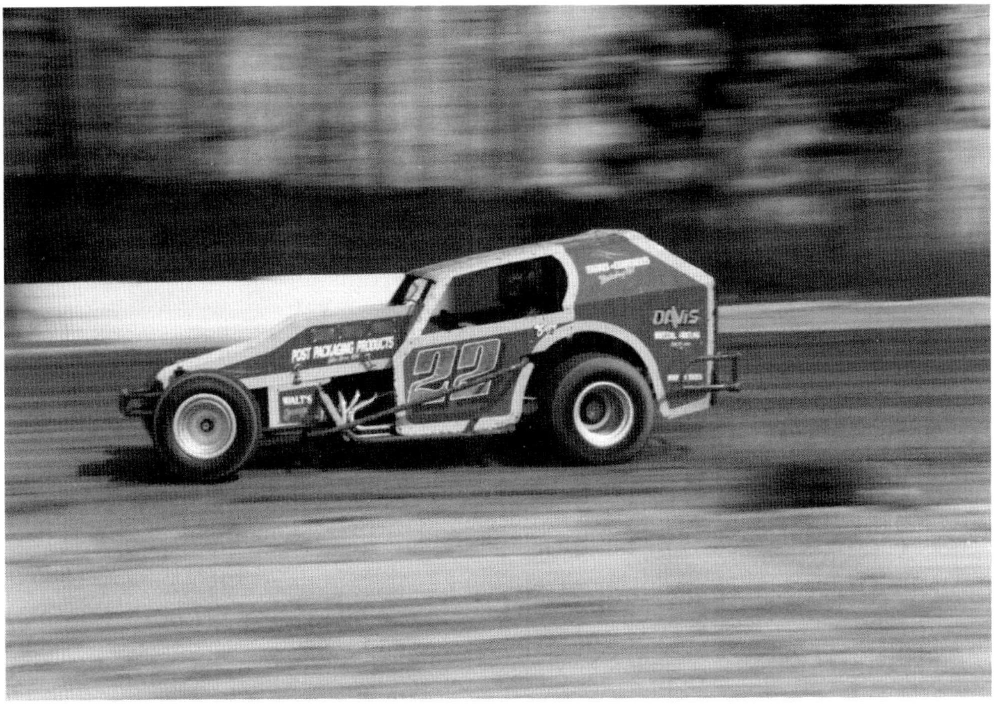

Bobby Walls (No. 22) had one of the best-looking Modifieds in Delaware. With performance to match the car's looks, Walls won 18 features at Delaware International Speedway and captured the Modified points championship at Georgetown Speedway in 1980. (Courtesy of D&L Photos.)

A.J. Foyt (left) attends the races at Georgetown Speedway with Melvin Joseph in August 1977. Foyt is the only driver to ever win the Indianapolis 500 (four times), the Daytona 500, the 24 hours of Le Mans, and the 24 hours of Daytona. Named one of NASCAR's 50 greatest drivers, Foyt's roots began on dirt tracks like the one at Georgetown. (Courtesy of Melvin Joseph Jr.)

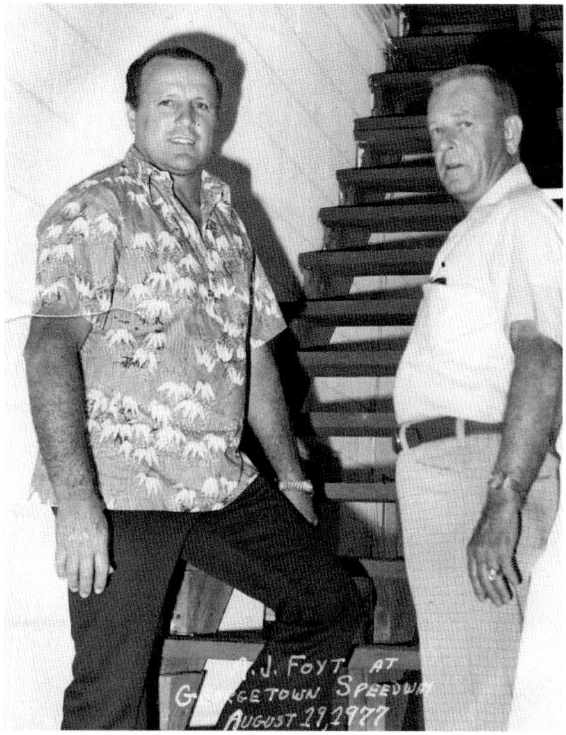

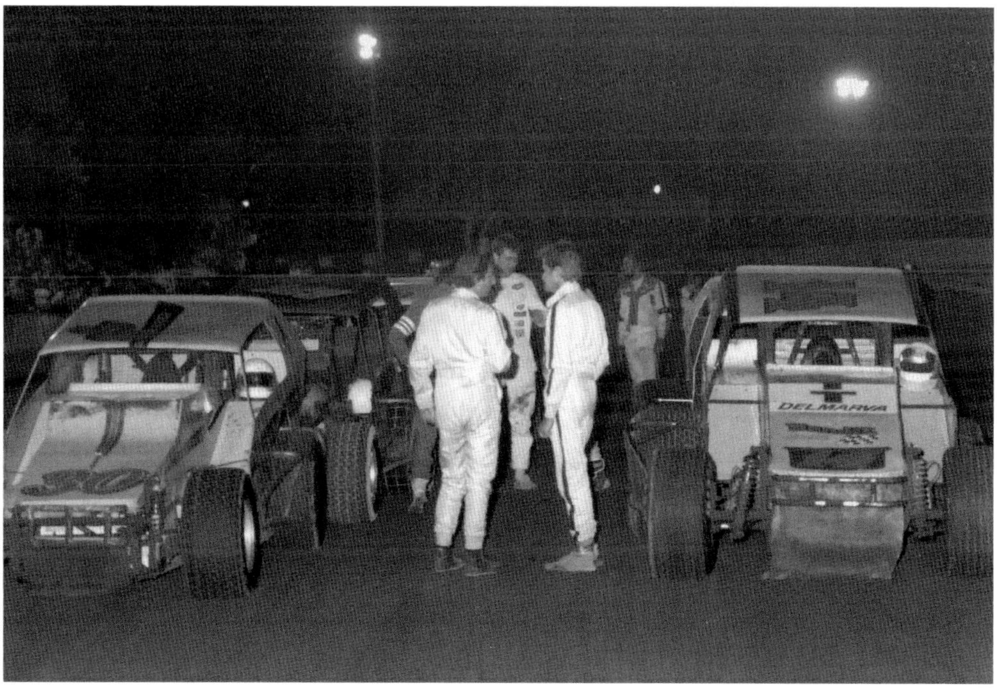

At the big Delaware State Fair race, drivers are caught in conversation just before driver announcements. Though they might be friendly before the race, when the helmet goes on, drivers focus on completing the job at hand—winning. (Courtesy of Helen Banks.)

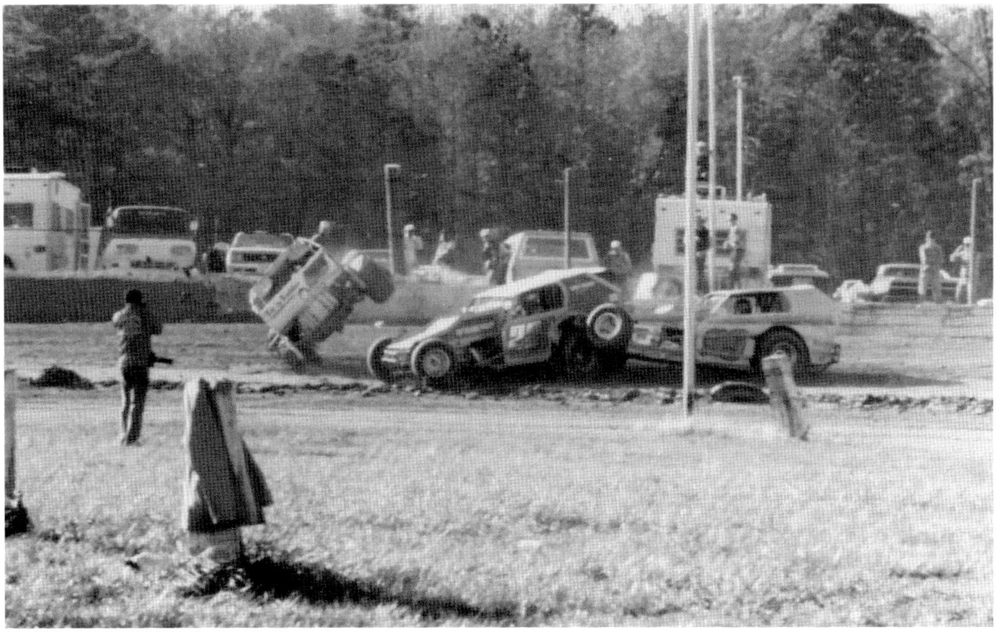

Freddy Brightbill (No. 25) flips wildly as Bobby Walls (No. 22) and No. 99 slam on the brakes to avoid contact. Photographing the race could be just as dangerous as driving. Photographer Don Allen captured photographer Ace Lane Jr. (at left) dangerously close to the action, with little protection between himself and the track. (Photograph by D&L Photos, courtesy of Helen Banks.)

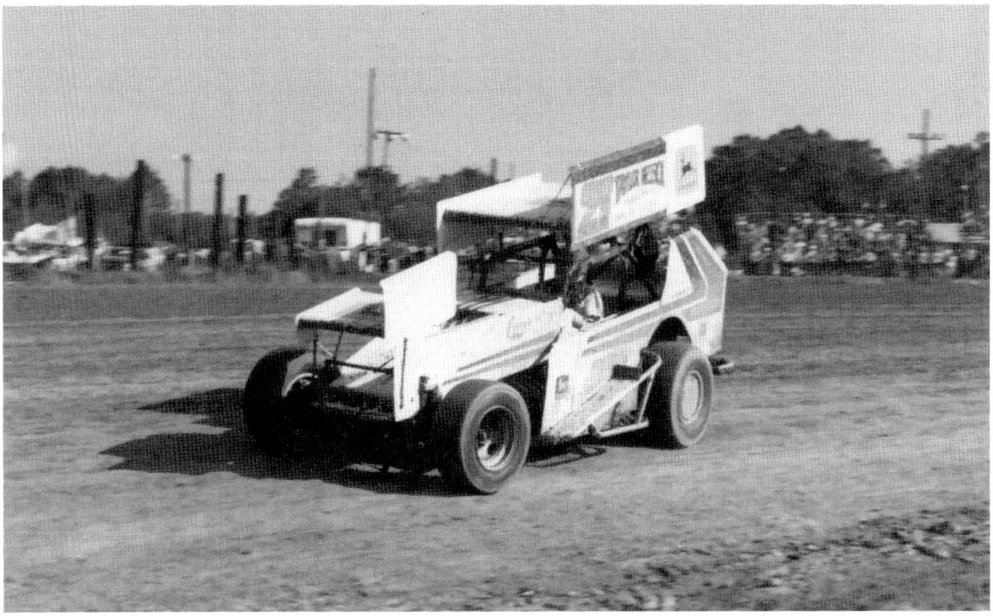

Open Competition Shows, or "Run What Ya Brung" races, were extremely popular at Delaware speedways. With no rules, competitors showed up with some wild-looking creations ready to take every chance at gaining valuable speed. With all those wings, Gary Gollub's car looks more like a plane than an automobile. (Courtesy of the Chad Culver Collection.)

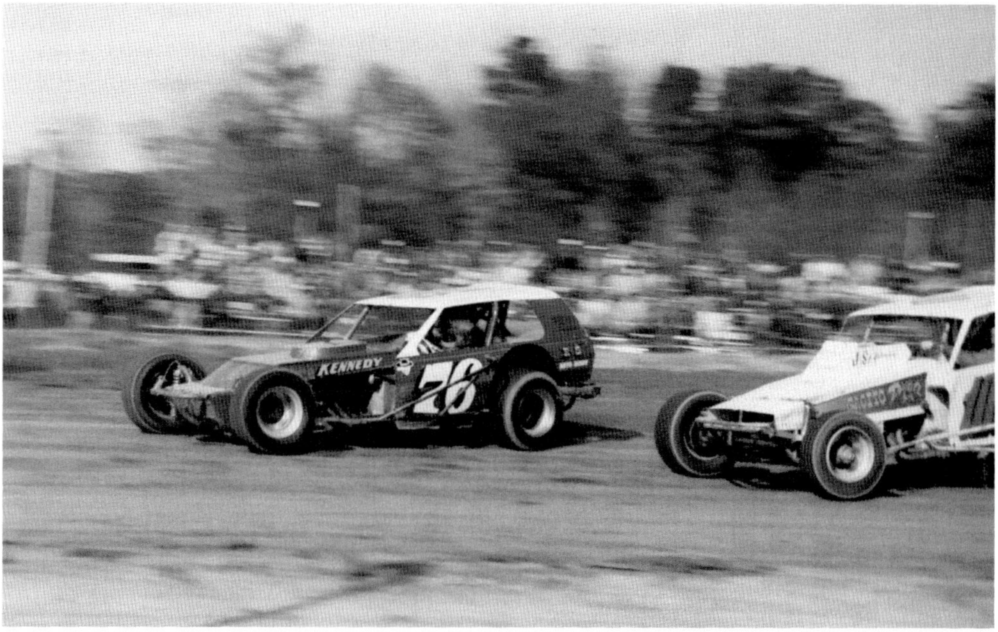

Gerald Chamberlain, in the No. 76, makes a rare appearance at Delaware International Speedway near the end of his historic racing career. Chamberlain had the second highest win total of all Modified drivers during the 1970s, with 140 wins. Only Kenny Brightbill had more, with 175 wins. (Courtesy of D&L Photos.)

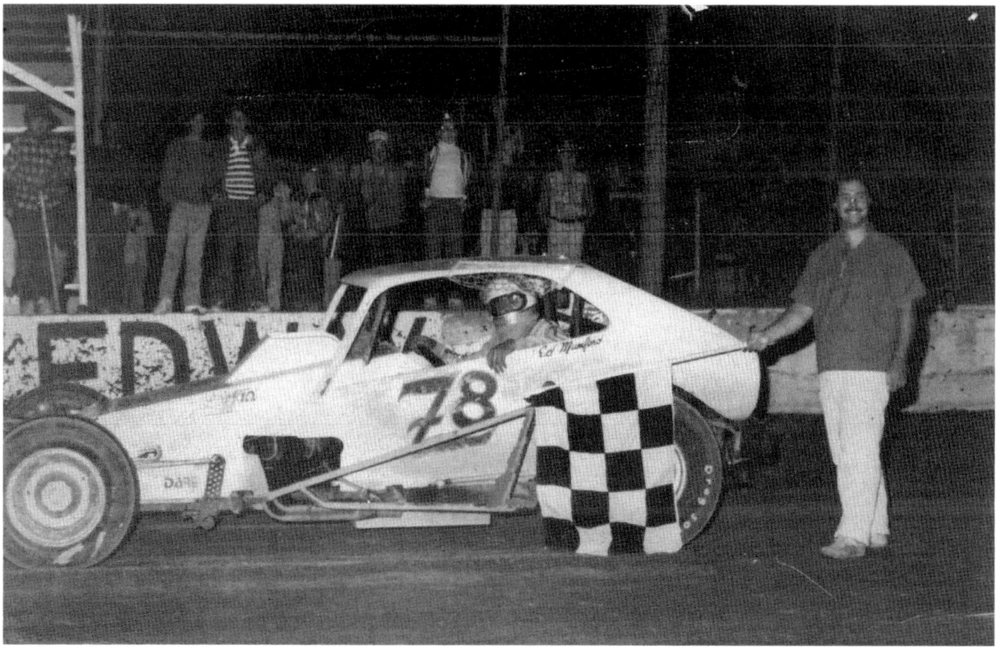

Ed Mumford poses in the victory lane in the No. Z8 Modified. Running against the larger Big Block engines, Mumford always ran a 314-cubic-inch small block engine. His choice of engine proved to be successful, as he won at Georgetown several times. (Courtesy of Melvin Joseph Jr.)

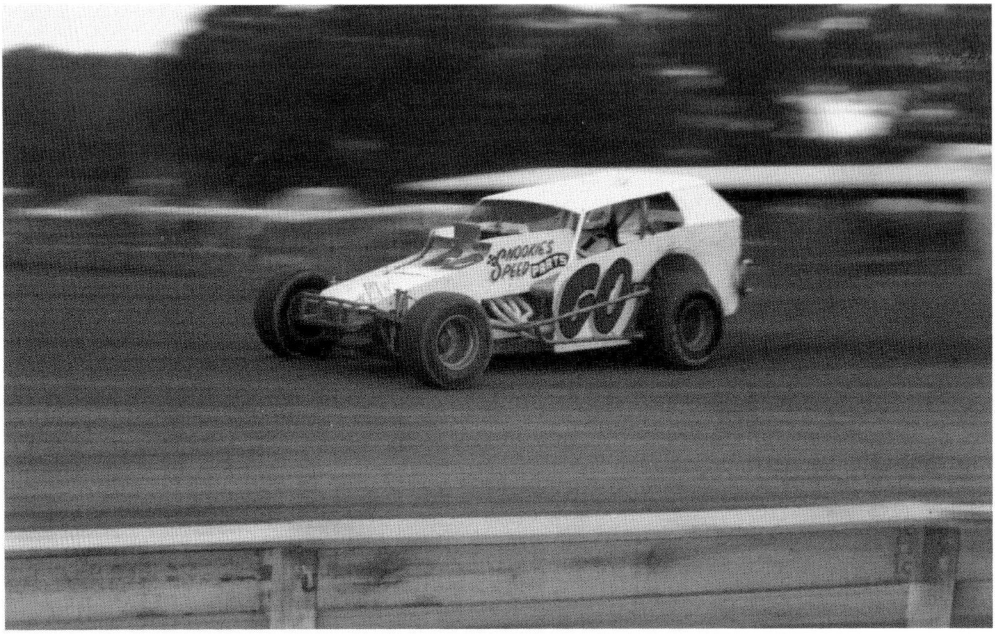

Jack Sapp, from Milford, was one of the first Delaware drivers to venture outside the state and race at places like Nazareth, Pennsylvania; East Windsor, New Jersey; and Reading, Pennsylvania. Sapp is pictured here in one of his last cars, No. GO. (Courtesy of D&L Photos.)

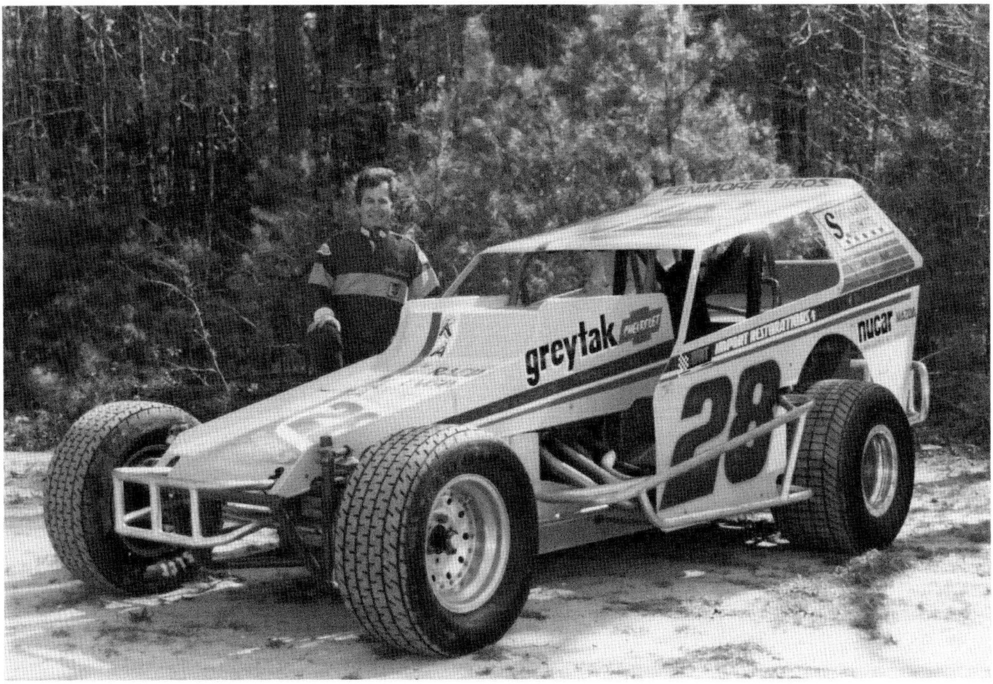

John Pinter proudly stands beside his No. 28 Modified. Pinter was the 1985 Georgetown Speedway Modified Points Champion. During his career, he also scored seven feature wins at Delaware International Speedway. (Courtesy of D&L Photos.)

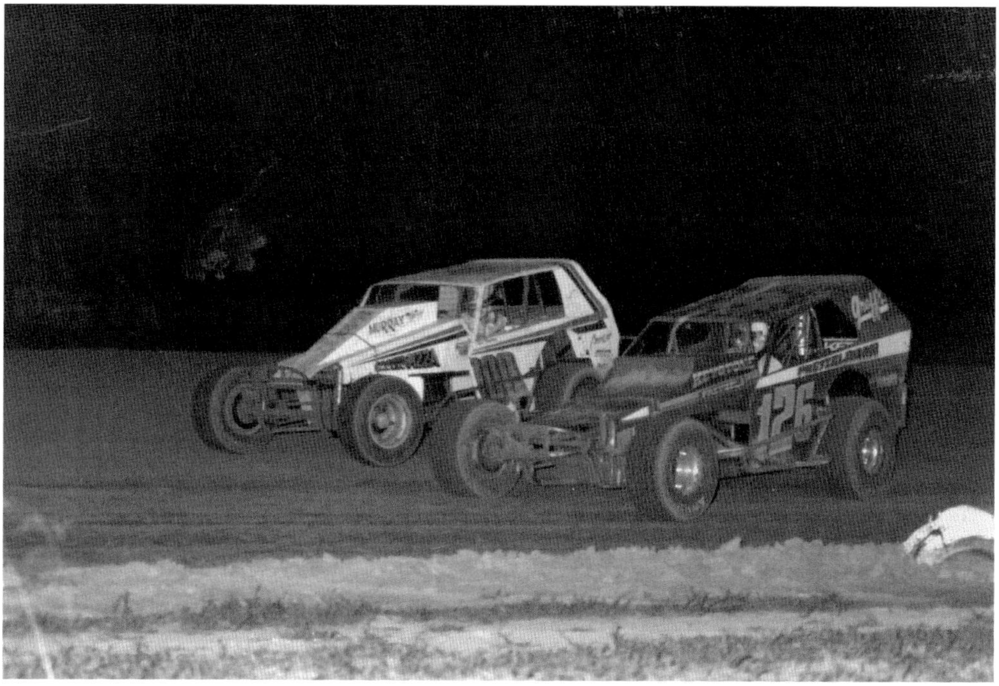

Local Hal Browning (No. 100) and invader Craig Von Dohren (No. 126), race side by side at Georgetown Speedway. Von Dohren had a very good year in 1986, with four victories at Georgetown. (Courtesy of D&L Photos.)

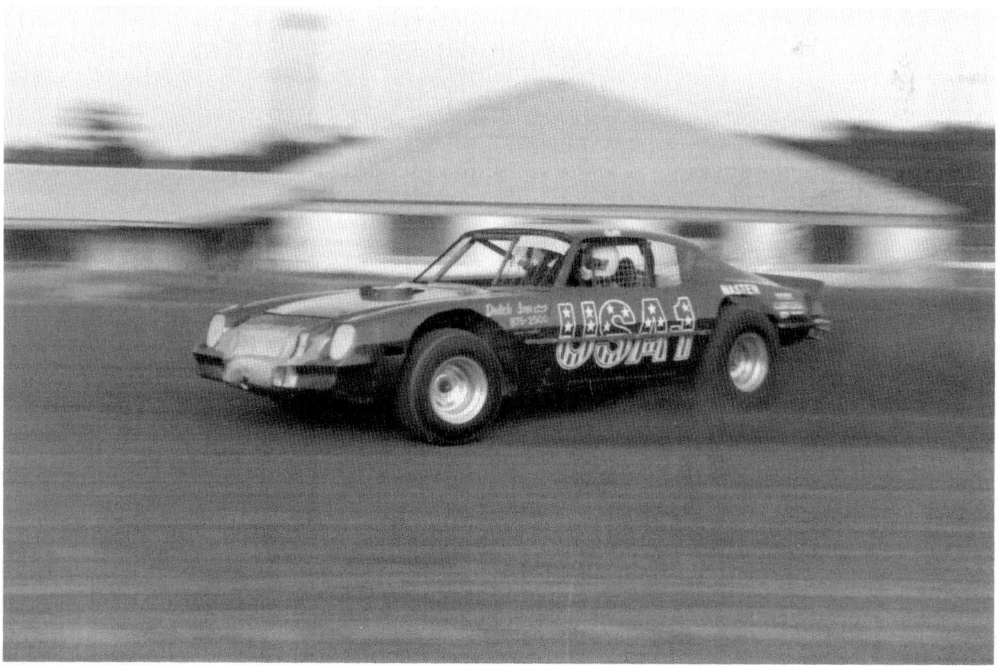

Jeff Turpin, pictured at the Delaware State Fairgrounds Speedway, drives the popular USA-1 Street Stock car. Note how close the horse barns are to the track. (Courtesy of D&L Photos.)

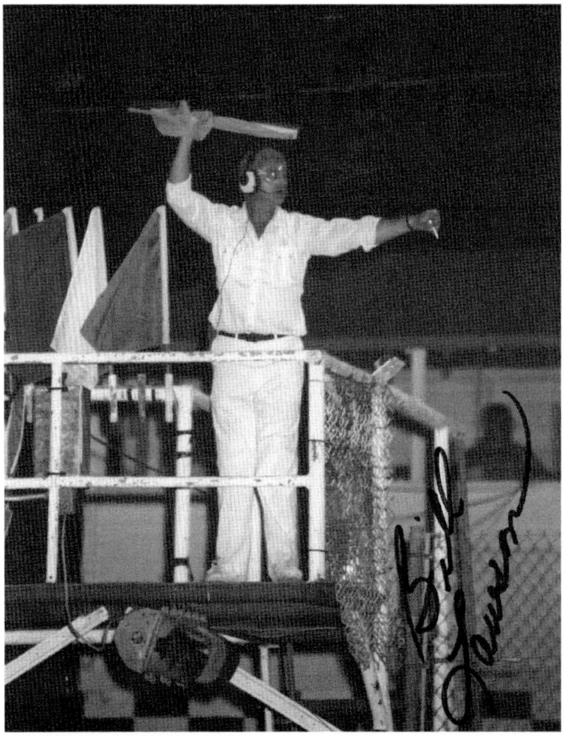

Bill Lawson, of Georgetown, Delaware, directs traffic as the field prepares to go green. Lawson had a unique style of flagging—he would throw one leg over the flag stand rail and hook his other leg on the side rail of the stand, leaning dangerously over the track to give commands to the racers. (Courtesy of D&L Photos.)

Seven-time United Racing Club feature-winner Billy Ellis (No. 27) tries to slide his Sprint Car under No. 26, Glenn Fitzcharles. Fitzcharles has the most URC wins in history, with 80 victories; he also won five URC championships. (Courtesy of D&L Photos.)

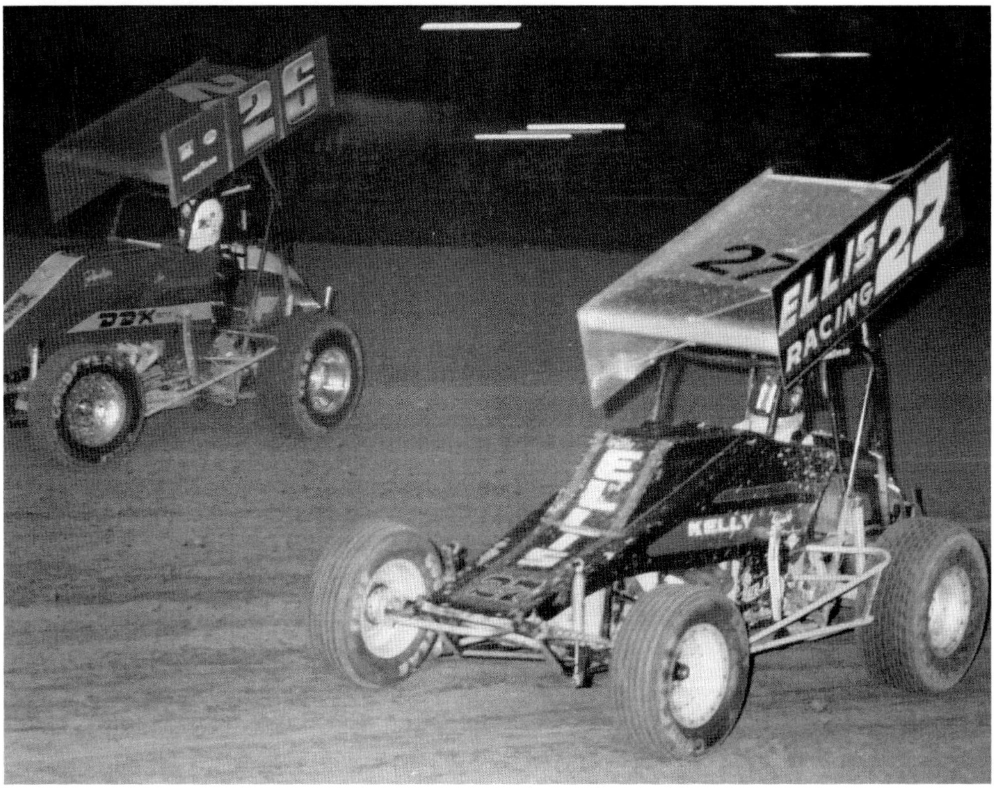

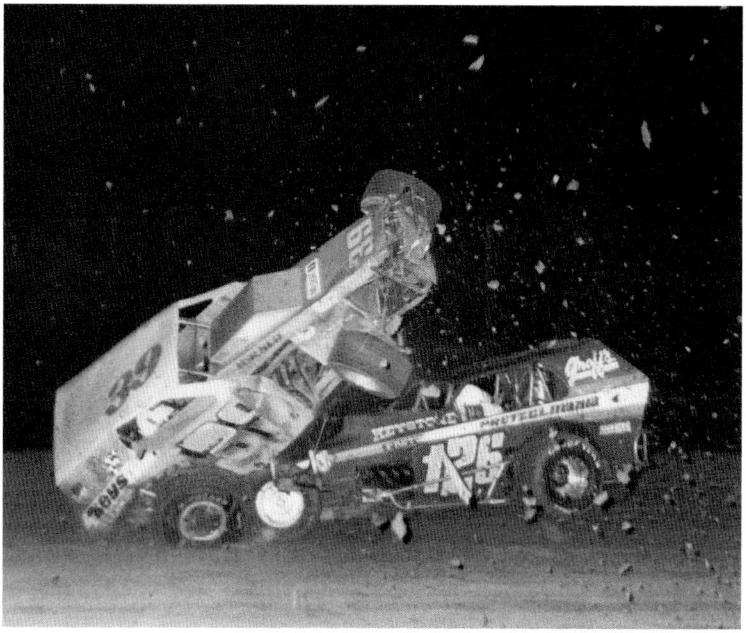

Ron Keys (No. 39) gets drilled by Craig Von Dohren (No. 126). By this point, Modifieds had made huge advances in construction and safety. Thanks to these improvements, both drivers were able to continue their racing careers after this nasty wreck. (Photograph by Jim Ritchie, courtesy of D&L Photos.)

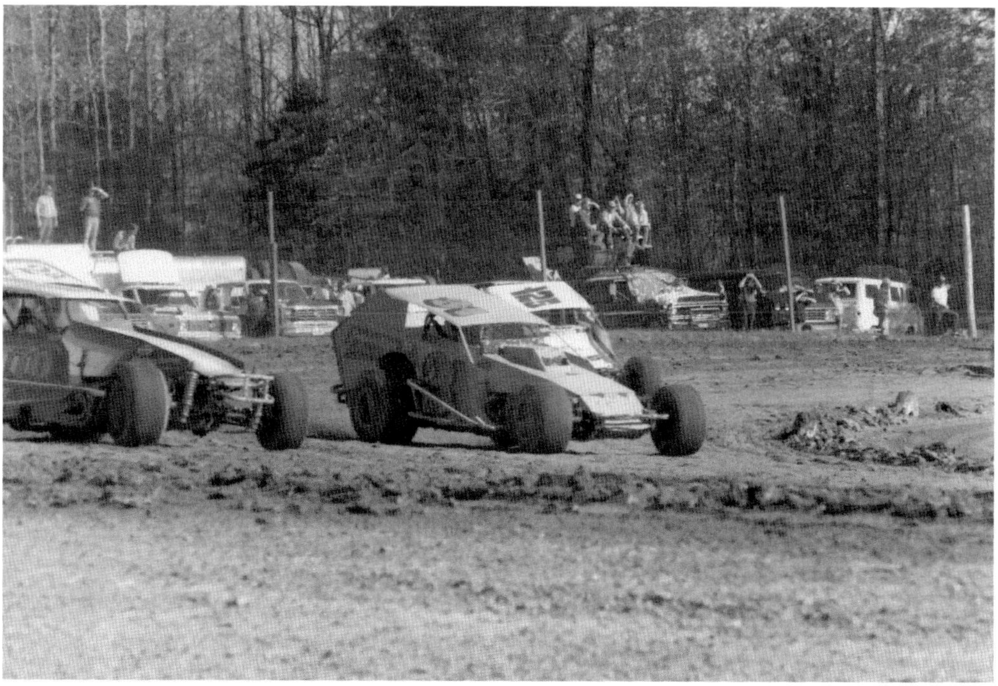

Modifieds start to form a cushion of thick clay around the top of the corner at Delaware International Speedway. Unlike asphalt tracks, dirt tracks are always changing, and racers must constantly alter the setup on the cars to remain fast. Experienced racers know how the track will change before it happens; this is called staying ahead of the track. (Courtesy of D&L Photos.)

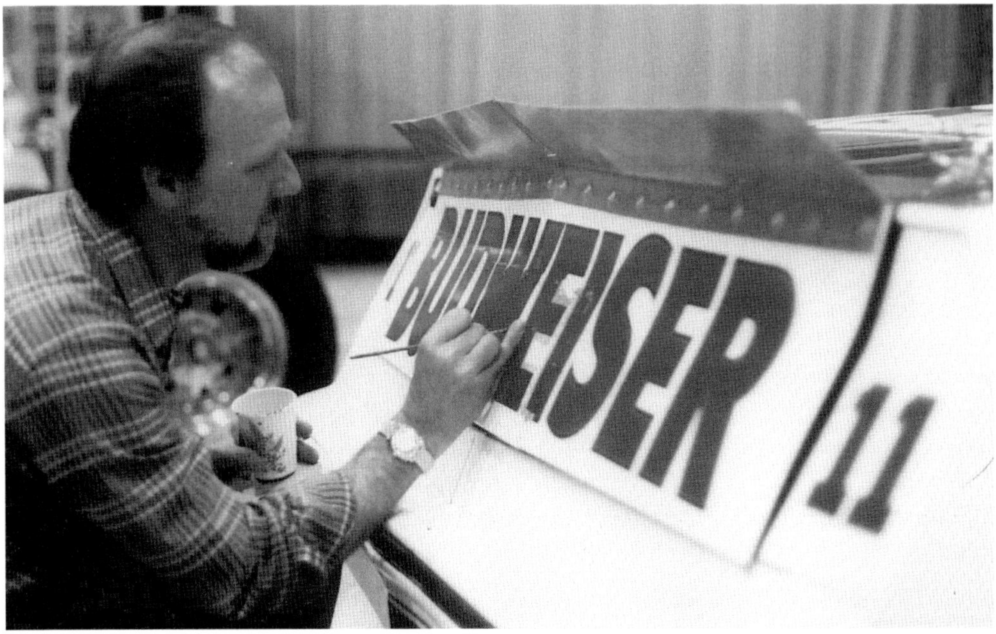

Before computer-printed graphics became the norm, artists hand-painted and lettered race cars. In this photograph, Richard Dix puts the finishing touches on Darrell Waltrip's No. 11 Budweiser car, owned by Junior Johnson. Artists like Dix and Don Penuel turned cars into works of art. (Courtesy of Betty Wyatt-Dix.)

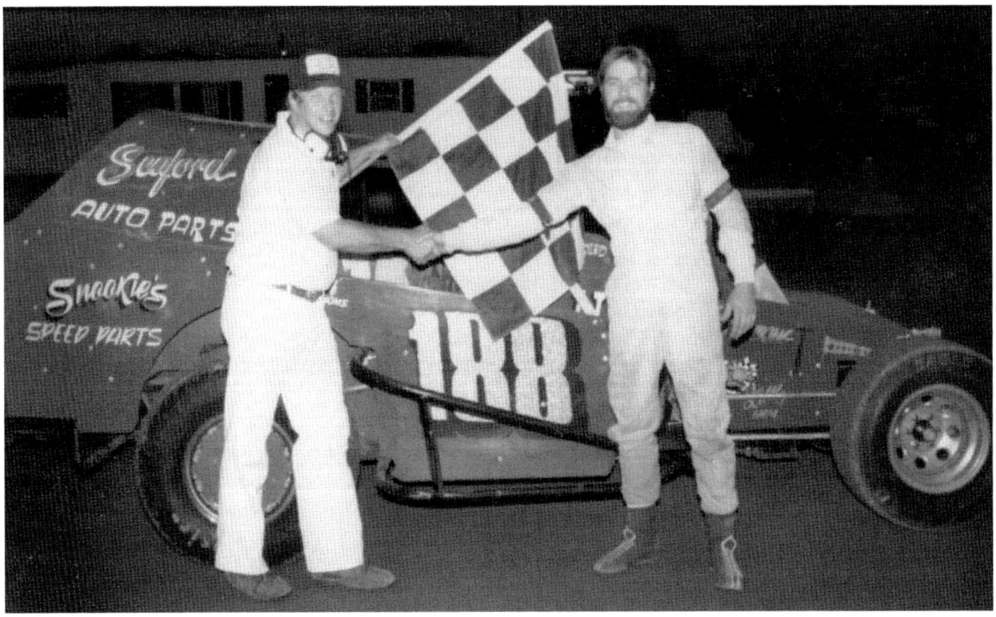

Bobby Wilkins (right) accepts the checkered flag from Bruce Webb at the Delaware State Fair. Wilkins and crew chief Andy Anderson partnered with car owner Harry Dutton to field the No. 188. Wilkins won the 1983 Delaware State Fair Stock Car Championship. (Courtesy of the Chad Culver Collection.)

In this 1978 photograph, Norris "Speedy" Reed (left) and Walter Messick stand on pit road at Georgetown Speedway. Both men loved racing and made lasting contributions to the sport. (Courtesy of Taylor and Messick Inc.)

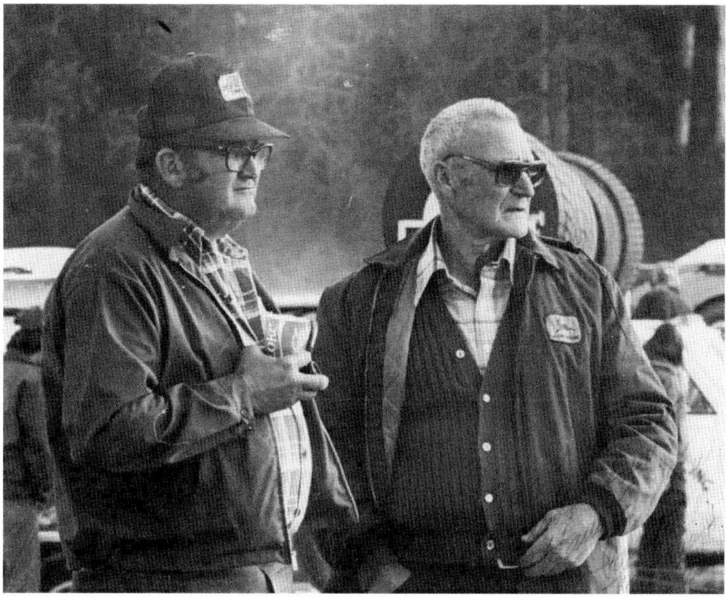

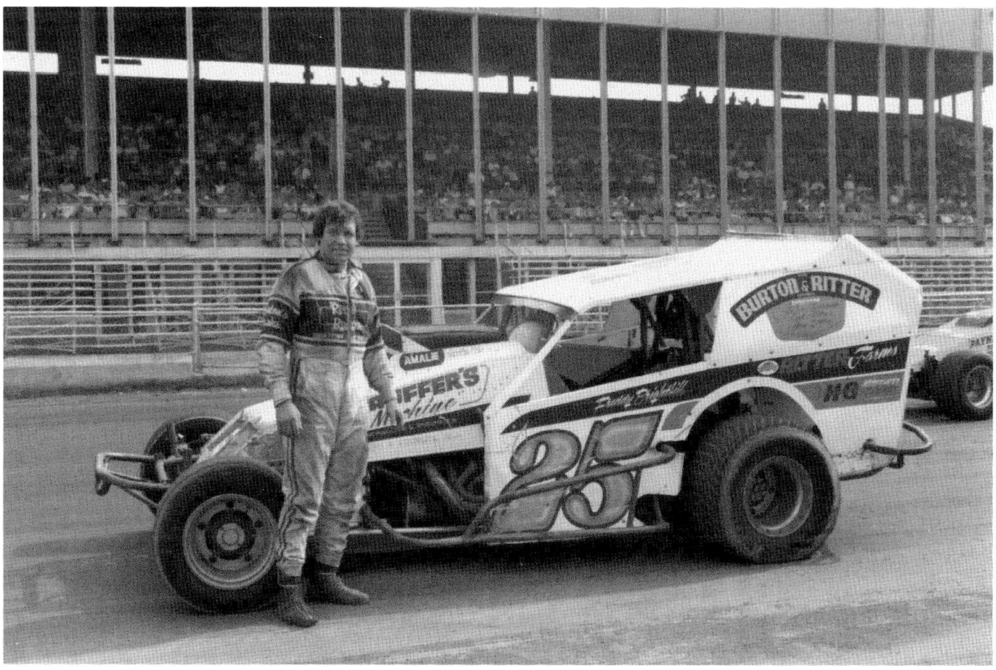

Freddy Brightbill stands on the front stretch of the Delaware State Fairgrounds Speedway next to his Ritter Farms–sponsored Modified. Note the massive rear tire and how it crinkles from low air pressure. (Courtesy of D&L Photos.)

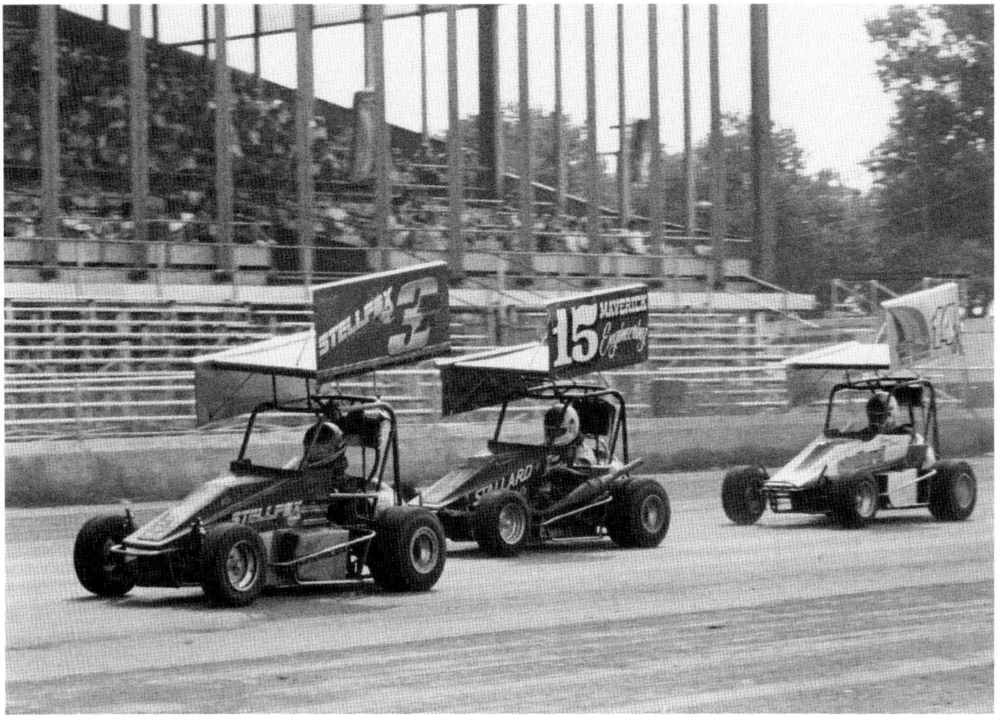

Micro Sprint Cars run at the Delaware State Fair. These cars are scaled-down versions of the larger Sprint Cars. Although smaller, they are just as quick and dangerous as full-size race cars. There are two main tracks in Delaware for Micro Sprints: Airport Speedway, in New Castle, and Middleford Speedway, in Seaford. Both are still in operation today. (Courtesy of D&L Photos.)

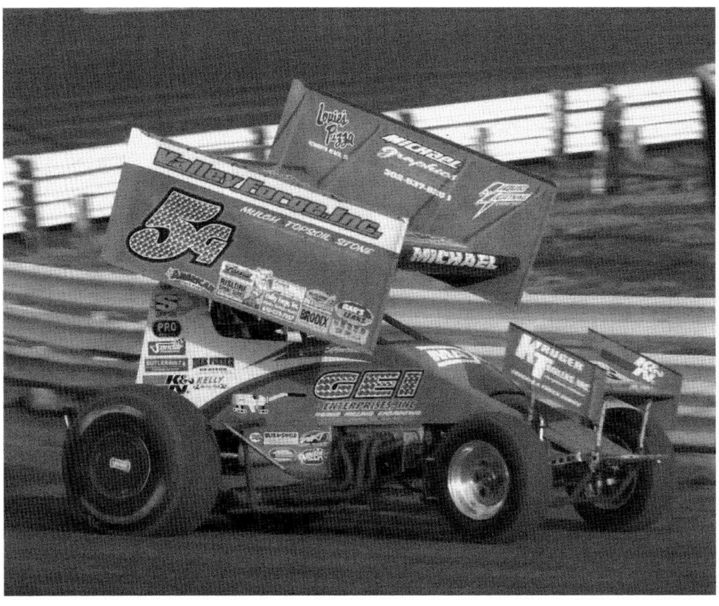

Curt Michael, of Ocean View, Delaware, is an eight-time United Racing Club Sprint Car Champion. No other driver in the long and storied history of the URC has ever won as many championships. Michael was also the first driver to win five championships in a row. (Courtesy of Curt Michael.)

4

DOVER DOWNS SPEEDWAY

"The Monster Mile," as Dover Downs Speedway is affectionately called, is a one-mile concrete oval that sits in the middle of Delaware. Holding NASCAR races since 1969, it has become known as one of the toughest tracks in existence. It is unique in that it is a year-round racing facility that has both horse and auto racing.

In the mid-1960s, David P. Buckson, a lawyer and politician, wanted to build a track for horse racing in Dover. At the same time, construction contractor and racing enthusiast Melvin L. Joseph wanted to build a track for big-time auto racing in Delaware. Together, the men, along with industrialist John W. Rollins, purchased a 204-acre tract of farmland owned by Thomas Murray. The idea was to have a dual-purpose facility with a .625-mile dirt track for horse racing and a high-banked, one-mile oval for auto racing. The one-mile length came about not by design but because that was the maximum they could fit on the land. The design of the track came from Melvin Joseph, who was aided by Richard E. Haber, former chief engineer of the Delaware State Highway Department. The track had 24-degree banked turns and 9-degree banked straightaways. Also, the walls were uniquely constructed—Joseph installed over 400,000 pounds of .375-inch thick boilerplate steel for the retaining walls, the theory being that it was cheap to install and slick, so when a car hit the wall, it would simply slide down the boilerplate.

In 1969, construction was completed at a cost of $12.5 million. Dover Downs held its first NASCAR race—the Mason-Dixon 300—on July 6, 1969. Richard Petty won the race, to the delight of about 20,000 fans. Continually expanding and growing, Dover Downs continues to host harness racing, as well as two weekends of NASCAR racing per year. The grandstands now hold over 135,000 people and completely encircle the track.

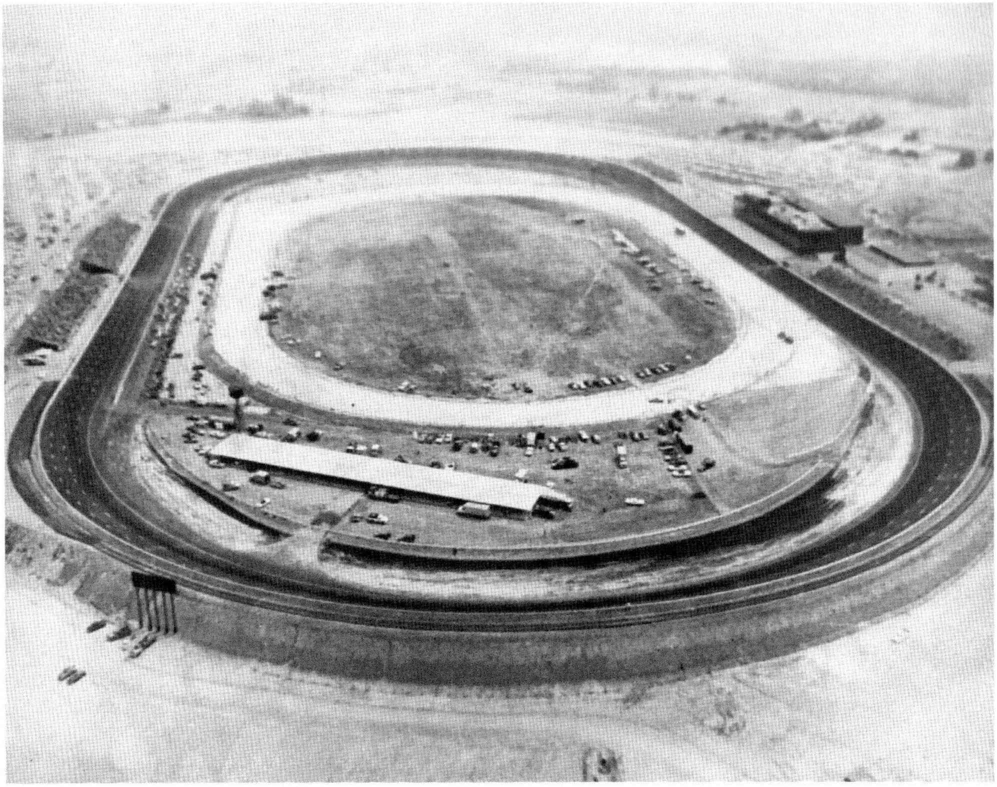

In this early aerial photograph of Dover Downs Speedway, the .625-mile horse track is visible inside the one-mile, 24-degree banked speedway. For the first race, in 1969, Dover had 10,333 bleacher seats. Today, Dover has seating for well over 100,000, including a unique "Monster Bridge" that allows fans to sit directly over the track on the backstretch. (Courtesy of Joe Ann Adams, representing the Melvin Joseph family.)

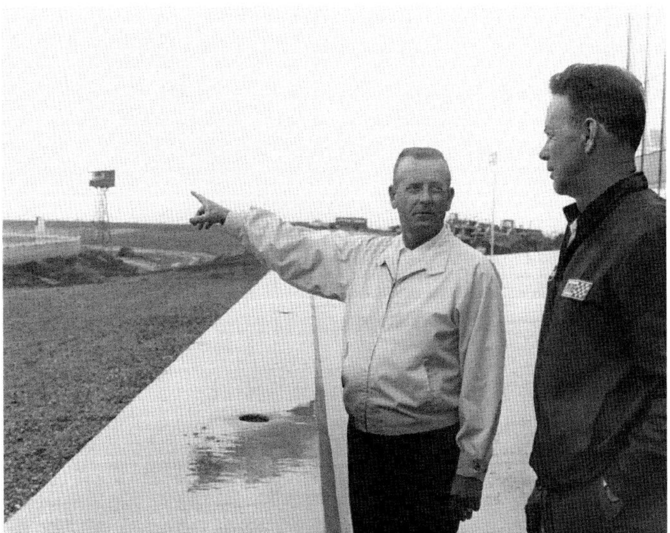

Melvin Joseph (left) points out some features of an unfinished Dover Downs to Ralph Moody. Construction of the one-mile track was a huge challenge. Headed by Joseph and his superintendent, Leroy Betts, it lasted for nearly two years and was completed just in time for the first race in July 1969. (Courtesy of Joe Ann Adams, representing the Melvin Joseph family.)

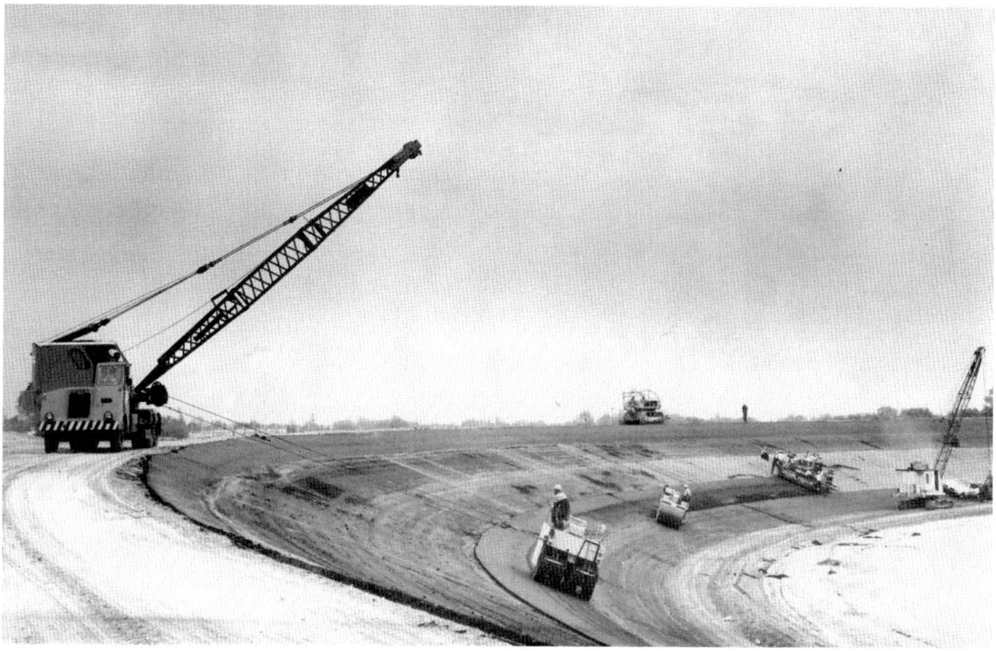

Building a track with 24-degree banking that was five stories tall provided quite a challenge for Melvin Joseph and his construction team. The biggest problem was how to hold the heavy equipment needed for construction on the high banks. Joseph came up with the simple, cost-effective solution of using cables to tether the equipment to a 35-ton crane that sat on top of the banking. After the track was graded, Joseph added four layers of asphalt to complete the racing surface. (Both, courtesy of Joe Ann Adams, representing the Melvin Joseph family.)

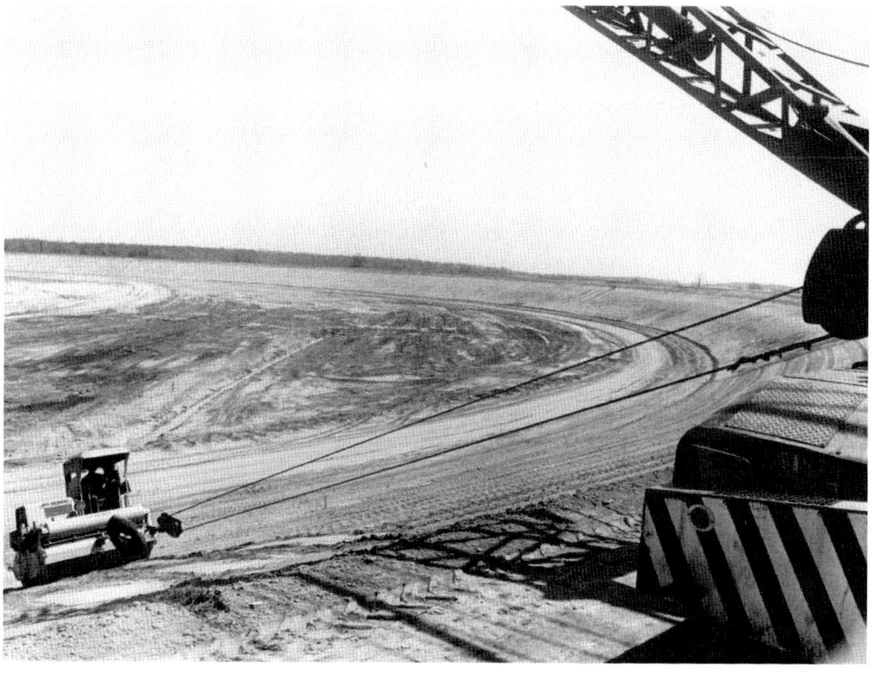

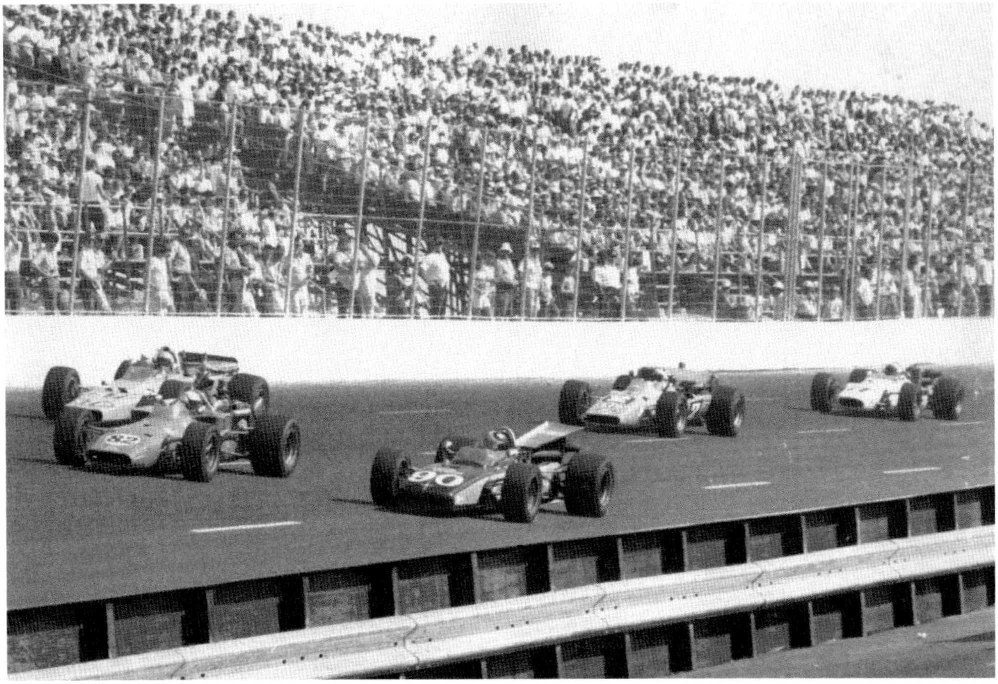

USAC Indy cars roar down the front stretch at Dover Downs in August 1969. Art Pollard (No. 57) went on to win the crash-marred race in a Plymouth-powered car; to date, this was the only victory for a Plymouth in Indy-car history. The high banks and high speeds proved to be too dangerous for the open-wheel Indy cars; as a result, they did not return to Dover until 1998. The Monster Mile proved once again that it was too tough to tame, as only 10 of 22 starters finished the race that year. (Courtesy of Joe Ann Adams, representing the Melvin Joseph family.)

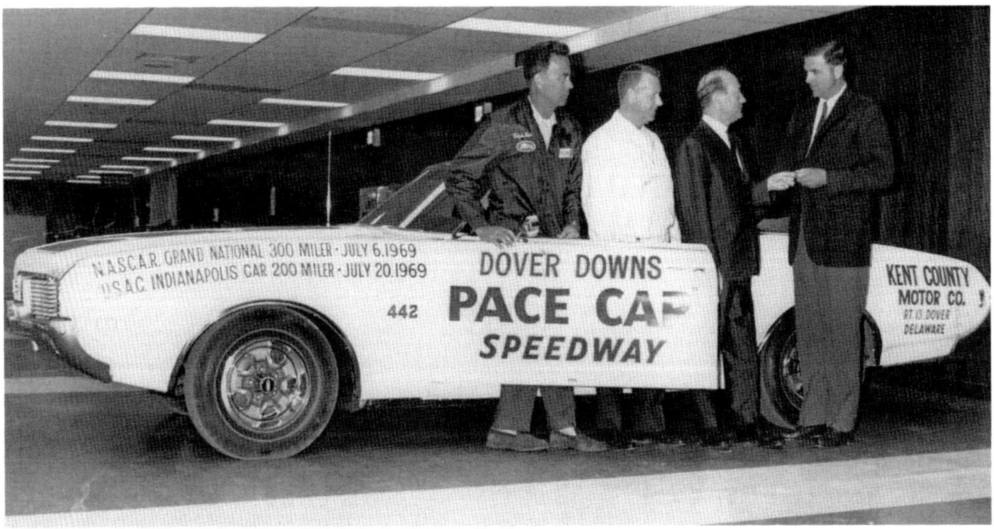

Standing in front of the Oldsmobile 442 pace car are, from left to right, Ralph Moody, Melvin Joseph, David Buckson, and Jack Whitby. The two biggest races of the track's inaugural year are listed on the front of the car. (Courtesy of Joe Ann Adams, representing the Melvin Joseph family.)

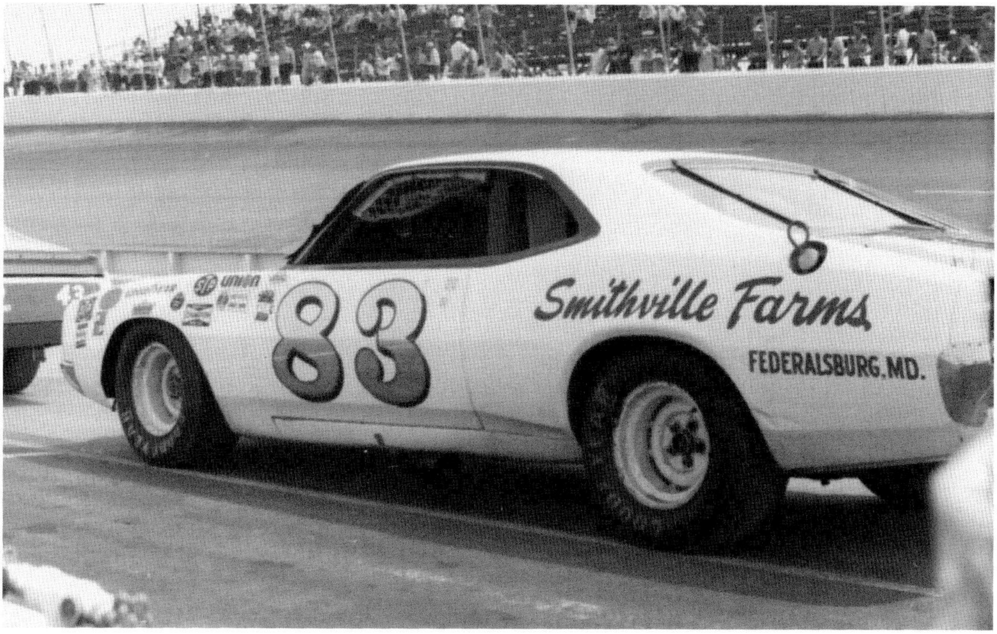

Local car owner Norris "Speedy" Reed fielded a Mercury at Dover in 1973 for driver Paul Tyler. After having engine problems, the Smithville Farms–sponsored car finished 23rd. (Courtesy of Charlie Brown.)

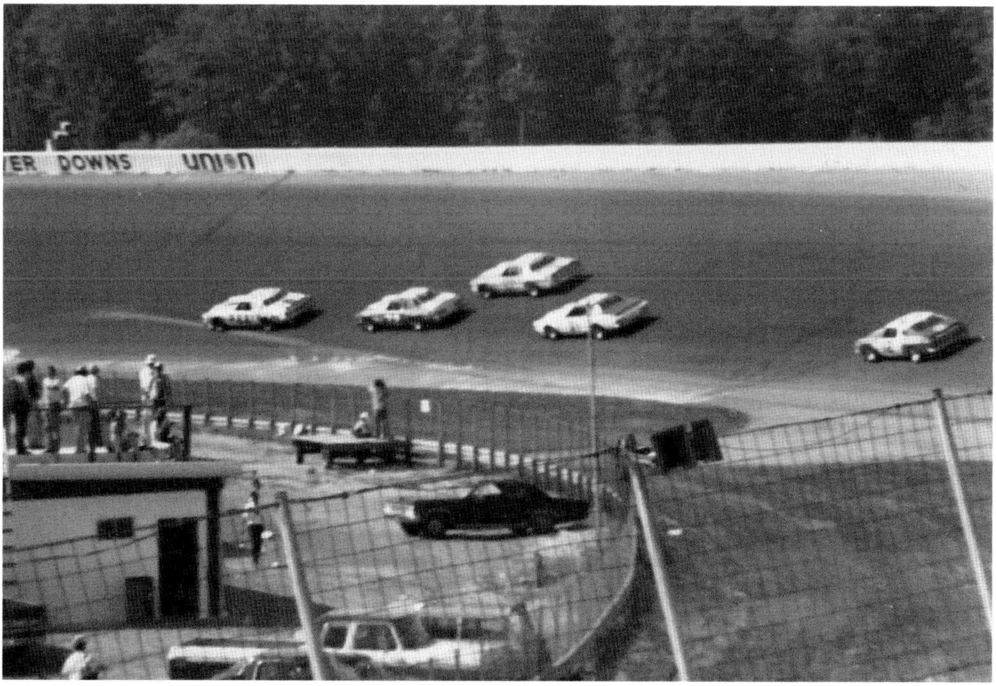

Darrell Waltrip leads the pack around Dover Downs in the 1977 Delaware 500. Benny Parsons eventually went on to win the grueling race. The trees in the background are now gone, as grandstands completely encircle the track. (Courtesy of D&L Photos.)

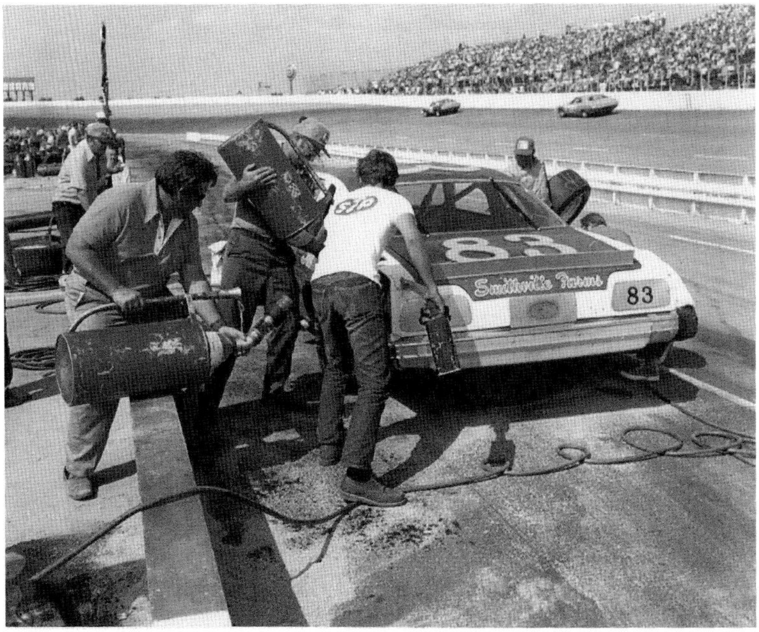

Norris "Speedy" Reed fills his car with gas at Dover Downs. Long before NASCAR-regulated fire suits and helmets, crew members simply wore everyday clothes when servicing the car on pit road. (Courtesy of Taylor and Messick Inc.)

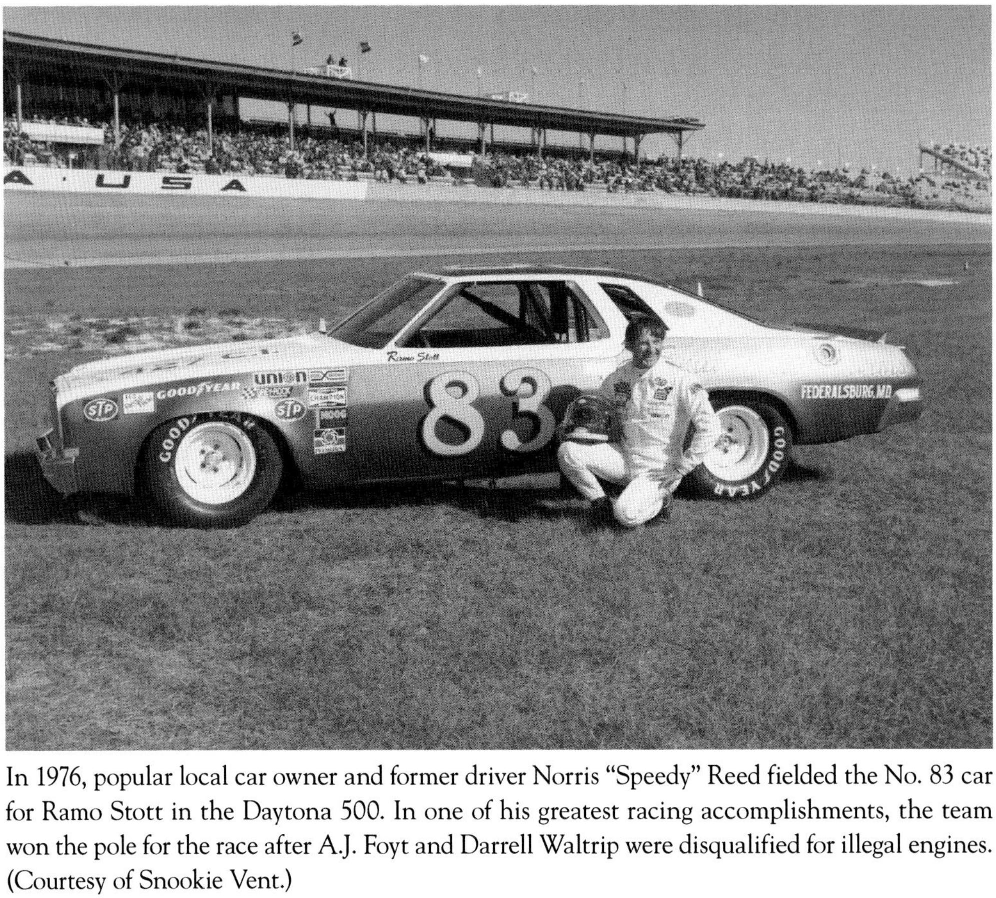

In 1976, popular local car owner and former driver Norris "Speedy" Reed fielded the No. 83 car for Ramo Stott in the Daytona 500. In one of his greatest racing accomplishments, the team won the pole for the race after A.J. Foyt and Darrell Waltrip were disqualified for illegal engines. (Courtesy of Snookie Vent.)

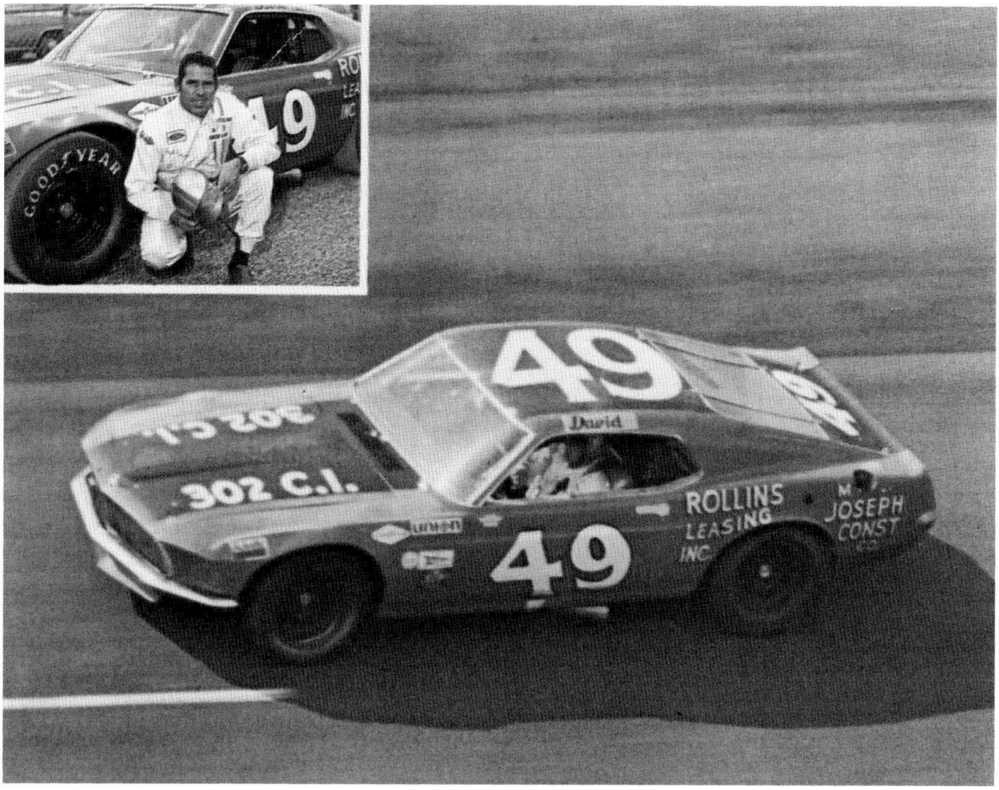

When NASCAR made the decision to allow Grand American cars to compete with Grand National cars on the short tracks, many teams took advantage. Bobby Allison is most famous for driving the No. 49 Mustang owned by Rollins Leasing of Wilmington, Delaware, and Melvin Joseph Construction of Georgetown, Delaware. A little-known fact is that David Pearson (inset) also drove the famous No. 49. (Courtesy of Melvin Joseph Jr.)

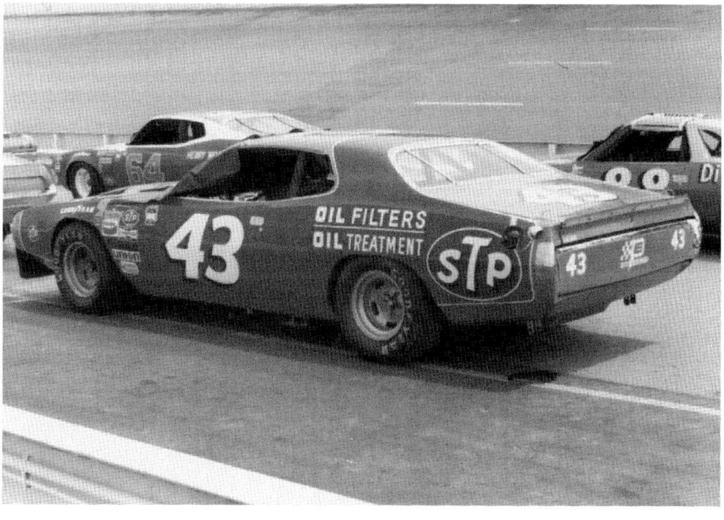

"The King" Richard Petty's car sits on pit row before the start of NASCAR's Dover Downs race in 1973. Petty not only won the first race in 1969, he won a total of seven times at Dover Downs, a feat only equaled by fellow NASCAR champion Bobby Allison. (Courtesy of Charlie Brown.)

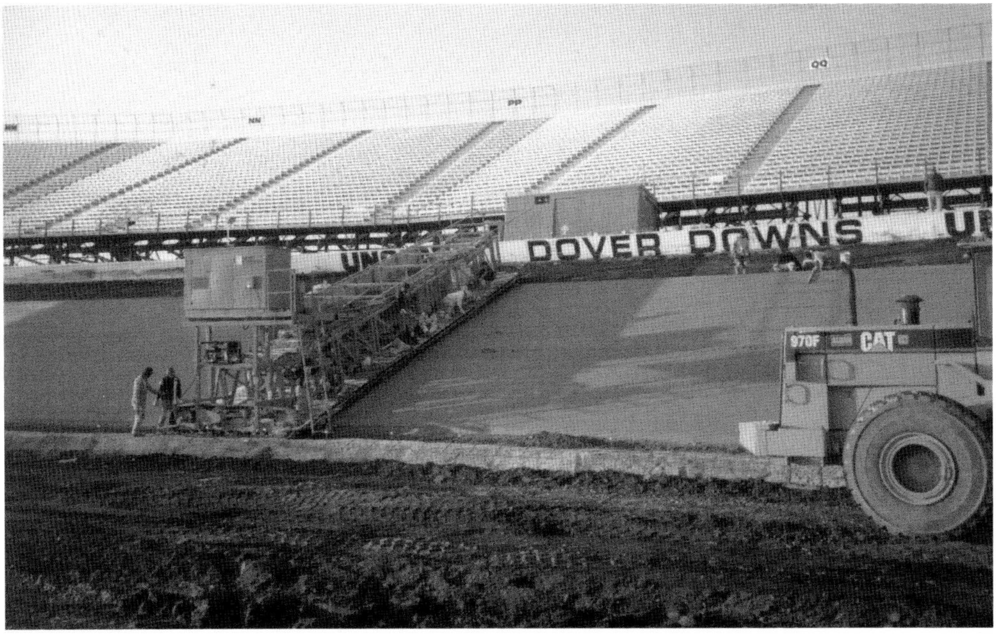

Dover Downs Speedway was converted from asphalt to concrete in 1994 and 1995. As the first super speedway to have a concrete racing surface, the project required special equipment. Melvin Joseph oversaw the construction, including the use of this slip-form paver that was specially modified to span 44 feet of racetrack. (Courtesy of Joe Ann Adams, representing the Melvin Joseph family.)

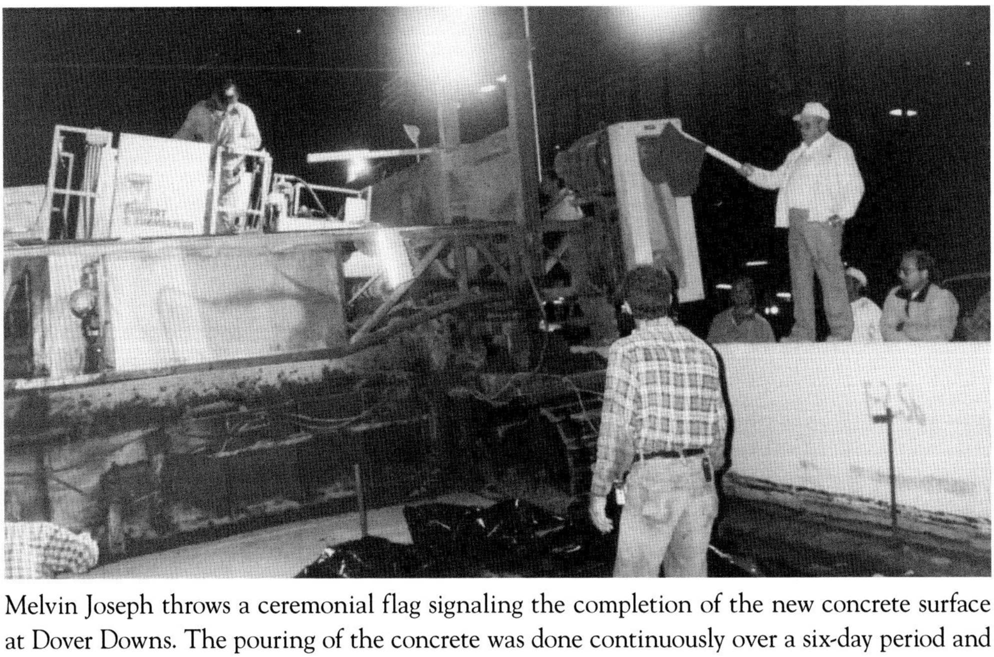

Melvin Joseph throws a ceremonial flag signaling the completion of the new concrete surface at Dover Downs. The pouring of the concrete was done continuously over a six-day period and produced a unique seamless design with no top-to-bottom joints. (Courtesy of Joe Ann Adams, representing the Melvin Joseph family.)

5

Delaware International Speedway

No track in Delaware has stood the test of time like Delaware International Speedway, the only dirt track that holds weekly auto racing events to this day. Although the name and layout of the speedway have changed through the years, it has remained in continuous operation by the Cathell family since 1965. In 1963, the Cathell family purchased land on the west side of US 13 in Delmar, Delaware, for a quarter-mile drag strip. Bill Cathell and his son, Charlie, were avid drag-racing fans and wanted to build a drag strip that would be safer than the popular one-eighth-mile drag strip at Georgetown, Delaware.

The first dirt oval was constructed in 1965 on the west side of the US 13 Dragway. From 1965 to 1968, the Delmarva Auto Racing Association leased and ran the track. The next year, the Cathells moved the dirt oval to the east side of the drag strip and started to manage the operation themselves. This first racecourse was a one-third-mile oval with a figure-eight track inside. This was eventually expanded into the half-mile clay oval that still hosts races today.

Delaware International Speedway has a rich history of producing some of the best drivers and racing in the business. Current promoter Charlie Cathell is well known for his meticulous track preparation and ability to attract some of the most famous drivers from the East Coast to race at Delaware International Speedway. DIS is the southernmost track in the country in which the Big Block Modifieds compete on a weekly basis. With no limits on engine size, the Modifieds provide plenty of exciting action every Saturday night. A top-notch facility run by a great family has not gone unnoticed. In 2004, Charlie was recognized as Promoter of the Year by *Racing Promotions Monthly*, as selected by the readers, and he was inducted into the NHRA Northeast Division Hall of Fame in 2003.

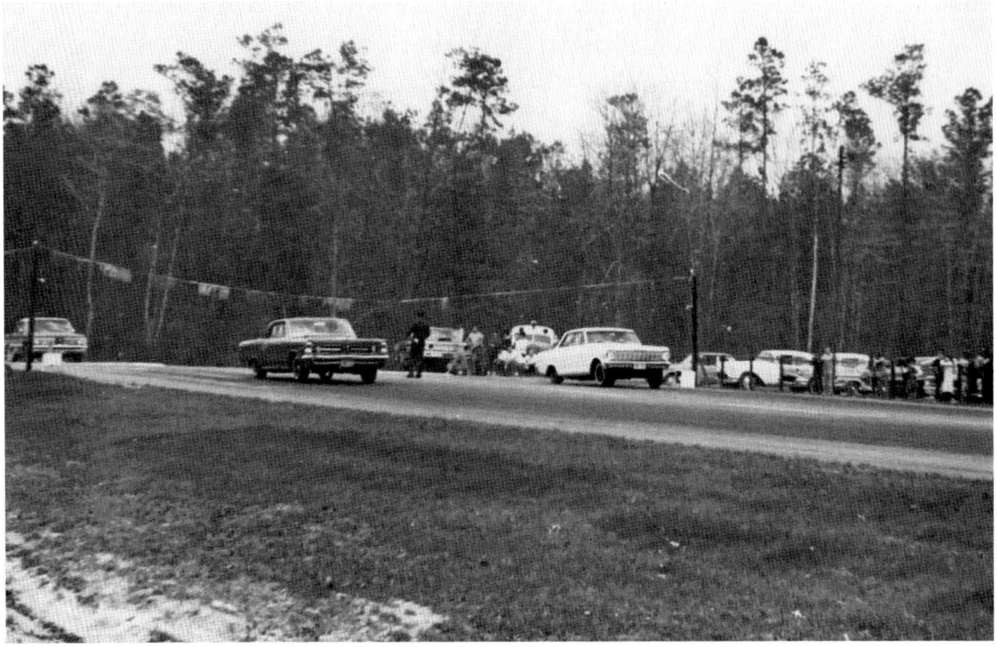

The US 13 Dragway first saw action in 1963. The first dirt track was built on the west side of the dragway in 1965. Grandstands were put on rollers and towed back and forth from the dragway to the speedway. In this photograph, two racers line up to find out who is faster (Courtesy of Betty Wyatt-Dix.)

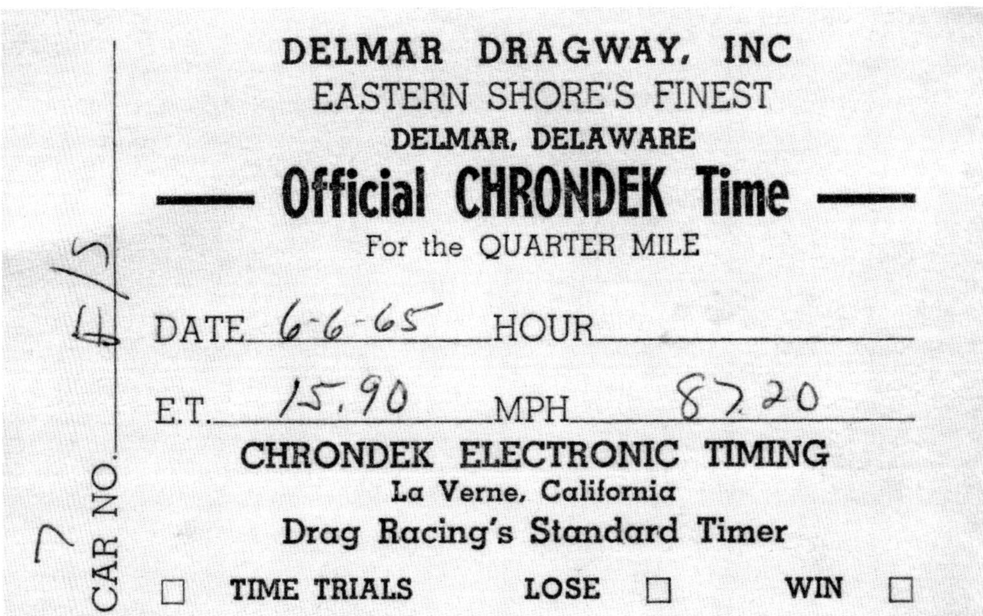

DELMAR DRAGWAY, INC
EASTERN SHORE'S FINEST
DELMAR, DELAWARE
— Official CHRONDEK Time —
For the QUARTER MILE

DATE 6-6-65 HOUR ______

E.T. 15.90 MPH 87.20

CHRONDEK ELECTRONIC TIMING
La Verne, California
Drag Racing's Standard Timer

☐ TIME TRIALS LOSE ☐ WIN ☐

CAR NO. 7 F/S

This early drag-racing time slip from the US 13 Dragway shows the racer's statistics for the quarter-mile run. The dragway, located in Delmar, Delaware, offered racers a safe quarter-mile track with a state-of-the-art timing system. (Courtesy of Betty Wyatt-Dix.)

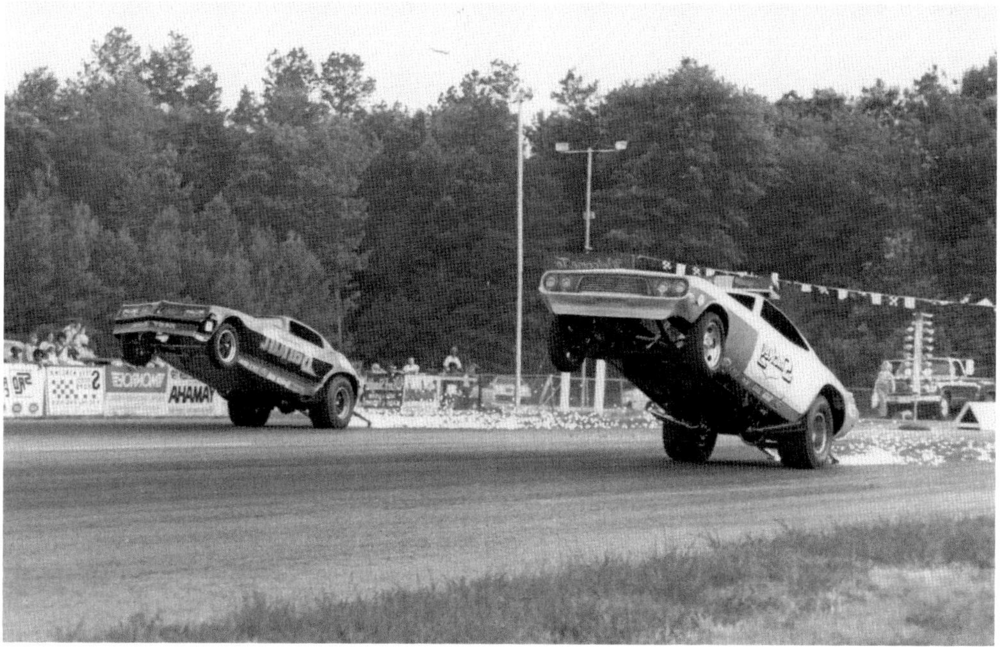

Wheel-standing exhibition drag cars cast showers of sparks behind them as they take off down the quarter-mile at the US 13 Dragway. The Delaware Motorsports Complex is second only to the beaches as a popular tourist attraction in Sussex County. (Courtesy of Charlie Cathell.)

From 1965 through 1968, the Delmarva Auto Racing Association leased and ran the dirt track at the Delaware Motorsports Complex. This first track was on the west side of the drag strip and was moved to its current location, on the east side of the complex, the following year. This photograph shows racers on the original track. (Courtesy of Charlie Cathell.)

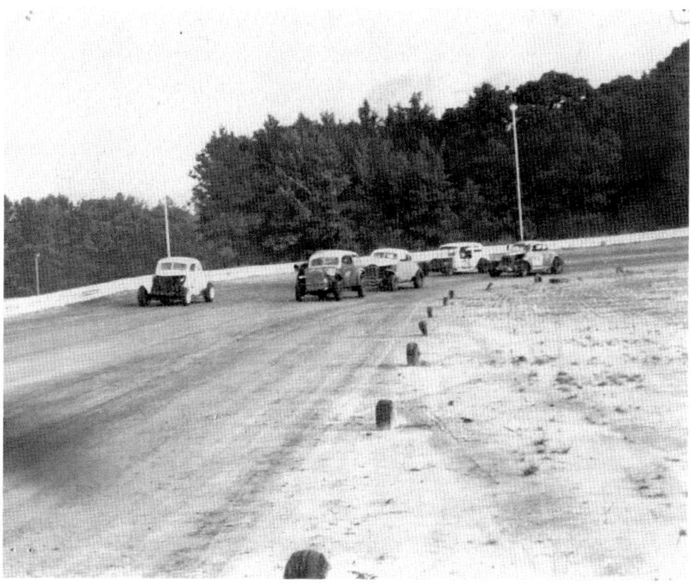

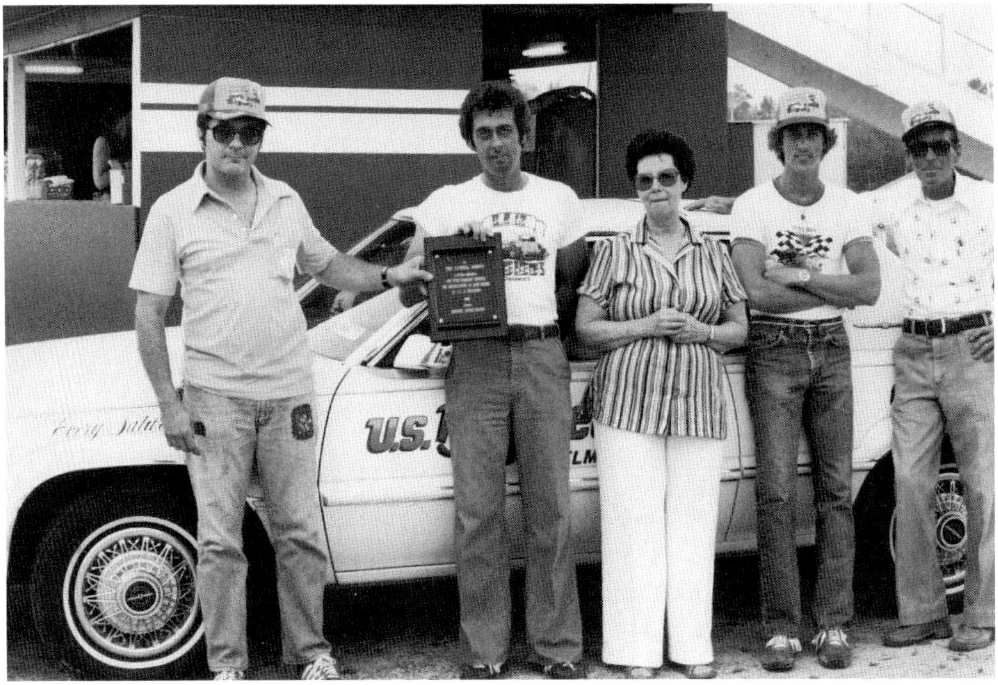

Standing in front of the US 13 pace car are, from left to right, Bruce Barmore, Charlie Cathell, Juanita Cathell, Hal Cathell, and Bill Cathell. The Delaware Motorsports Complex has always been in the Cathell family and currently houses a quarter-mile drag strip, half-mile banked dirt track, and a Kart track. (Courtesy of Charlie Cathell.)

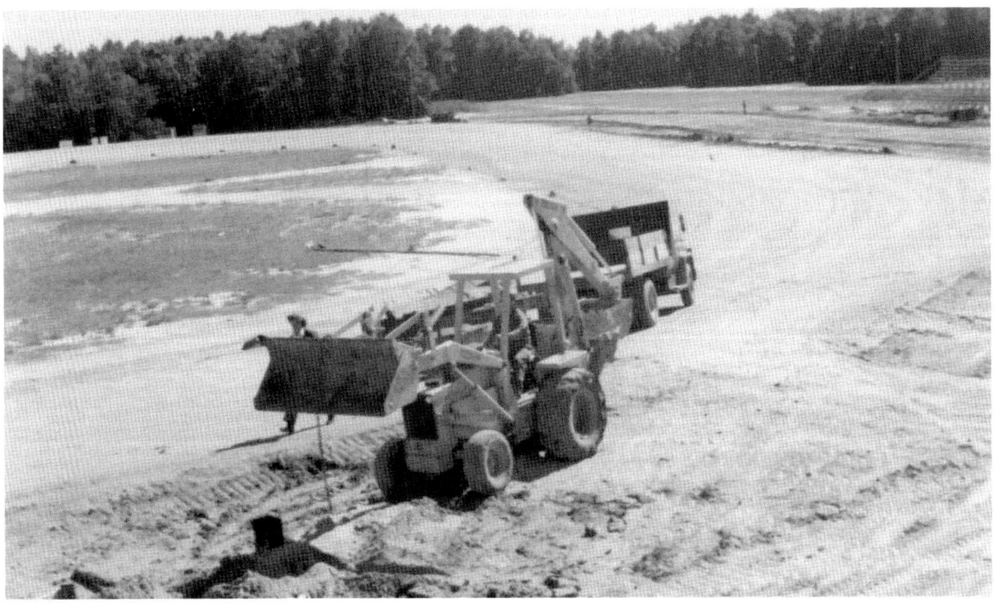

The track located to the east of the Delmarva Motorsports Complex was originally one third of a mile in length. In this 1976 photograph, the track is being expanded into the half-mile oval that racers use today. (Courtesy of Charlie Cathell.)

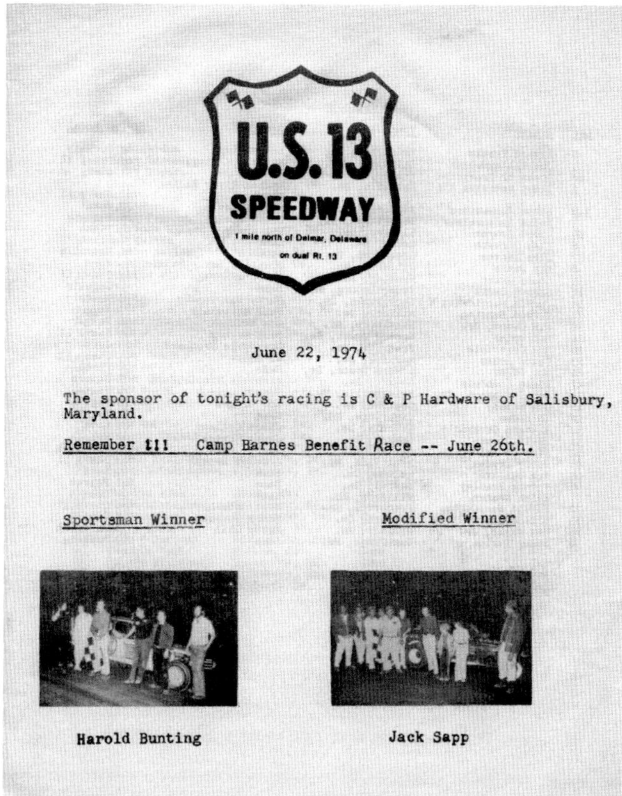

U.S. 13 SPEEDWAY
1 mile north of Delmar, Delaware
on dual Rt. 13

June 22, 1974

The sponsor of tonight's racing is C & P Hardware of Salisbury, Maryland.

Remember !!! Camp Barnes Benefit Race -- June 26th.

Sportsman Winner — Harold Bunting

Modified Winner — Jack Sapp

Before its name was changed to Delaware International Speedway, the half-mile clay oval in Delmar was known as US 13 Speedway. This track program from 1974 shows the previous week's winners: Harold Bunting (Sportsman race) and Jack Sapp (Modified race). (Courtesy of the Don Allen Collection.)

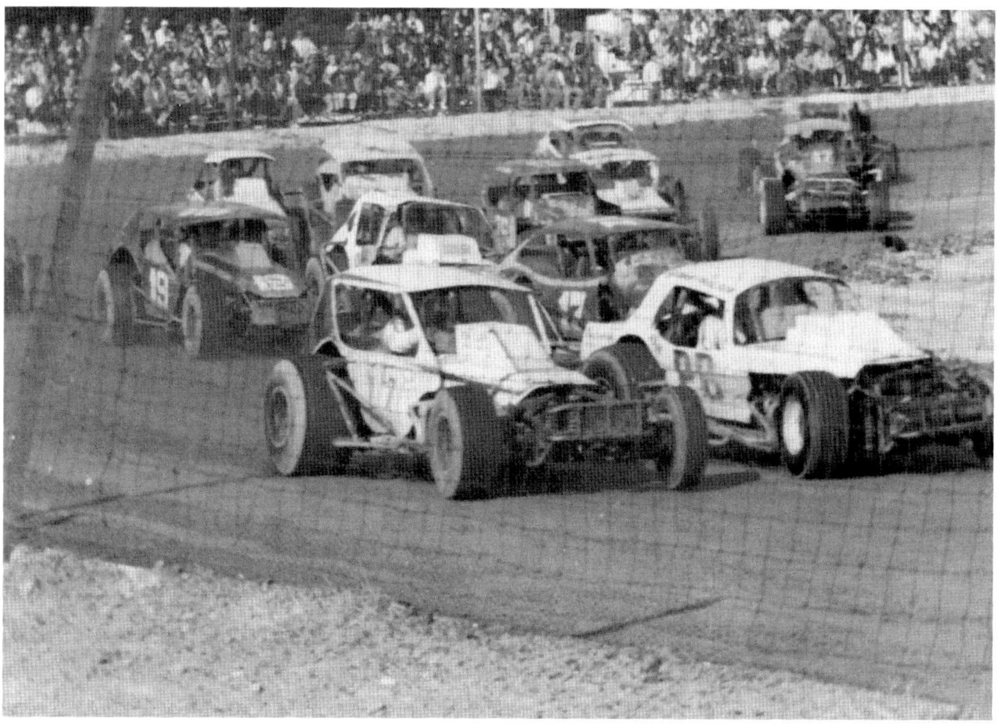

Taking the green flag in the 1977 Twin 40 Championship races at Delaware International Speedway are Dave Kelly (No. 17), Ron Paulson (No. PB), Toby Tobias (No. 17), and Harold Bunting (No. 19). Kelly won both of the 40-lap events. (Courtesy of D&L Photos.)

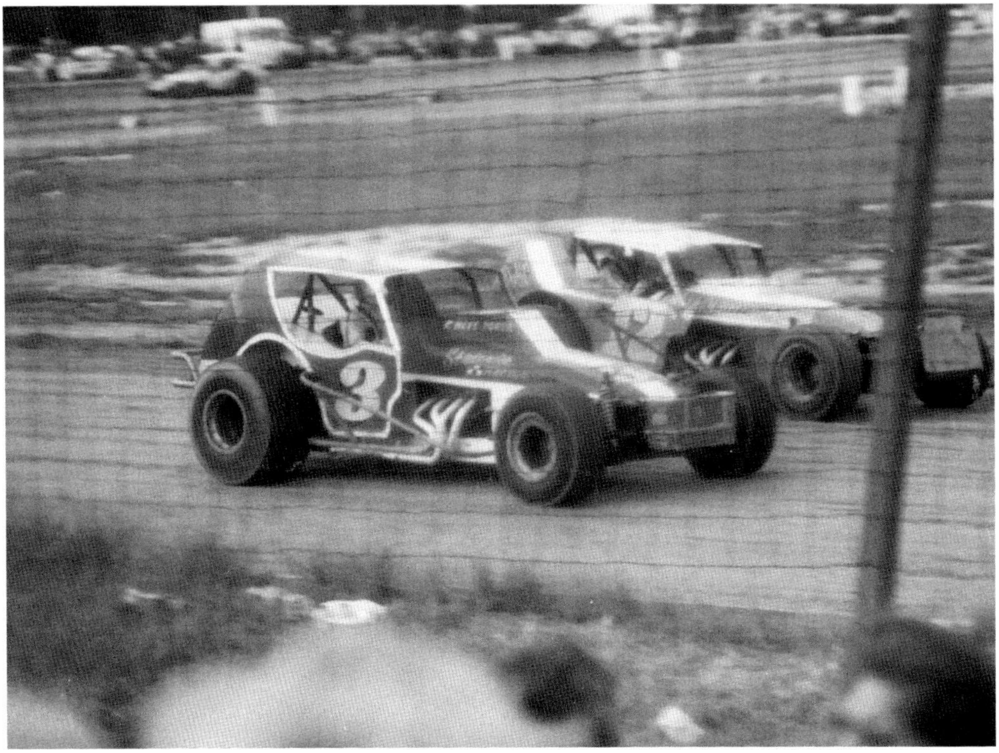

When Delaware International Speedway held special races and big money was on the line, "invaders" would come from other states and tracks and attempt to snatch the prize. Delaware racers held their own against these racers from out of state. Pictured here are two of the top invaders— Jimmy Horton (No. 3) and Kevin Collins (No. 12), racing in the 1978 Diamond State 50. (Courtesy of D&L Photos.)

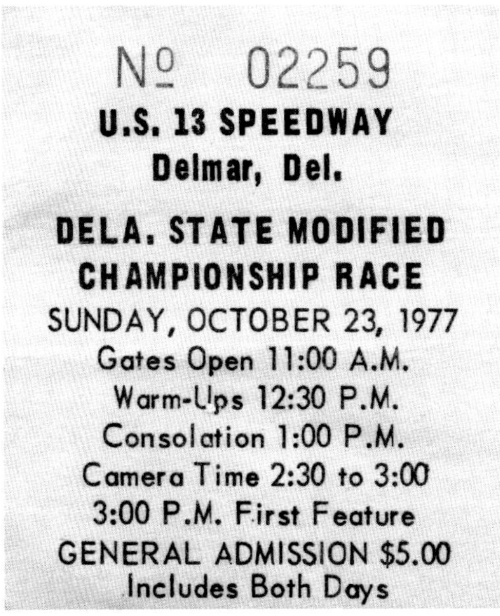

No 02259
U.S. 13 SPEEDWAY
Delmar, Del.
DELA. STATE MODIFIED
CHAMPIONSHIP RACE
SUNDAY, OCTOBER 23, 1977
Gates Open 11:00 A.M.
Warm-Ups 12:30 P.M.
Consolation 1:00 P.M.
Camera Time 2:30 to 3:00
3:00 P.M. First Feature
GENERAL ADMISSION $5.00
Includes Both Days

In 1977, racing was one of the biggest entertainment bargains in the state of Delaware. For $5, spectators got two days of championship racing featuring longer-than-normal 40-lap races. These events were normally standing room only, as the grandstands were filled to capacity. (Courtesy of the Don Allen Collection.)

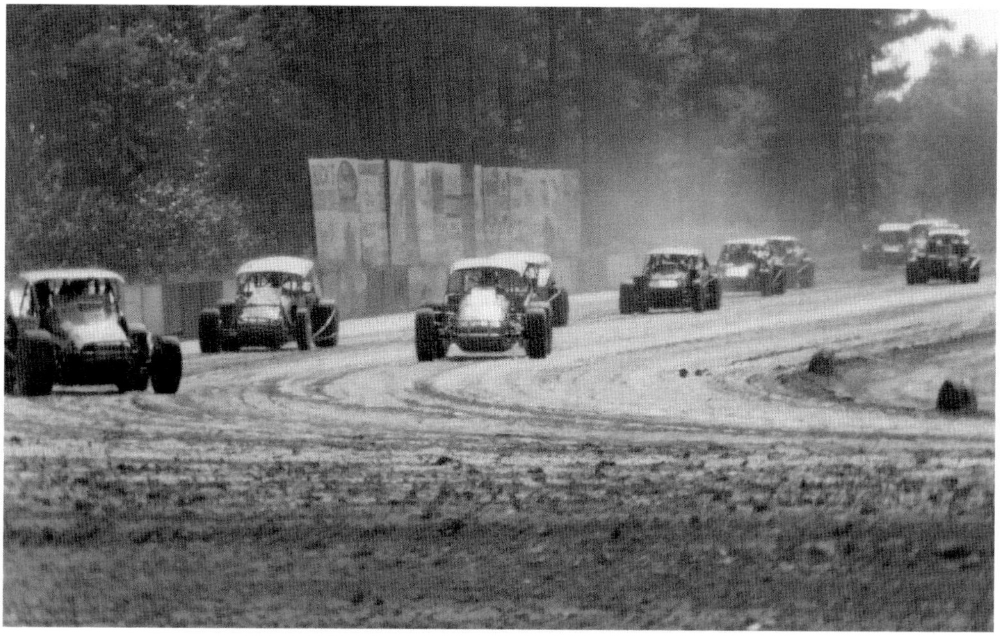

Gremlin-bodied Modifieds race down the backstretch at Delaware International Speedway. The extreme stagger in the rear tires is visible here; the outer tire is much taller to help cars turn through the corner. (Courtesy of D&L Photos.)

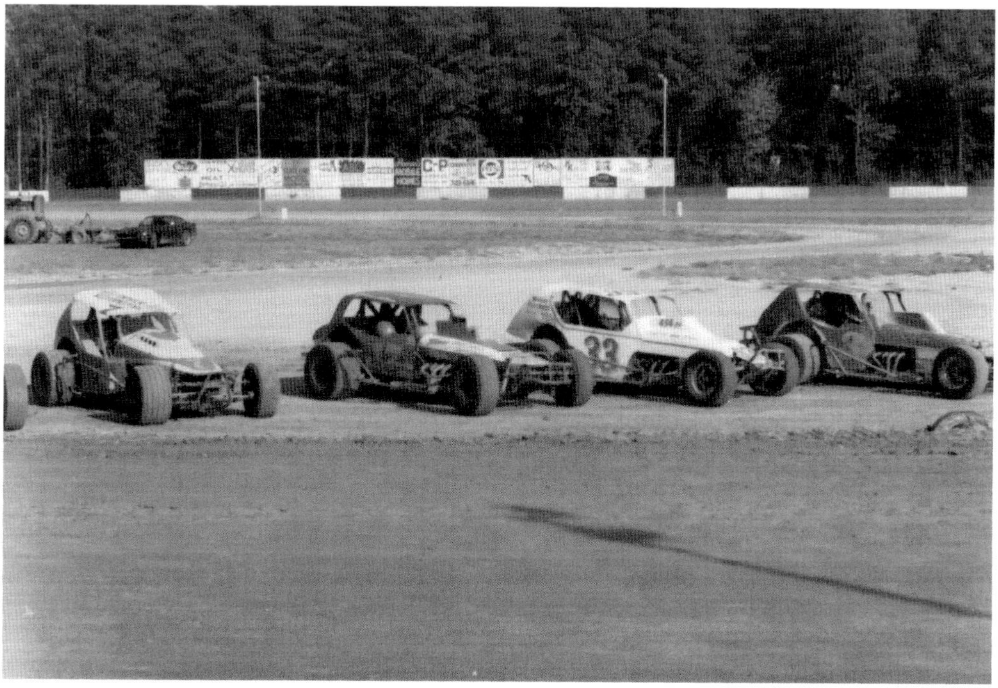

At the 1979 Delaware Modified Championship, drivers line their cars up on the front stretch before drawing numbers for starting positions. From left to right are Jim Martin (No. 7), Ronnie Tobias (No. 17), Gary Trice (No. 33), and Jimmy Horton (No. 3). (Courtesy of D&L Photos.)

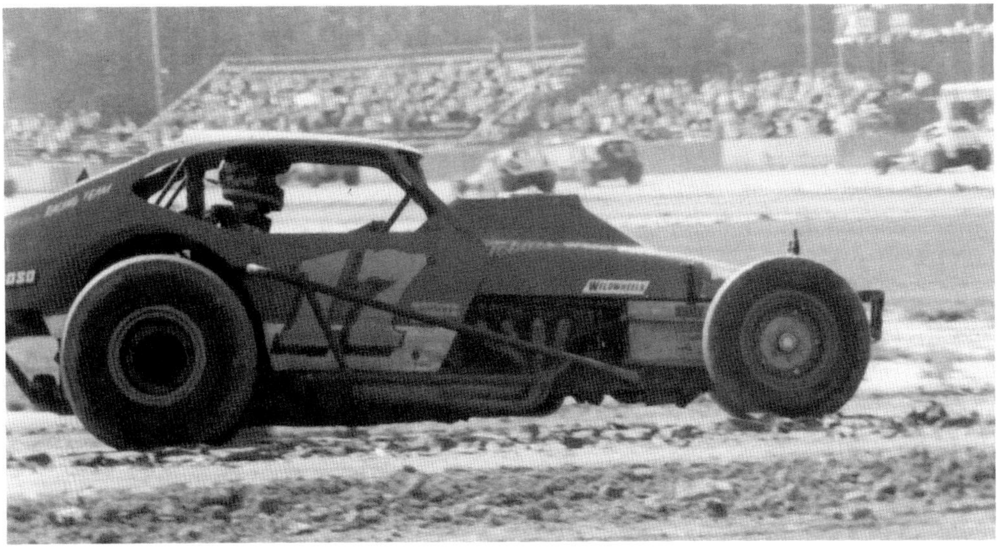

Dick "Toby" Tobias was a racing legend. Tobias produced the first Modified chassis that was not based on a production car frame. After winning over 300 races, he was tragically killed in a USAC Sprint Car accident in 1978. His sons, Scott and Ronnie, carried on the Tobias family racing tradition. Pictured here is Scott Tobias at the 1979 Delaware Modified Championship. (Courtesy of D&L Photos.)

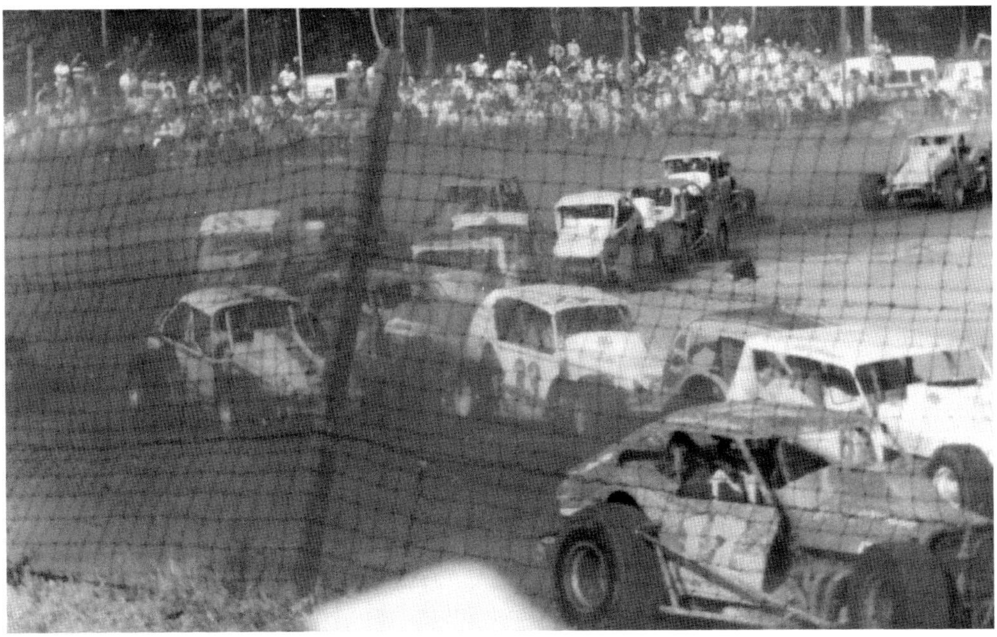

Many would consider the 1970s the peak of Modified racing. With extremely large car-counts and record crowds, racetracks everywhere were bursting with activity. Today, development, noise, and the economy threaten local racetracks across the country. Delaware International Speedway is one of the few that have not only survived, but also flourished. This photograph is a great example of the best era in Modified racing. (Courtesy of D&L Photos.)

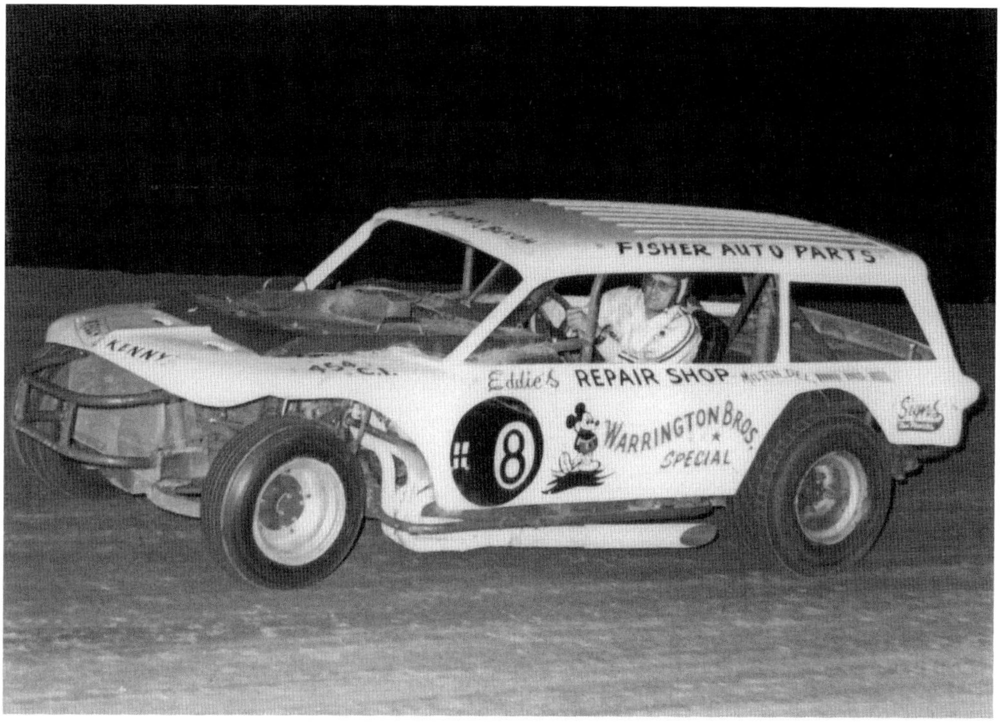

Almost every attendee at US 13 Speedway in the early 1970s saw this car in Victory Lane. Note the 454-cubic-inch Chevrolet motor stuffed into a small Corvair body. Driver Eddie Pettyjohn seems to have a smile on his face as he pilots the car toward another victory. (Photograph by Tri-State Racing Photographs Inc., courtesy of Keith Short.)

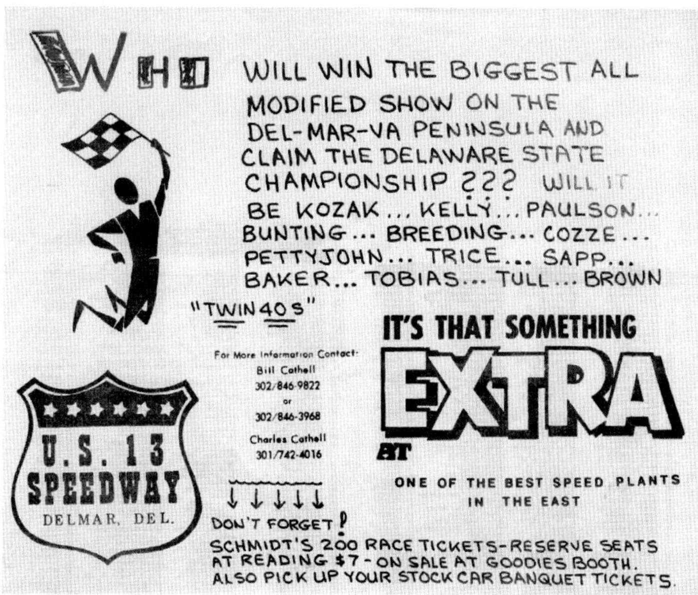

The Delaware International Speedway, formerly called US 13 Speedway, has always attracted the biggest stars in Modified racing. This pamphlet promoting the Delaware State Championship lists all the top names in the sport. The twin 40-lap format gave racers two chances to win. (Courtesy of the Don Allen Collection.)

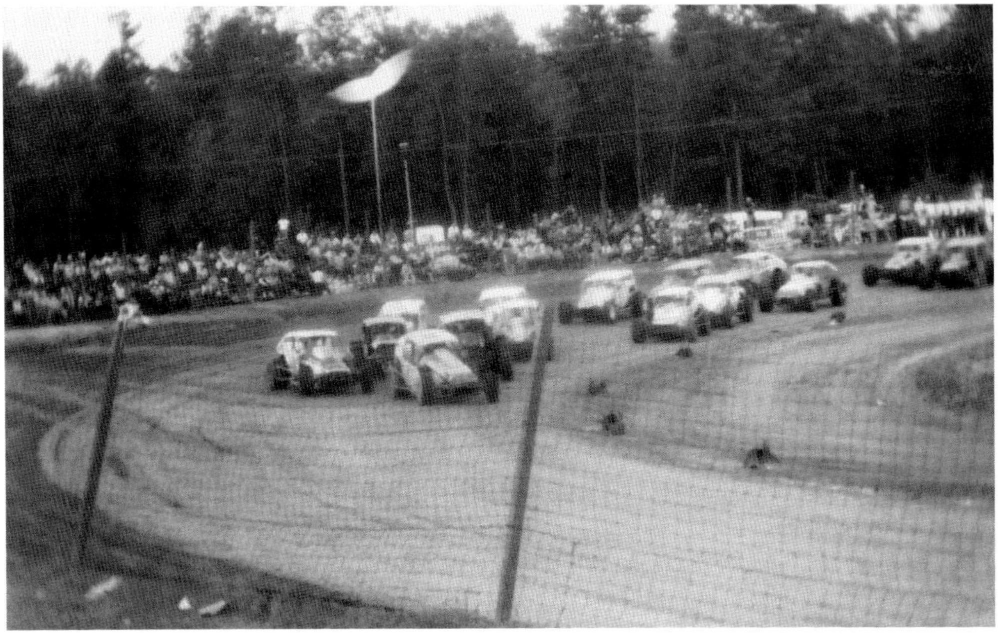

The Delaware double-file restart was the idea of promoter Charlie Cathell. Tired of penalizing drivers for jumping the restart from the front row, he put the leader alone in the front with the rest of the field double-wide. Since then, the idea has been used nationwide in numerous racing series. (Courtesy of D&L Photos.)

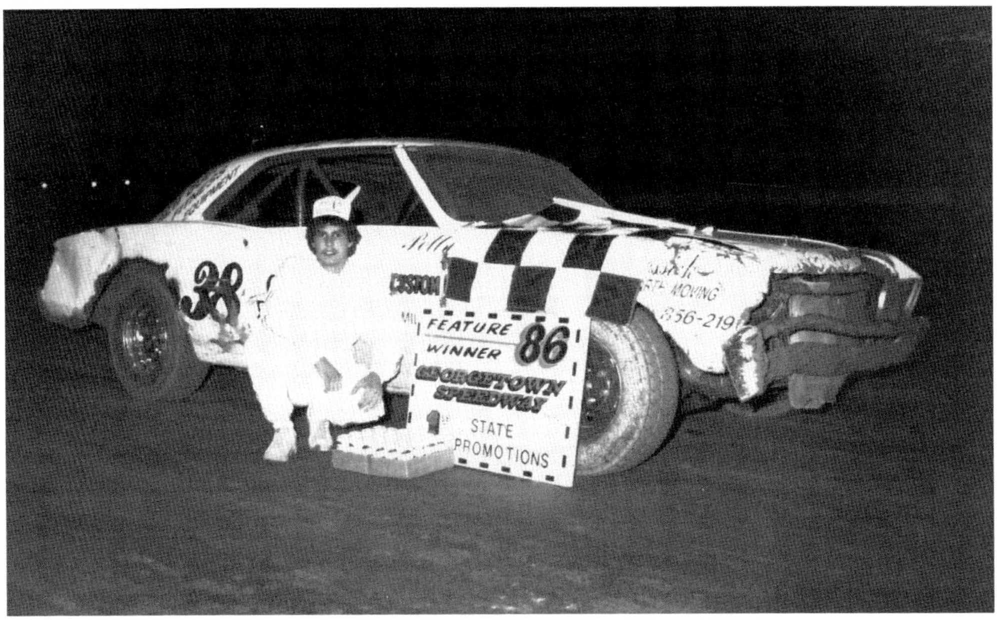

A young Kenny Pettyjohn is pictured in Victory Lane at Georgetown Speedway. Pettyjohn went on to win one track championship in the Street Modified division, as well as a record 10 Late Model Track Championships at Delaware International Speedway. Between the two classes, he has 144 victories and counting. (Courtesy of D&L Photos.)

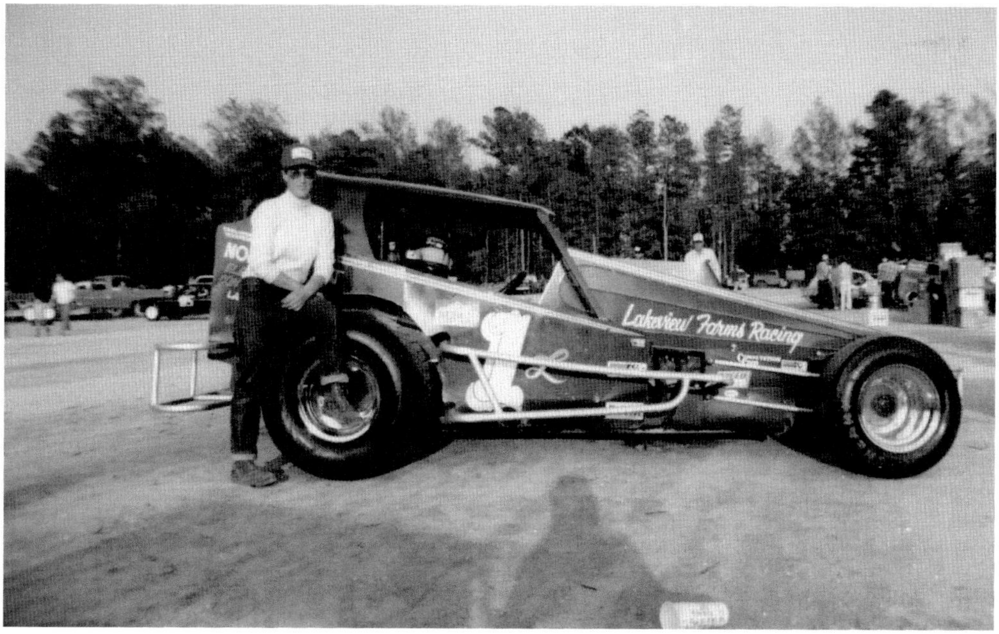

Racer Lacy Lafferty broke down barriers when she became the first female Modified racer to compete at Delaware International Speedway. Many have followed her example, as there are multiple female racers at DIS today. (Courtesy of D&L Photos.)

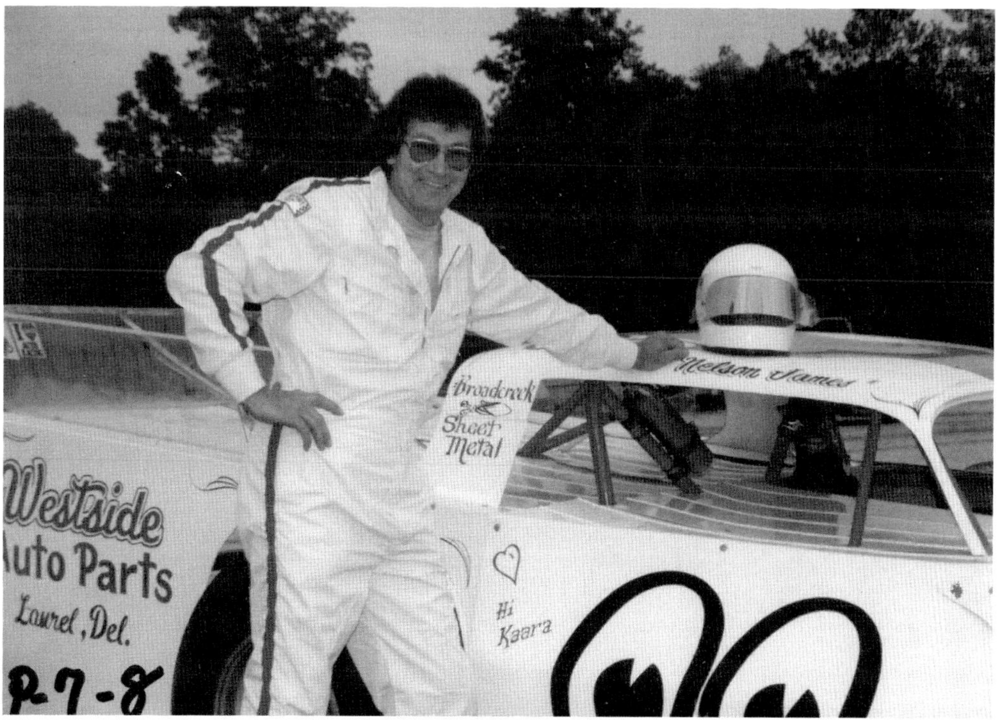

Gentleman driver Nelson James raced both Modifieds and Late Models. Here, he poses with the No. 00 Late Model owned by Minus Givins of Laurel, Delaware. (Courtesy of D&L Photos.)

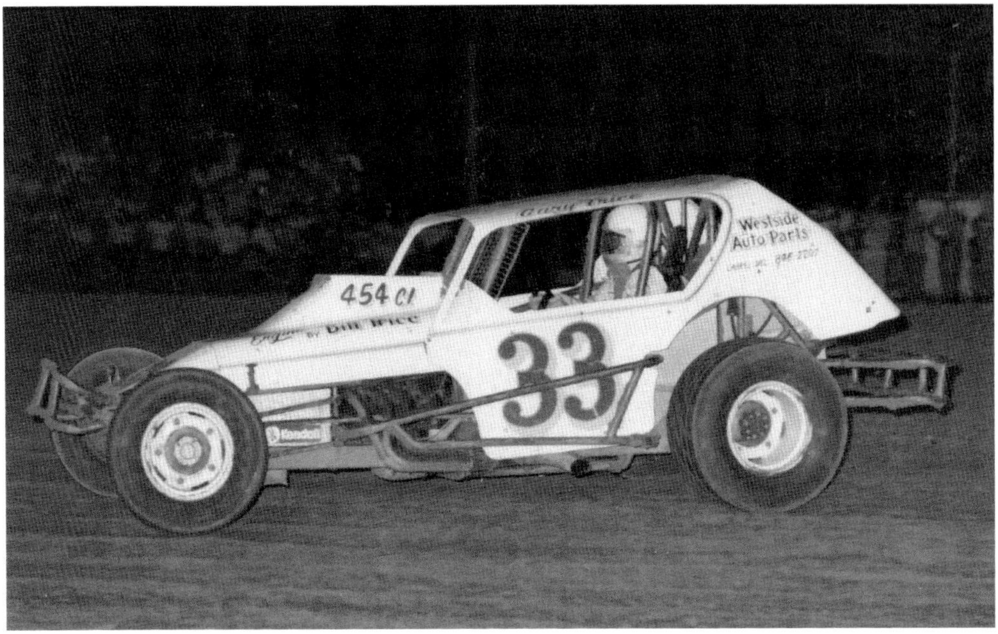

Gary Trice drives his No. 33 Modified at Delaware International Speedway. This car is the essential 1970s Modified, with Big Block Chevy power in a small, Gremlin-style body with large Firestone drag tires on the rear of the car. (Courtesy of David Grey.)

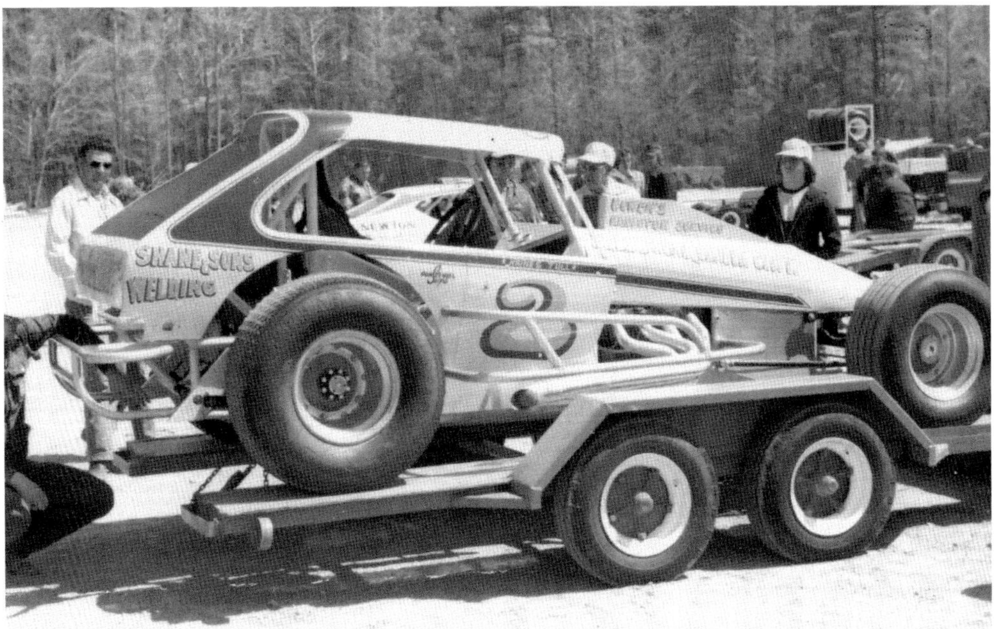

Before racers had fully enclosed trailers, which are basically workshops on wheels, they used open trailers—or whatever they could find—to get cars to the track. Here, Haines Tull's brand-new Chevette-bodied car sits on its trailer before the 1978 season. (Courtesy of D&L Photos.)

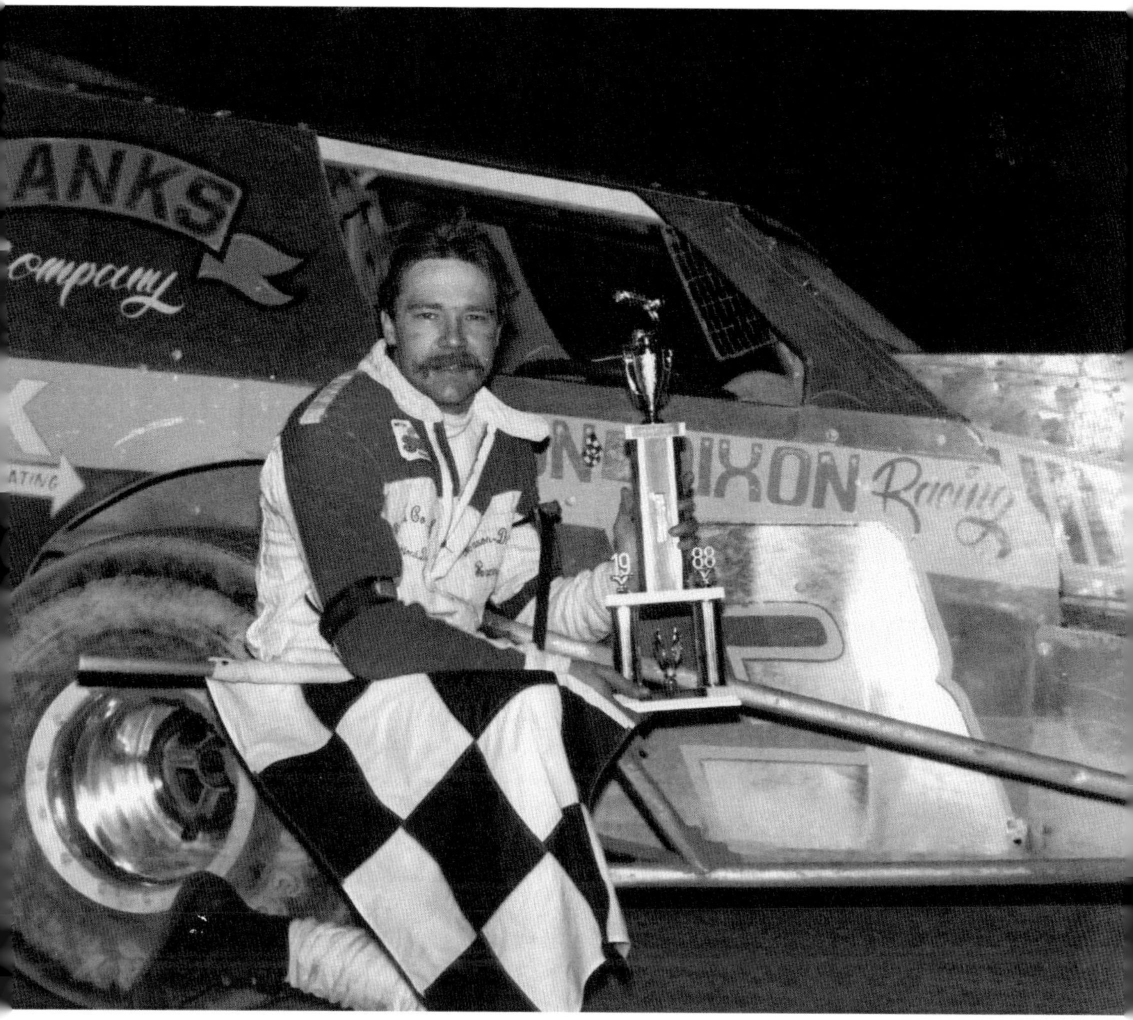

Bobby Wilkins has the most wins of any Modified driver in the history of Delaware International Speedway, with 118 victories and 7 track championships. Wilkins also won races and championships at Georgetown Speedway and Bridgeport Speedway. One of Delaware's most versatile drivers, he also took the checkered flag at races in a United Racing Club Sprint Car. (Courtesy of Helen Banks.)

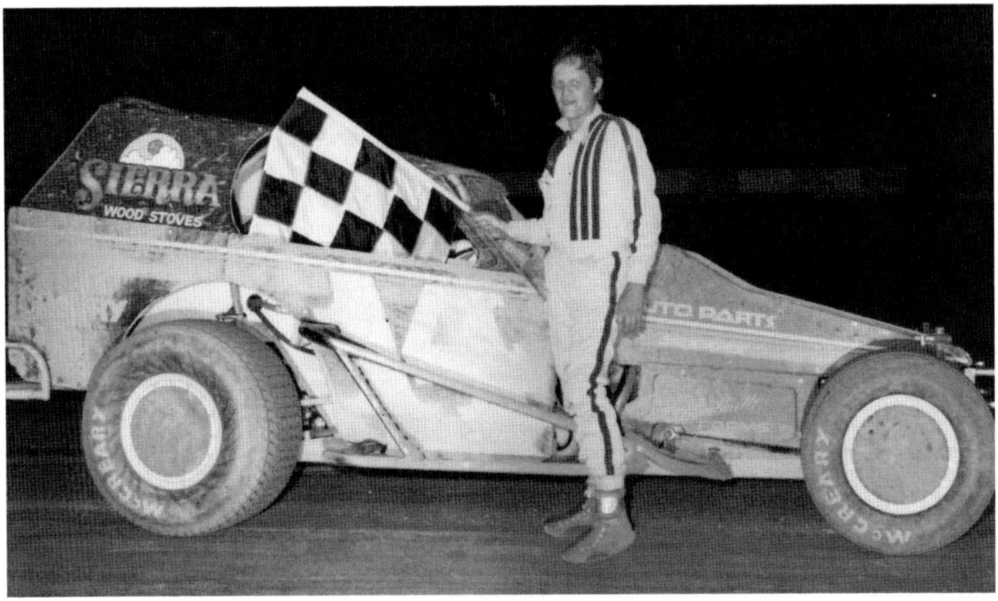

Bob Toreky's first win of the 1985 season was at Delaware International Speedway (then called US 13 Speedway). Toreky won 31 Modified races at DIS and captured the Modified championship three times—in 1982, 1987, and 1988. (Courtesy of Helen Banks.)

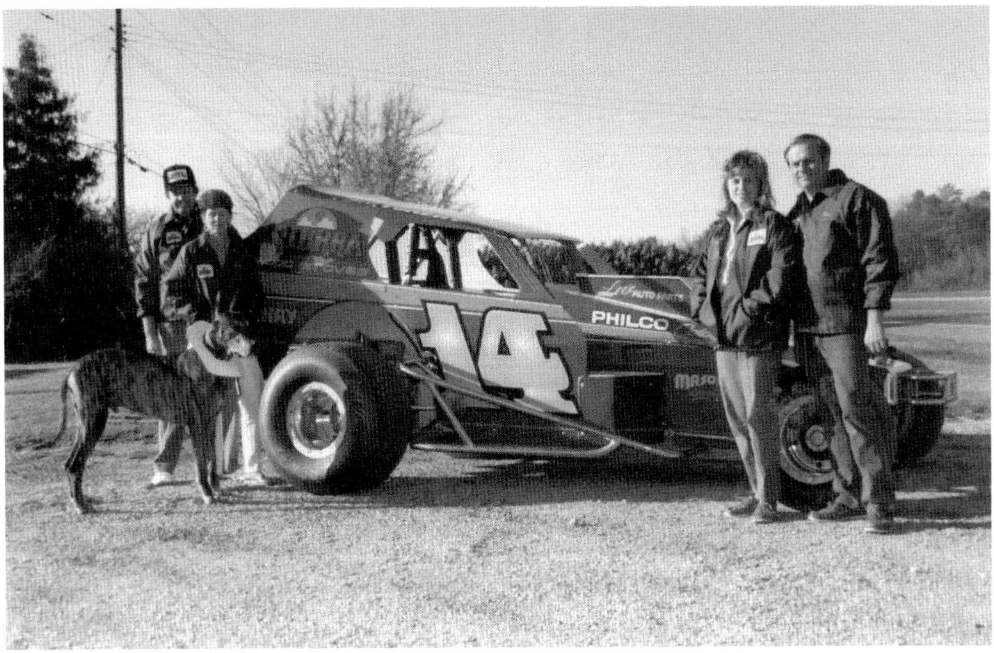

No. 14 owners Gerald and Helen Banks (left) and Gloria and Walt Breeding (right) always had one of the cleanest and most meticulously prepared cars around. The Banks owned the profitable Banks Company in Frankford, Delaware. Walt, a former driver, went on to become a successful fabricator and builder of the Modified Bandit chassis. Both Banks and Breeding had luck with the No. 3 driven by Bobby Wilkins and the No. 14 driven by Bob Toreky. (Courtesy of Helen Banks.)

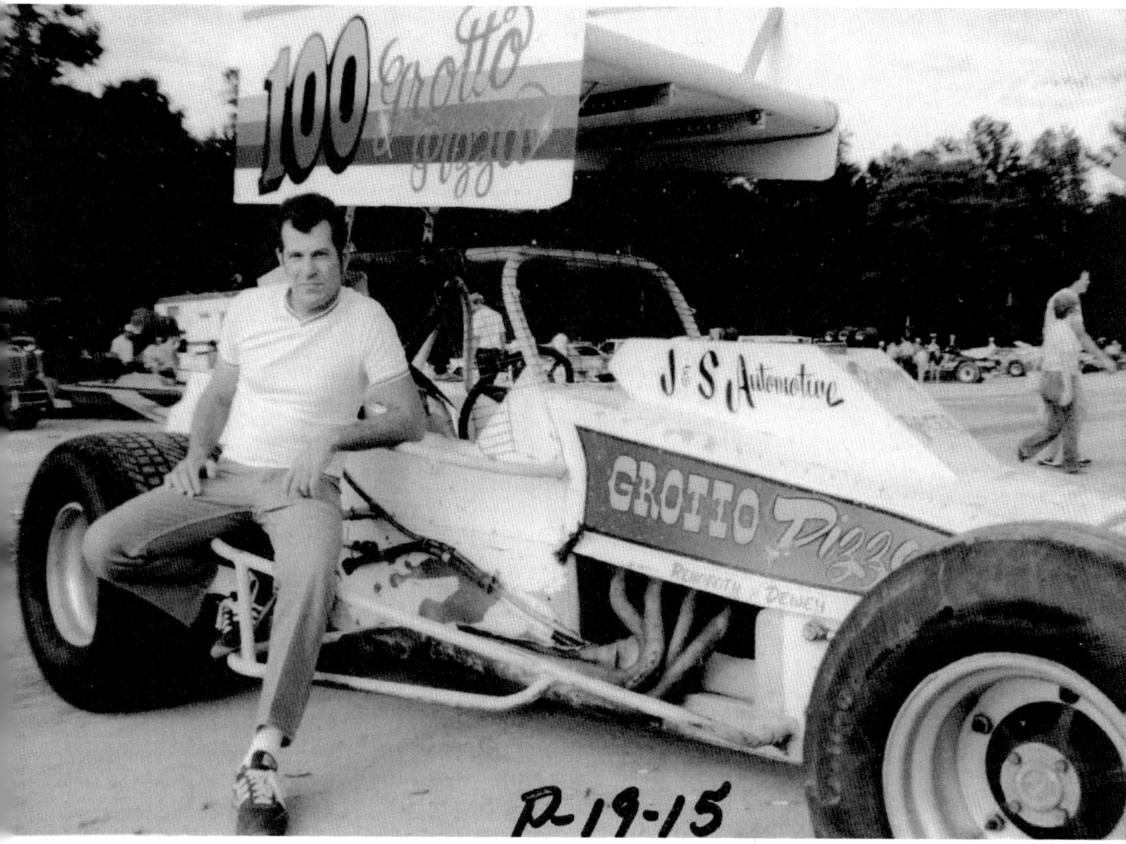

The ageless Hal Browning is a Delaware racing legend. Browning has been a winner in Sprint Cars, Late Models, and Modifieds. He has 23 Modified feature wins as well as 51 Late Model wins at Delaware International Speedway, plus two Delaware International Track Championships. (Courtesy of D&L Photos.)

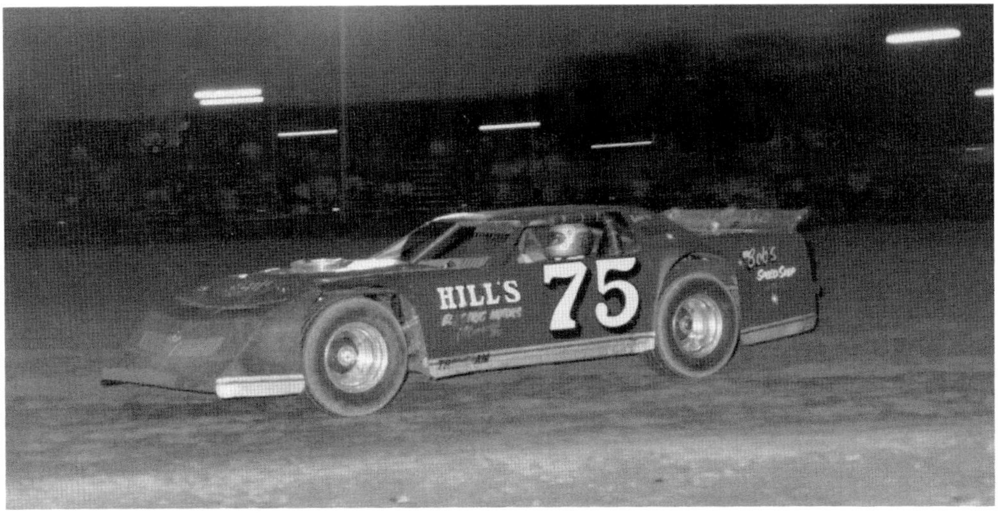

David Hill is the winningest Late Model driver in the history of Delaware International Speedway. With 140 and counting, he continues to add to his impressive resume of feature wins. David's father, Larry Hill, was a two-time DIS track champion, and David Hill has five track championships to his credit. (Courtesy of D&L Photos.)

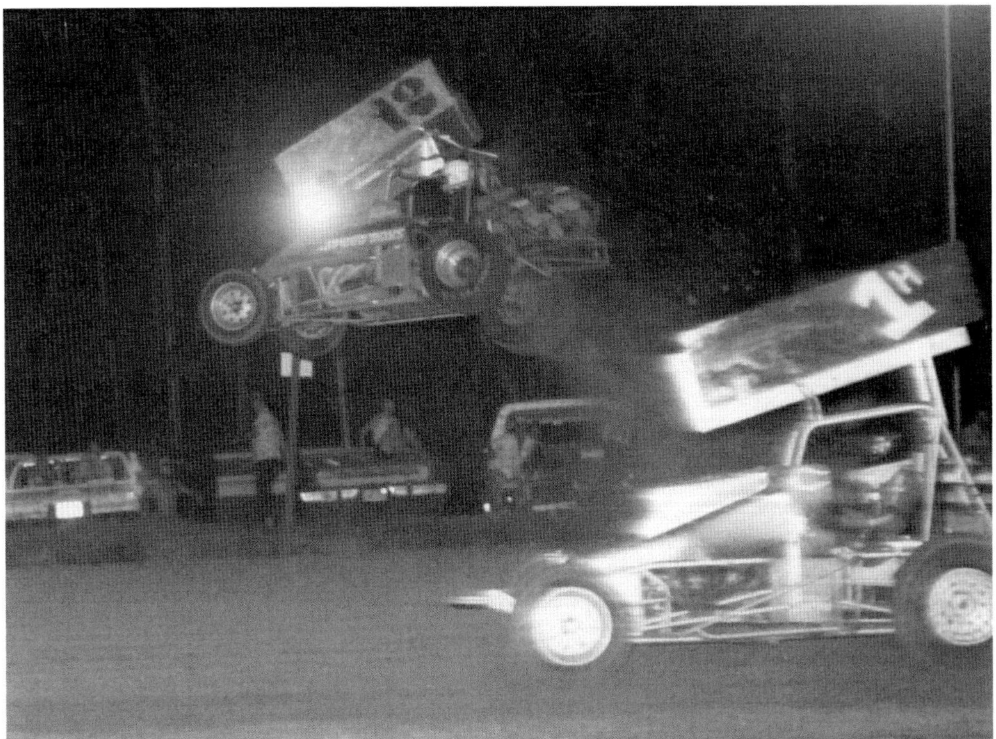

The United Racing Club Sprints always are exciting at Delaware International Speedway. Here, Kevin Collins (No. 12) gets some air while fans scramble away from the fence in the background. (Photograph by "Ears," courtesy of D&L Photos.)

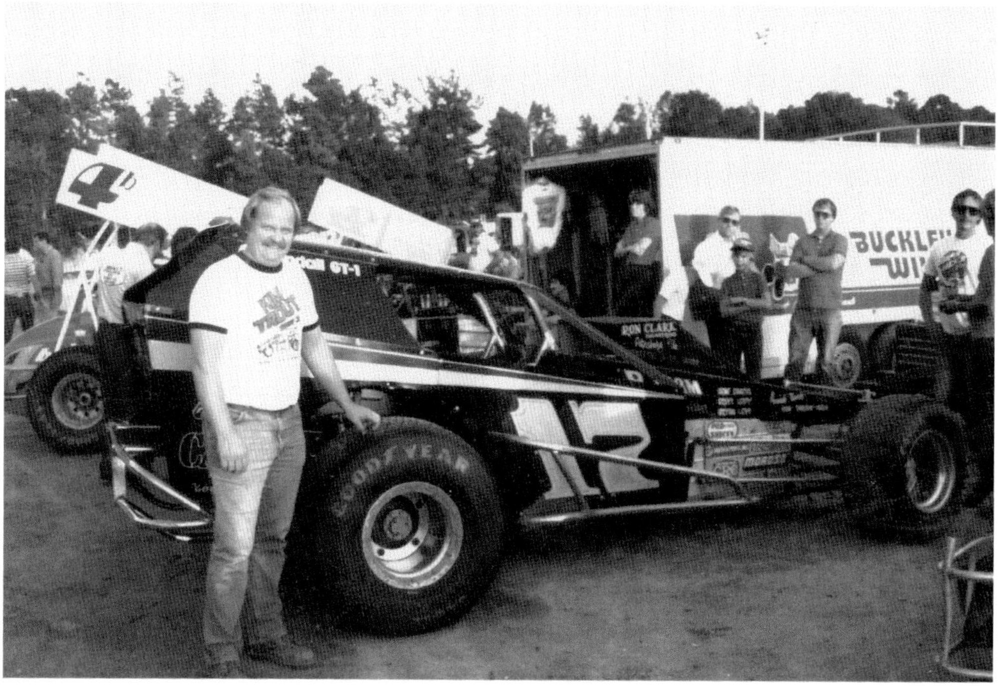

Dave Kelly was a beloved driver and fan favorite in the 1970s and 1980s. Kelly was a double threat: racing in the Modified division (above) and with the United Racing Club Sprint Cars (below). Kelly has won 51 Modified races, including the 1977 Delaware State Championship race at Delaware International Speedway. In 1978, he won the track championship at DIS and was always a threat during the popular "twin 20" races of the 1970s. With 76 career Sprint Car wins, Kelly went on to become a five-time URC Sprint Car champion. (Both, courtesy of D&L Photos.)

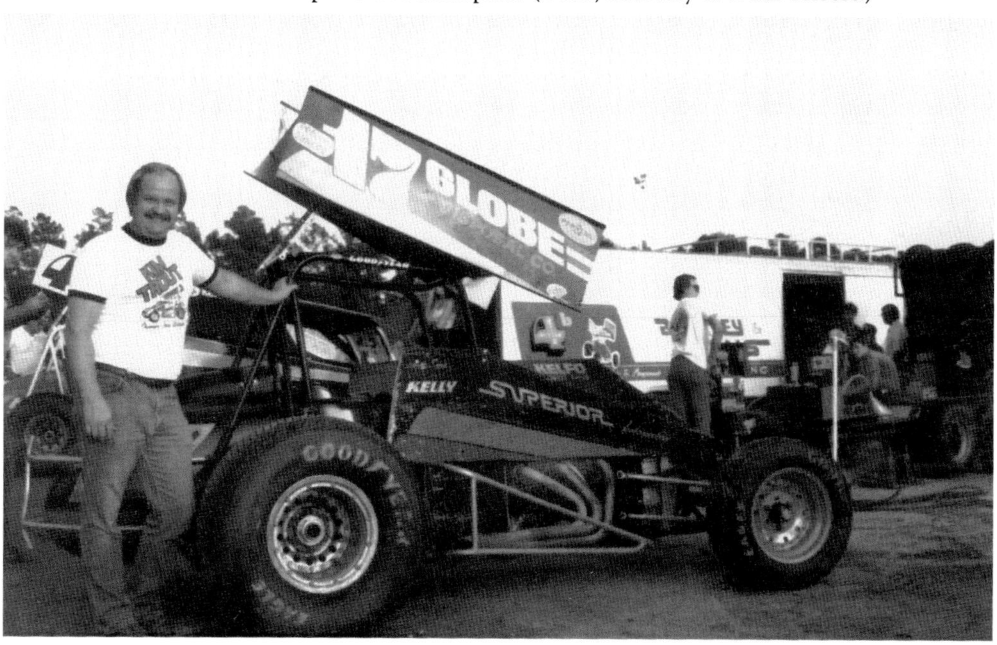

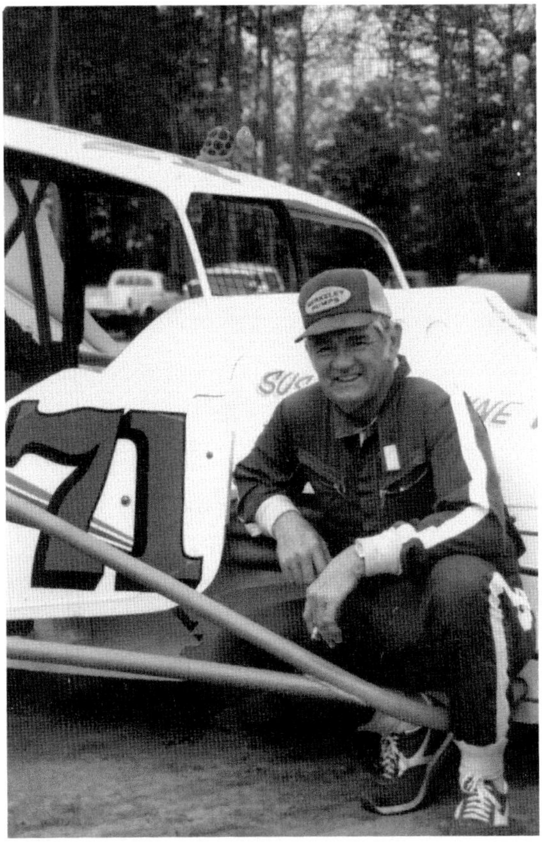

Charlie Phillips was always a favorite in the Modified division. The friendly Phillips always had a light-up green turtle on the top of his No. 71 Modified. (Courtesy of D&L Photos.)

Richard Jarvis, in the No. 680, powers around a turn at Delaware International Speedway. Using a Tony Feil–built Big Block motor for power, Jarvis's Modified was an absolute rocket on the track. Jarvis racked up 29 Modified wins and won the track championship in 1981. (Courtesy of D&L Photos.)

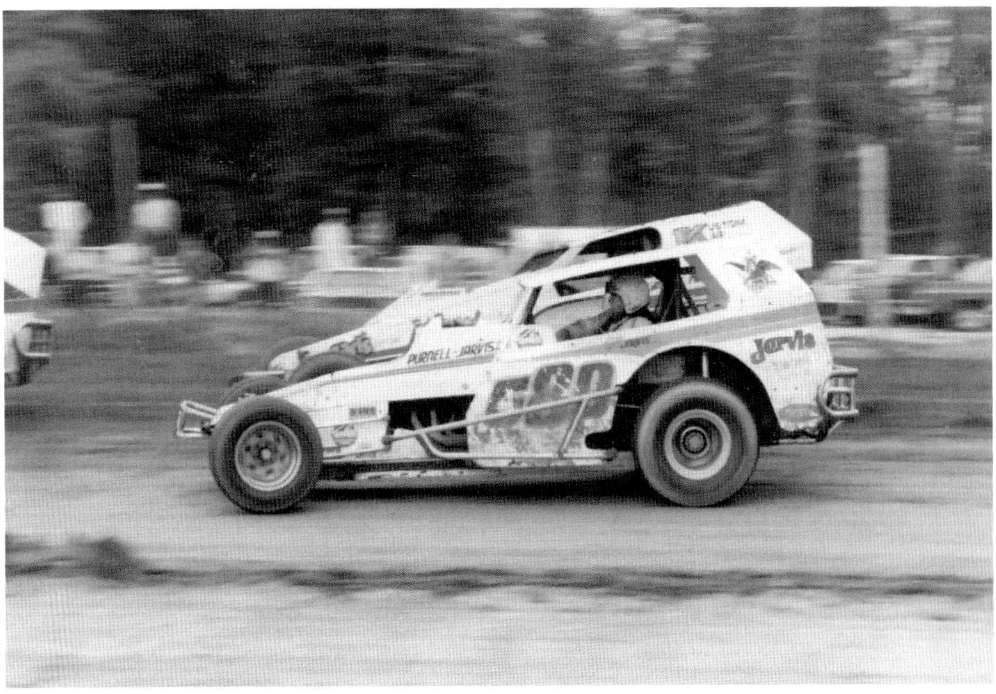

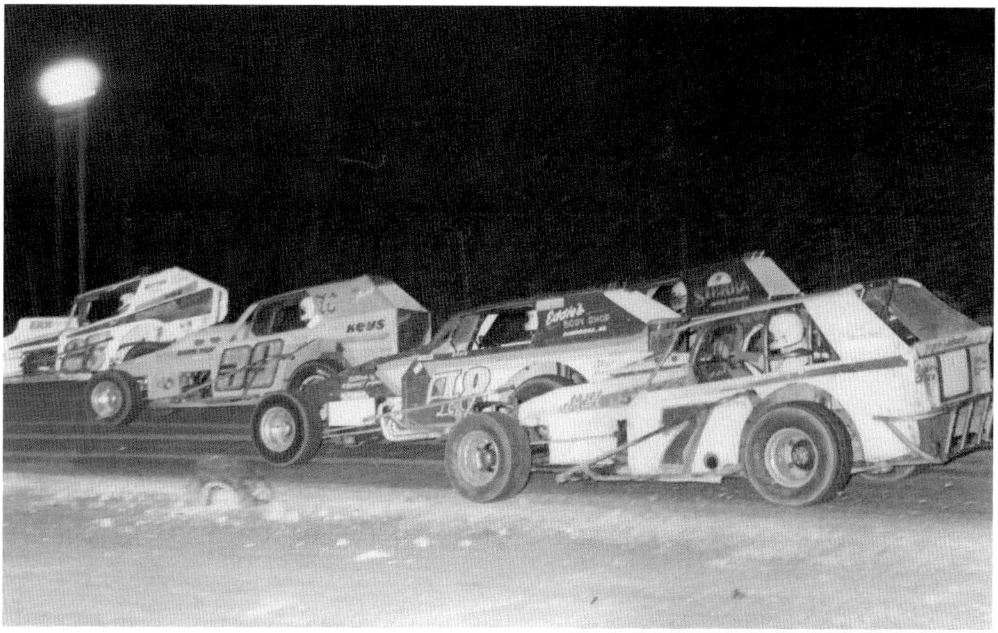

Close racing at Delmar always kept the crowd (and drivers) on edge. Pictured here are, from left to right, Freddy Brightbill (No. 25), Ron Keys (No. 39), Eddie Brown (No. 48), Bob Toreky (No. 14, behind No. 48), and Charlie Moore (No. 7). (Courtesy of Helen Banks.)

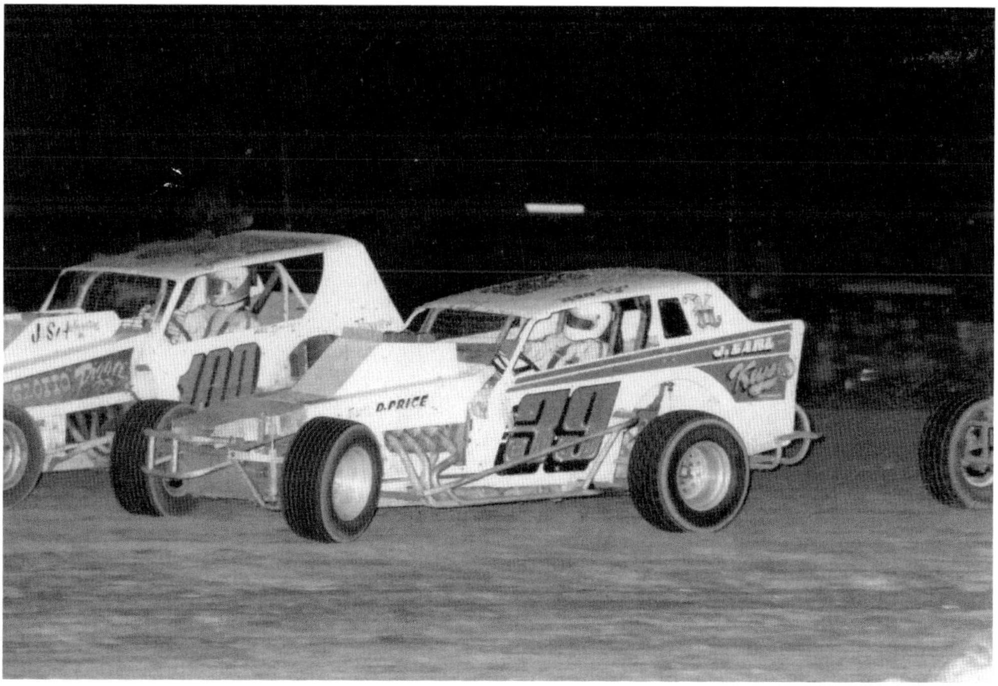

Ron Keys (No. 39) tries to get a nose under Hal Browning (No. 100) at Delaware International Speedway. Keys had eight feature Modified wins at DIS and was always a front-runner. (Courtesy of D&L Photos.)

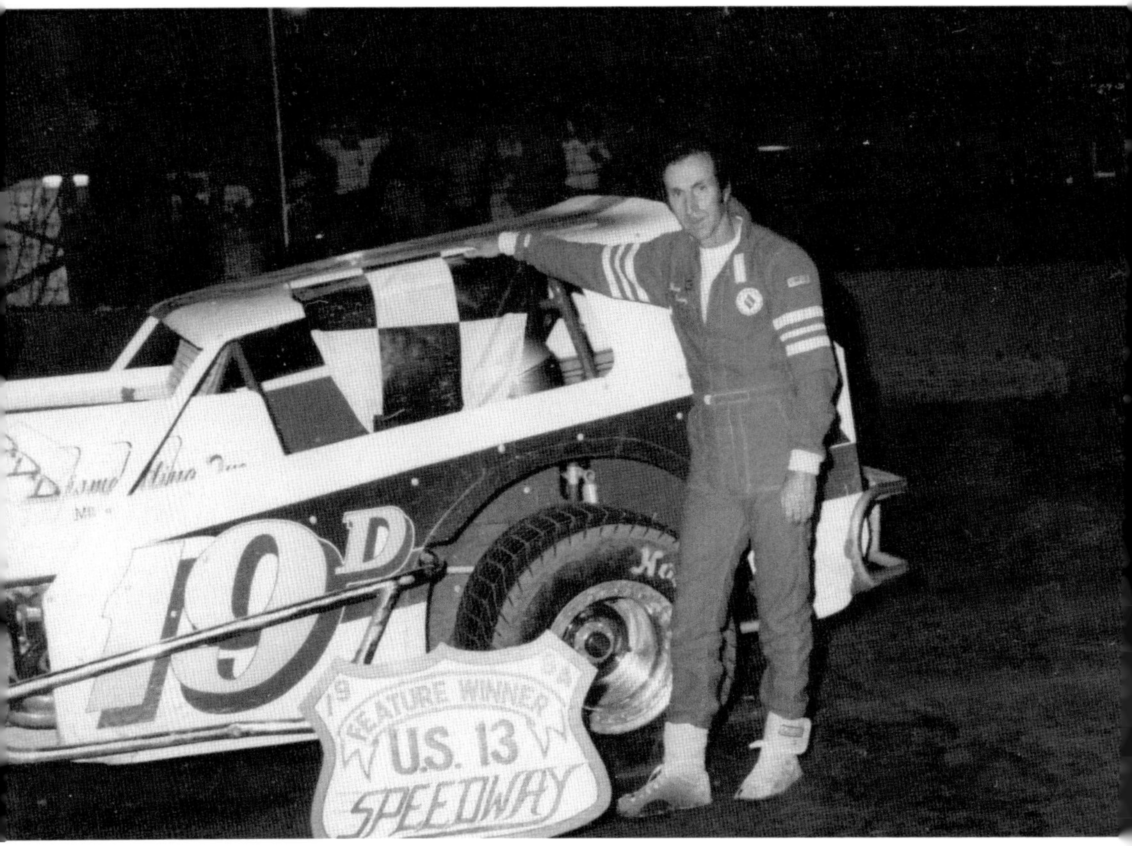

When Harold Bunting retired from racing at the end of the 1986 season, his statistics at Delaware International Speedway were impressive; he amassed 87 feature wins in the Modified division, along with four Modified track championships. (Courtesy of D&L Photos.)

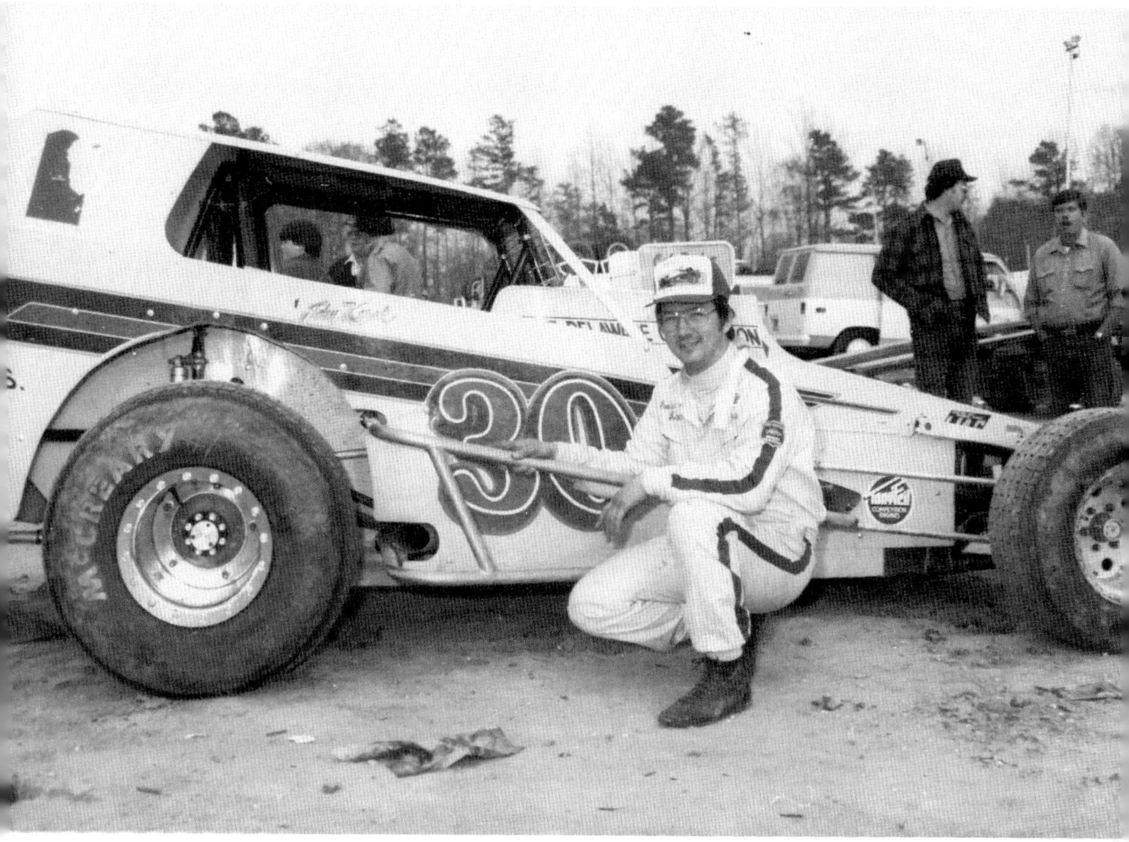

John Kozak had much success with Blue Hen Racing team at Delaware International Speedway. Kozak won the point title for Modifieds in 1979 and amassed 44 wins at DIS. (Courtesy of D&L Photos.)

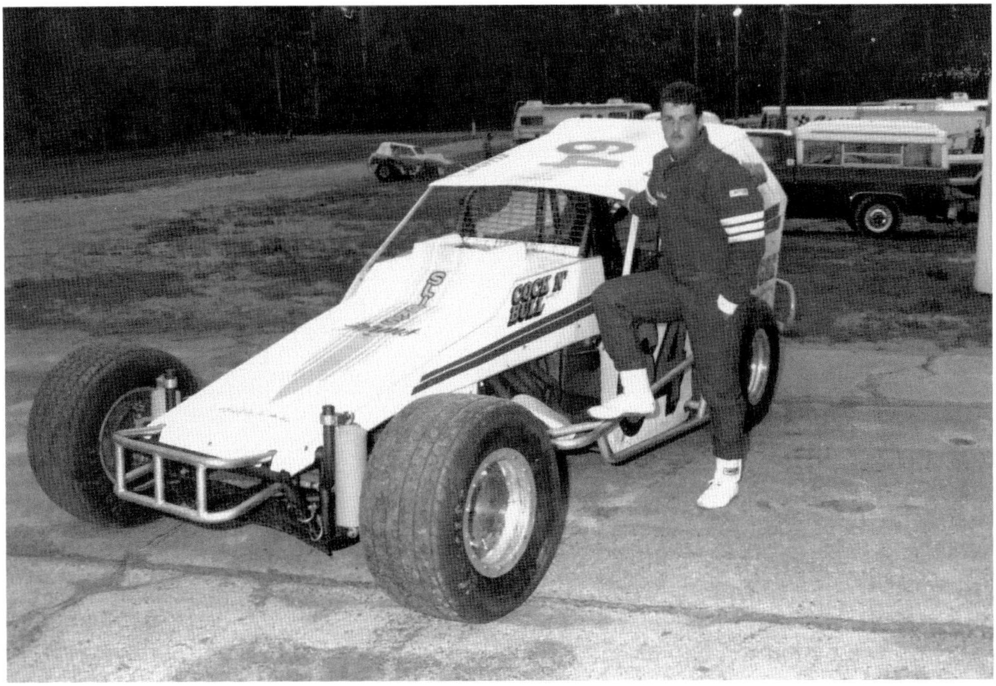

A young Ricky Elliott stands next to one of his first Modifieds. Elliott has won two Modified track championships, three Delaware State Championship Races, and has 60 wins and counting at Delaware International Speedway. (Courtesy of D&L Photos.)

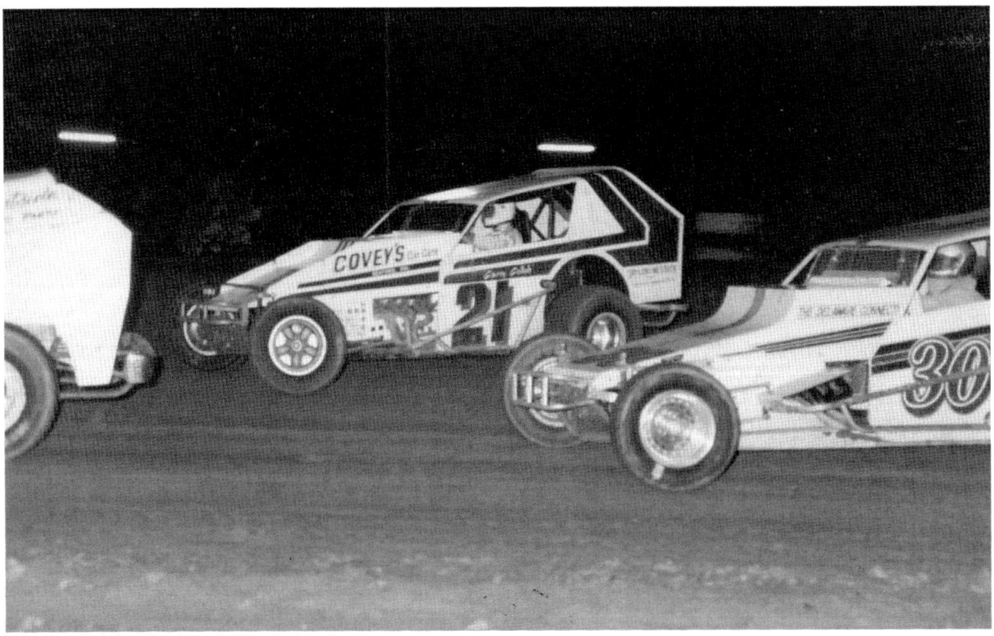

Gary Gollub drove the No. 21 Covey's Car Care–sponsored Modified to 24 wins for owner Ken Covey. Gollub won the United Racing Club Sprint Car Championships in 1975 and 1976 and has 19 URC wins. (Courtesy of D&L Photos.)

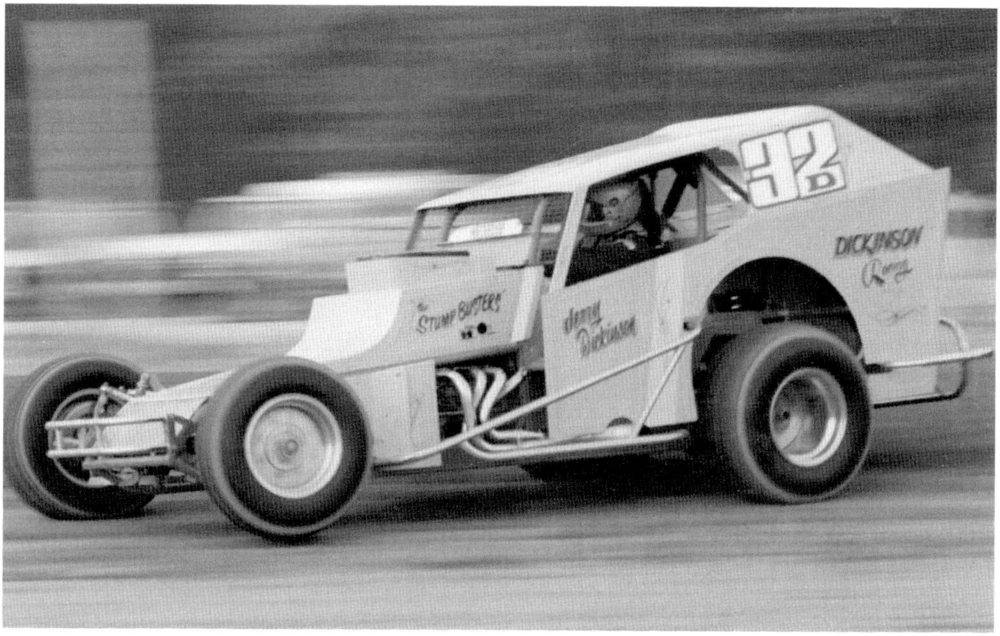

Jerry Dickinson is on the gas at full speed. With Modifieds no longer using bodies from production cars, new designs were tried out to gain every advantage possible. Dickinson's Modified is a great example of how a craftsman can turn a piece of sheet metal into rolling art. (Courtesy of D&L Photos.)

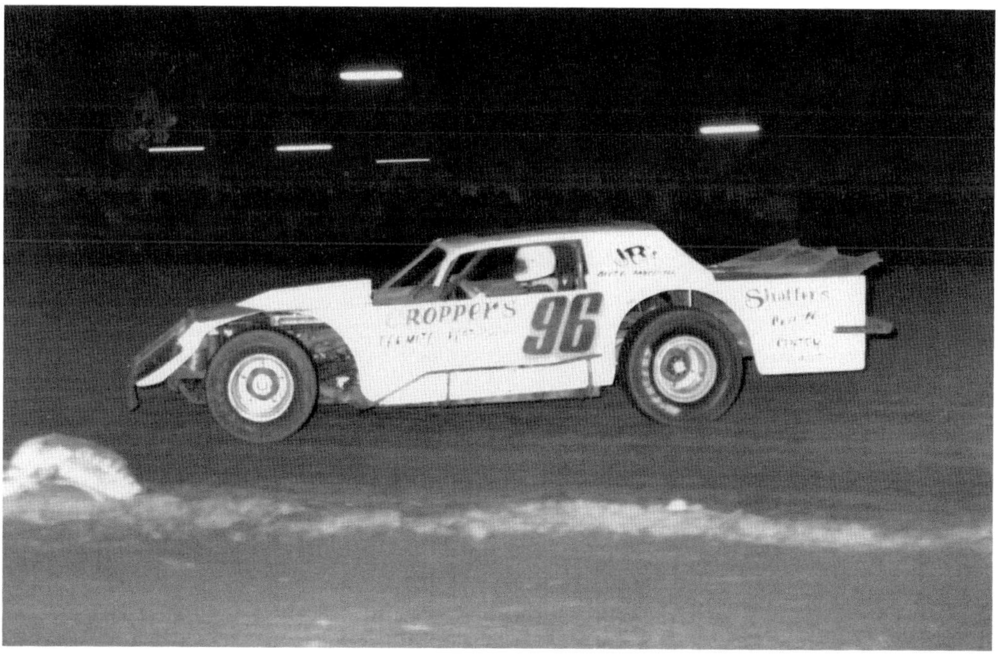

Lou Johnson is a five-time Late Model Track Champion at Delaware International Speedway. Over his career at DIS, he has 28 wins and counting. Johnson ranks fifth on the all-time Late Model win list at the speedway. (Courtesy of D&L Photos.)

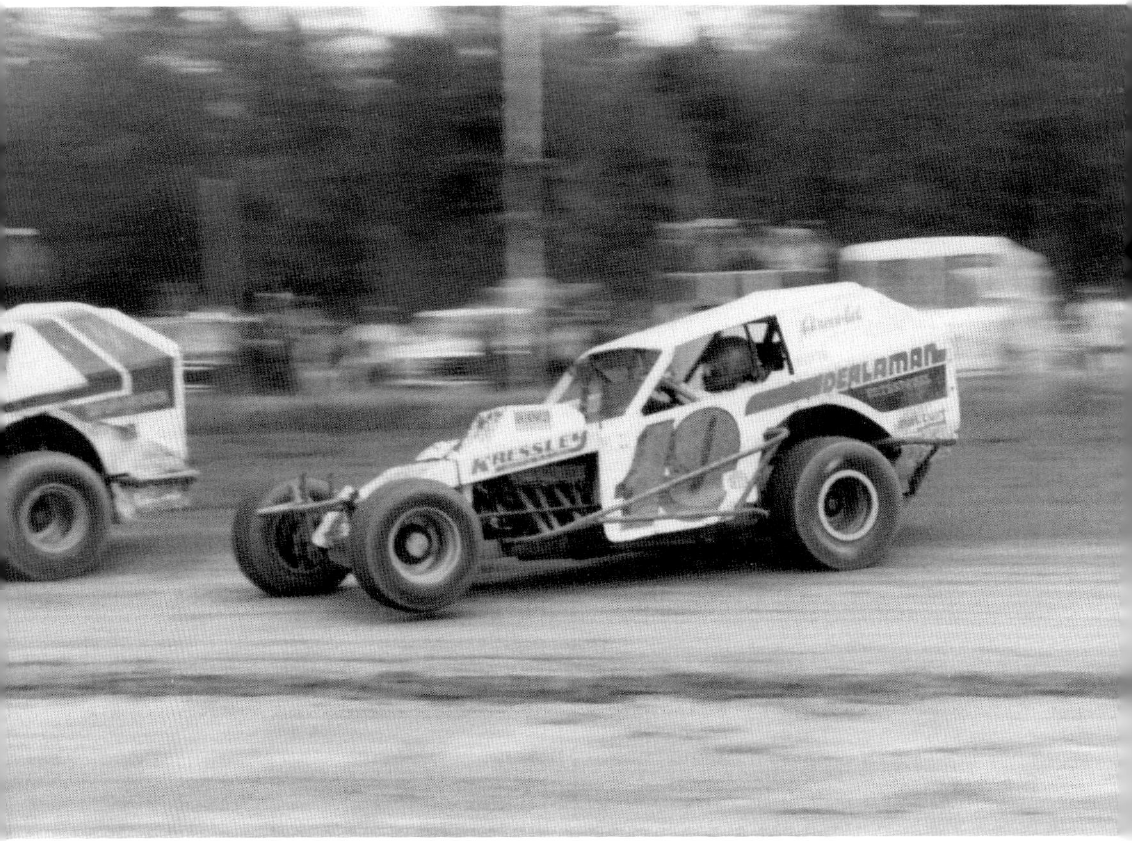

Kenny Brightbill, from Sinking Springs, Pennsylvania, always traveled to Delaware International Speedway to race in big events and won four Delaware State Championship races. A driver since 1969, he has won championships at Bridgeport, Flemington, Big Diamond, Penn National, East Windsor, and Delaware International Speedway. With over 430 feature wins, he is a master on the dirt track. In 1988, he won at Syracuse while driving for Eugene Mills of Delaware. In 2010, at the age of 62, he became Modified Track champion at DIS and continues to add to his win total. (Courtesy of D&L Photos.)

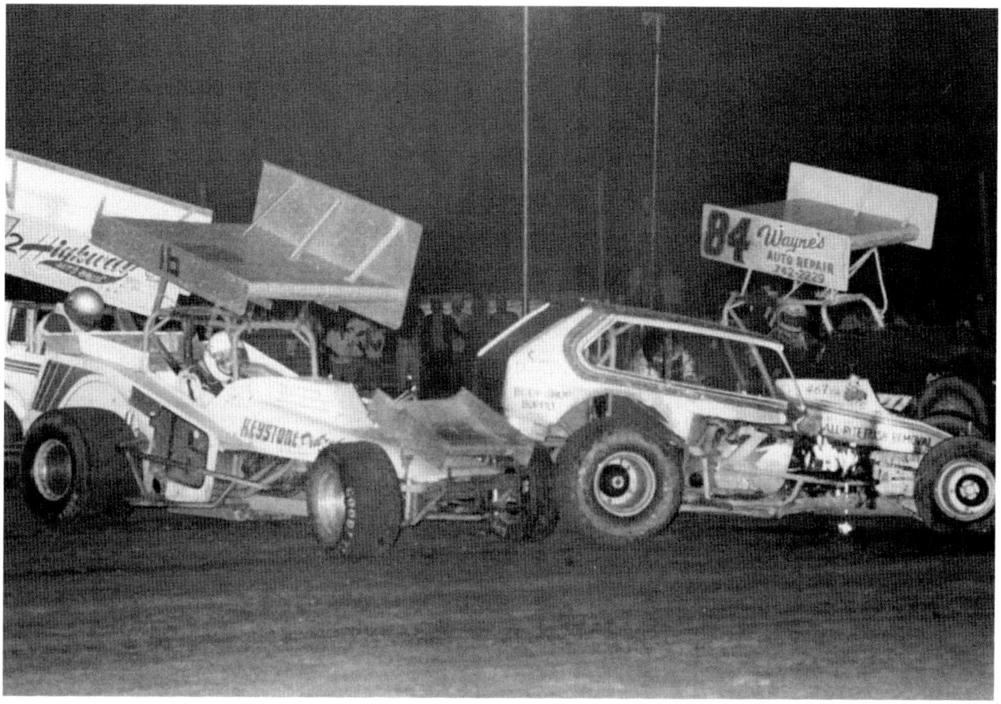

One of a driver's worst fears is fire. In this photograph, the engine on the No. 47 (at right) starts to catch fire during an Open Competition Show at Delaware International Speedway. Track rules require certain safety measures for each racing class in order to reduce the risk of injury. (Courtesy of D&L Photos.)

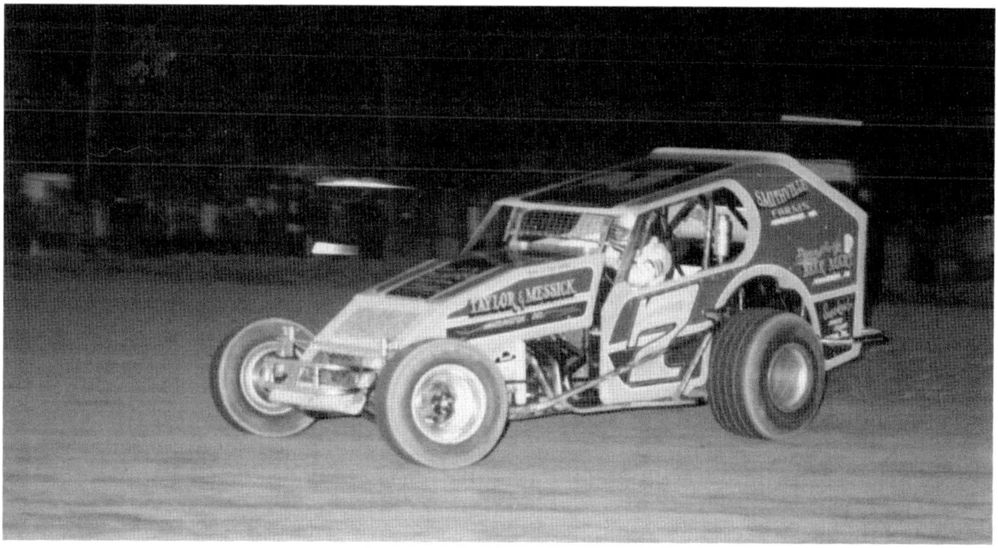

Walt Breeding has scored 44 career wins at Delaware International Speedway. Breeding was not only a great driver, but also a great fabricator, businessman, and promoter. Famous for driving the No. 1 Taylor and Messick and Smithville Farms cars, he is pictured here in the No. 7 Modified. (Courtesy of D&L Photos.)

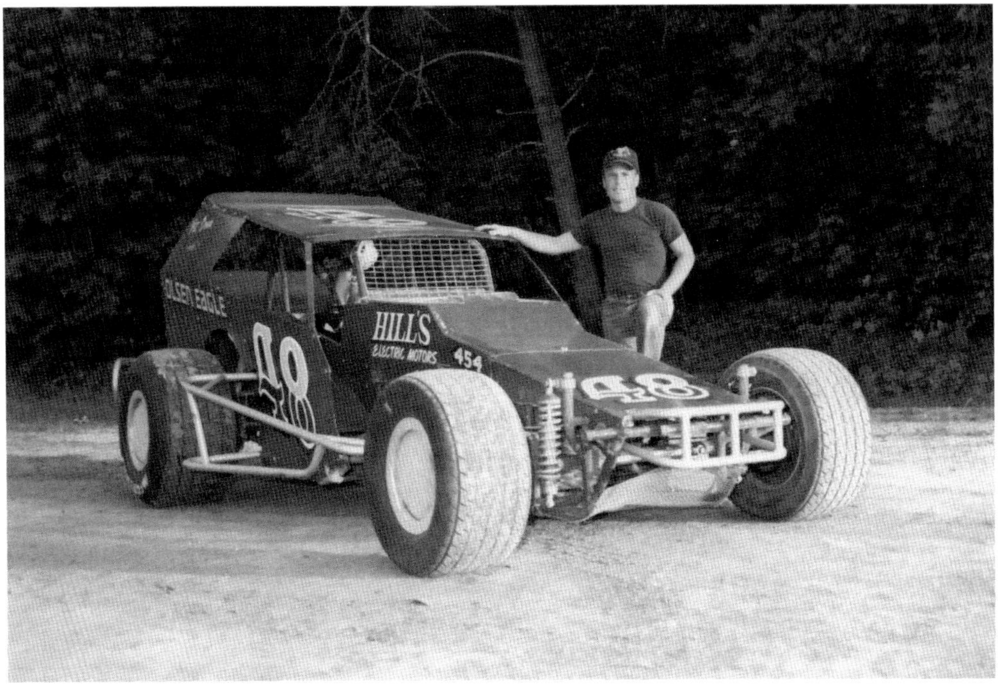

Ed Brown poses next to his Olsen Eagle–chassis Modified. This style of car was typical in the 1980s. Gone were the Gremlin and Pinto bodies of the 1970s as lighter, more aerodynamic sheet-metal bodies started to become the norm. Most Modified chassis used a unique setup of torsion-bar suspension in the rear and coil springs in the front. (Courtesy of D&L Photos.)

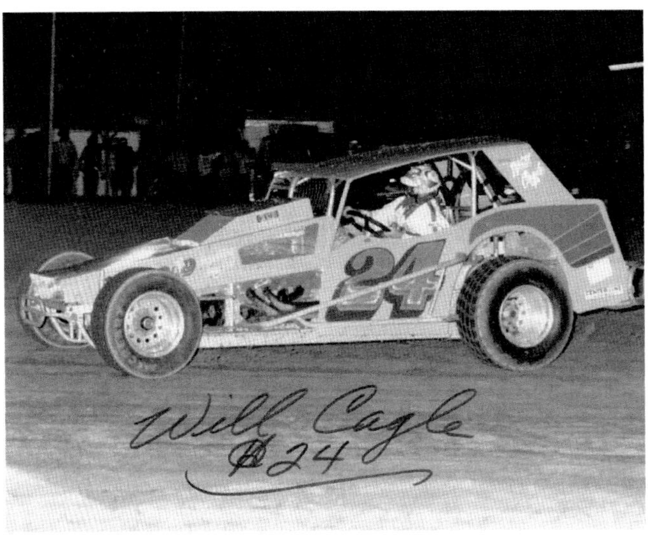

Although he never won a feature at Delaware International Speedway, Modified great Will Cagle invaded the track for a chance at big money when a special race was held. Cagle won 35 Modified races during the 1970s and was a threat everywhere he traveled. (Courtesy of D&L Photos.)

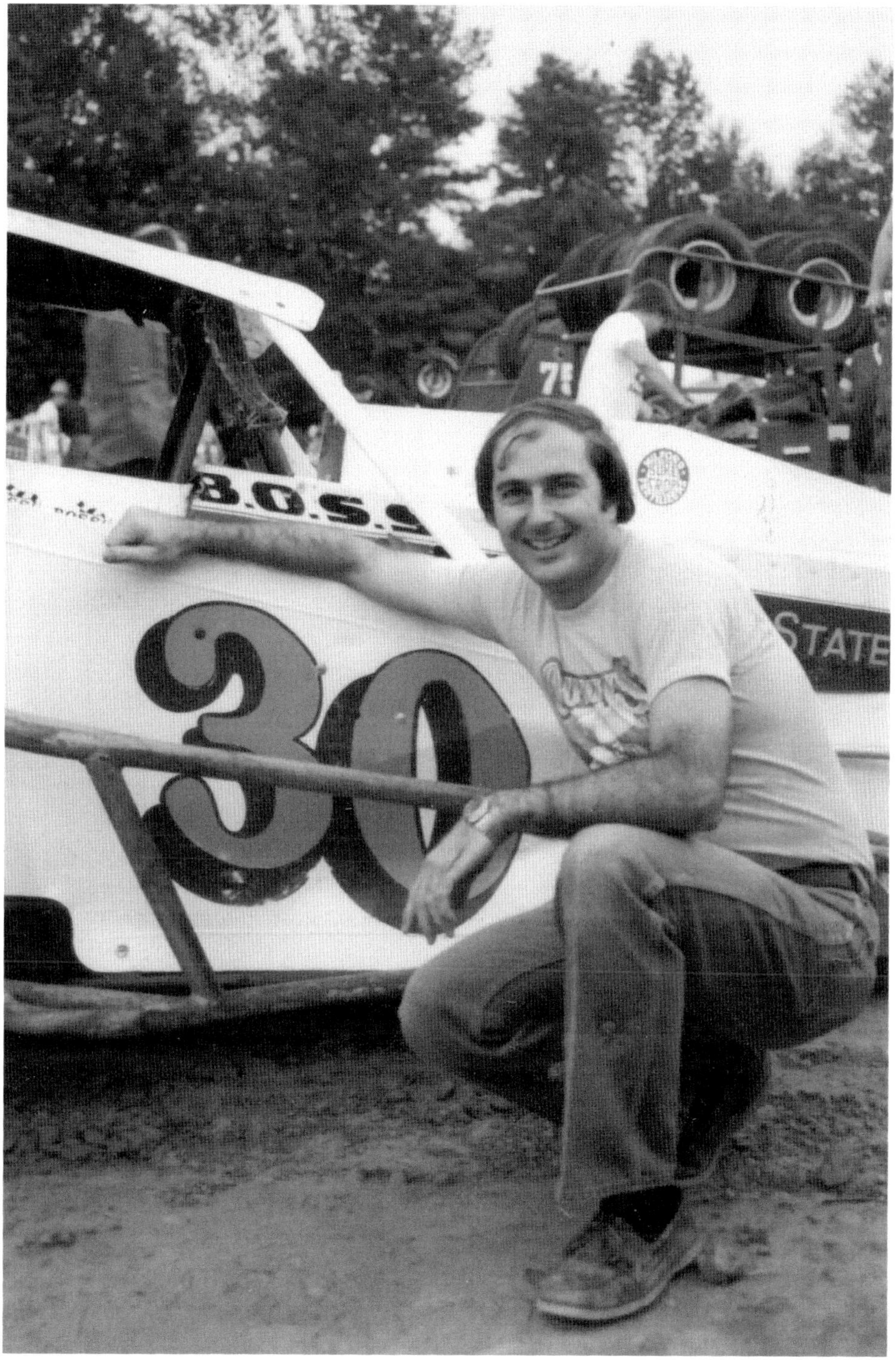

Beloved local racer Billy Towers has seen success in both the Modified and Late Model classes at Delaware International Speedway. Towers has a combined total of 27 feature wins. (Courtesy of D&L Photos.)

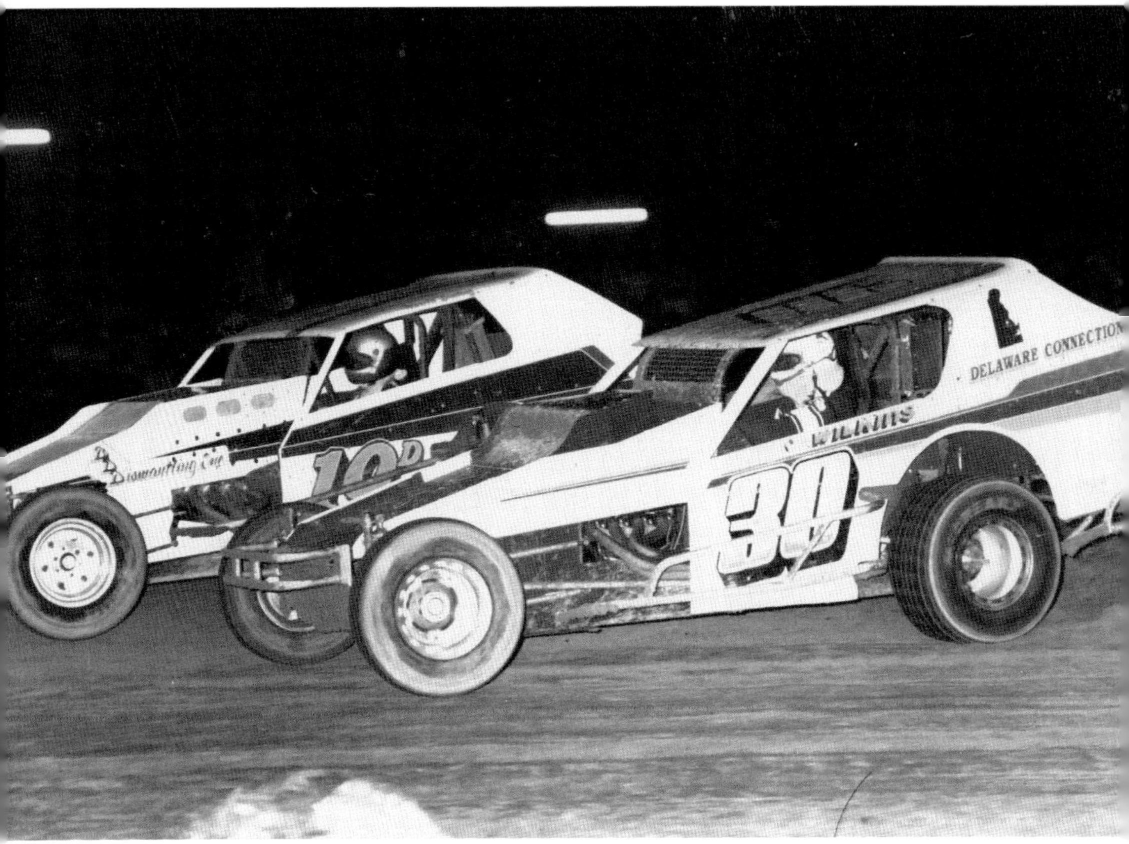

The two winningest Modified drivers in the history of Delaware International Speedway—Bobby Wilkins (No. 30) and Harold Bunting (No. 19D)—race side by side. Both drivers gave Delaware race fans some great memories. (Courtesy of D&L Photos.)

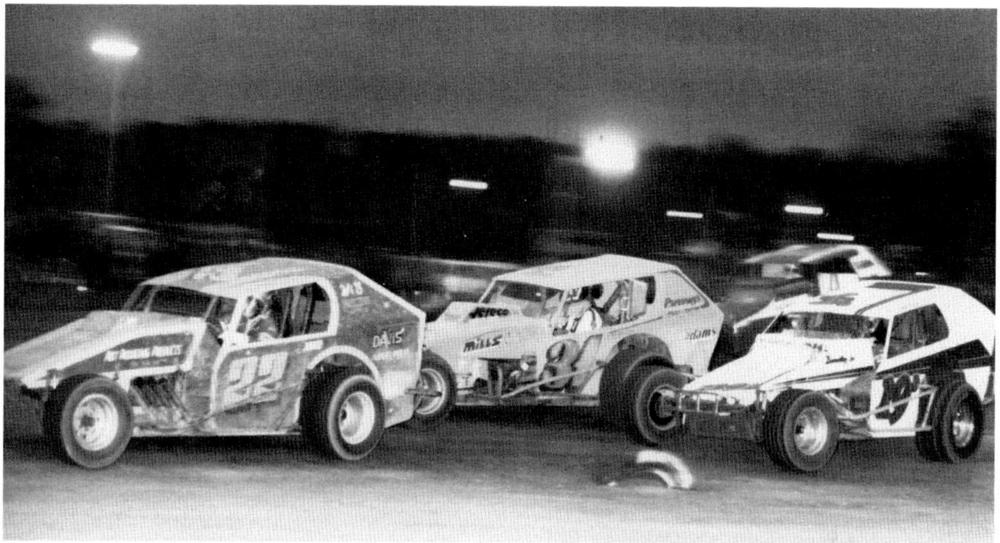

Saturday-night lights shine upon some close racing action. Battling it out in a feature event at Delaware International Speedway are, from left to right, Bobby Walls (No. 22), John Kozak (No. 31), and Harold Bunting (No 19D). (Courtesy of D&L Photos.)

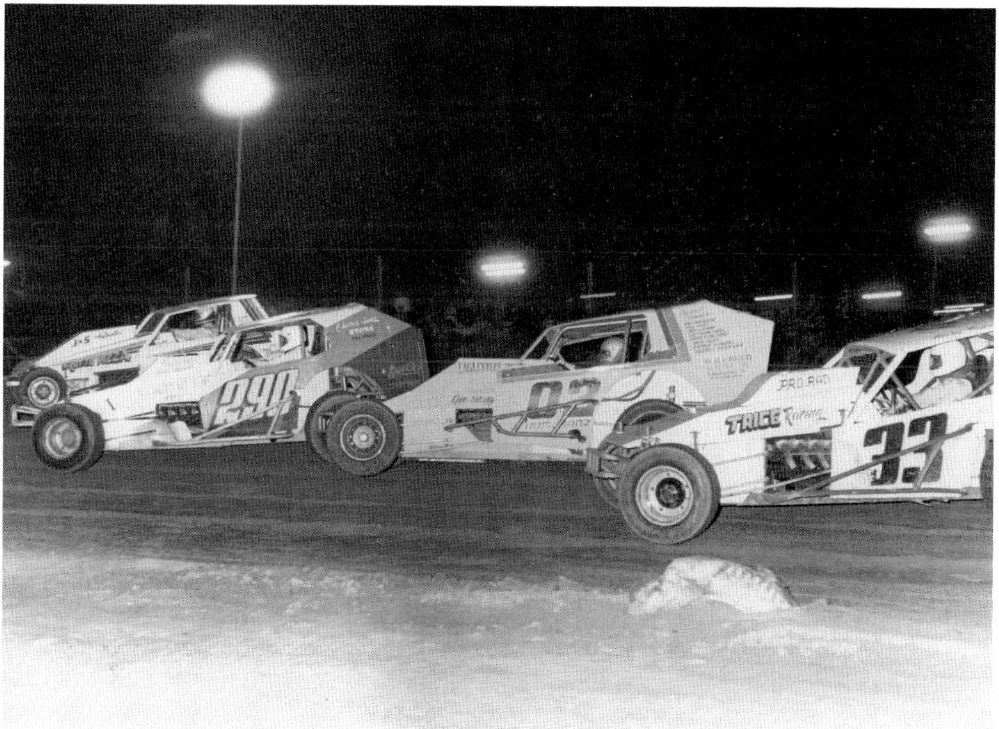

Running a track is a full-time job. The Cathell family works all week to meticulously prepare the half-mile dirt track for hundreds of race laps on Saturday nights. The effort pays off for competitors and fans, as racers are often able to go four-wide on the track surface. (Courtesy of D&L Photos.)